PART ONE

THE AMERICANS: A Brief History to 1877

PART ONE

THE AMERICANS

A BRIEF HISTORY TO 1877

HENRY F. BEDFORD

Phillips Exeter Academy

TREVOR COLBOURN

University of New Hampshire

Under the General Editorship of John Morton Blum
Yale University

Harcourt Brace Jovanovich, Inc.

New York   Chicago   San Francisco   Atlanta

COVER   *Cincinnati, 1838.* Public Library of Cincinnati
and Hamilton County.

© 1972 by Harcourt Brace Jovanovich, Inc.

ISBN: 0-15-502600-3

Library of Congress Catalog Card Number: 71-182337

Printed in the United States of America

SOURCES OF ILLUSTRATIONS

Ollie Atkins: pp. 472, 474
Bettmann Archive: pp. 191, 238, 250, 373
Brown Brothers: pp. 45, 346, 384
John Carter Brown Library, Brown University: p. 22
Culver Pictures: pp. 160, 167, 294, 326, 388, 401
Courtesy of Essex Institute, Salem, Mass.: p. 42
Michael Gregory/Pix: p. 481
The Historical Society of Pennsylvania: p. 30
Bern Keating/Black Star: p. 454
Library of Congress: pp. 17, 25, 36 (*top*), 52, 56, 69, 72, 100, 123, 149, 155, 168, 195, 196,
    197, 205, 217, 218, 222, 227, 231, 235, 268, 276, 279, 287, 299, 315, 322, 325, 331, 337, 349,
    355, 426
Mariner's Museum, Newport News, Va.: p. 126
The Metropolitan Museum of Art: pp. 63 (Gift of Mrs. Russell Sage, 1910), 77
    (Bequest of Charles Munn, 1924), 102 (Gift of Henry Marquand), 131 (Bequest of
    Seth Low), 142, 185, 211
Museum of the City of New York: pp. 140, 246 (*bottom*) (The Jacob A. Riis Collec-
    tion)
National Archives/Signal Corps: p. 342
National Maritime Museum: p. 36 (*bottom*)
National Portrait Gallery: p. 43
New York Historical Society: pp. 98, 111, 125, 127, 162, 258, 267, 364
New York Public Library: p. 310
Lloyd Ostendorf Collection: p. 209
Preservation Society of Newport County: p. 246 (*top*)
Public Library of Cincinnati and Hamilton County: p. 171
Ben Shahn, *The Passion of Sacco and Vanzetti.* Whitney Museum of American Art,
    New York: p. 366
Edward Sorel: p. 492
TVA: p. 397
United Press International: pp. 438, 445
Virginia Museum: p. 91
White House Collection: pp. 116, 312
Wide World: pp. 416, 420, 427, 434, 448, 455, 461, 488

A NOTE

ON THE TWO-VOLUME EDITION

This volume is part of a variant printing, not a new or revised edition, of *The Americans: A Brief History*. Many instructors have requested a two-volume version that would enable them to fit the text into the particular patterns of their teaching and scheduling. To meet that request, the publishers have prepared this printing, consisting of two separate volumes that exactly reproduce the text of the one-volume version of *The Americans: A Brief History*. The first of these volumes continues through Reconstruction. The second volume repeats the chapter on Reconstruction (Chapter 12), and carries the account forward to the present day. The variant printing, then, is intended as a convenience to those instructors and students who have occasion to use either one part or the other of *The Americans: A Brief History*. Consequently, the pagination and index of the one-volume version, as well as its illustrations, maps, and other related materials, are retained in the new printing. The difference between the one-volume and the two-volume versions of the book is a difference only in form.

PREFACE

Some four centuries ago an Elizabethan scholar pondered the importance of history: "Man without learning and remembrance of things past," concluded Sir William Dugdale, "falls into a beastlye sottishnesse and his life is noe better to be accounted of than to be buried alive." Two centuries later, David Hume thought history "the greatest mistress of wisdom," and Benjamin Franklin praised "Good History" because it could "fix in the Minds of Youth deep Impressions of the Beauty and Usefulness of Virtue of all kinds." More recently American Presidents have erected great stone shrines in which their papers might be cataloged for study by future generations of historians.

The importance of the American historical experience seems generally accepted, even if its relevance is not always appreciated. The most casual observer of the American scene cannot fail to notice the seemingly unceasing flow of historical books, periodicals, and monographs from the nation's presses. No other nation boasts such a profusion of textbooks that attempt to analyze, describe, and synthesize its history. In spite of this abundance there is a case to be made for a textbook that seeks brevity without lamentable omissions, succinctness without tantalizing allusions, interpretation without prejudice. We have written *The Americans: A Brief History* in the hope of providing such a book.

vii

As we were writing this book, young Americans in particular were questioning their national heritage: Have Americans constructed a racist society? Must Americans change the balance of nature and foul the environment? Can the American political system respond to human needs? Are Americans inherently greedy, imperialistic, conforming, prudish, and apprehensive? In raising such questions, many students implied a criticism of their earlier courses in American history, where they studied the details but gained little sense of historical perspective. This book reminds students of the facts and also tries to suggest, rather briefly, the dimensions of the relevant past.

The opening chapter discusses those values that have characterized the American people—the Puritan work ethic, thrift, the profit motive, emphasis on education, the belief in political solutions to problems—and these themes are addressed (often obliquely) throughout the book. We hope, for instance, that readers will better understand the nation's faith in its political process as they consider its political history; we hope to have made the aspirations of American industrial workers as clear as the chicanery of some of their employers; we hope the black American emerges as more than an unstated exception to generalizations about American ideals.

Any text must derive substantially from the learning and judgment of others. The authors are particularly indebted to John M. Blum, Yale University, and Donald B. Cole, Phillips Exeter Academy, for their helpful suggestions, and to Thomas A. Williamson and Virginia Joyner for their encouragement and patience. We owe thanks also to G. Wallace Chessman, Denison University, William W. Freehling, University of Michigan, and Robert Middlekauff, University of California, Berkeley, who read and commented on portions of the manuscript. Every historian cited at the end of each chapter is our unacknowledged collaborator, as are scores of others in the historical fraternity.

Henry F. Bedford
Trevor Colbourn

CONTENTS

APPENDIX, 499

INDEX, 525

THE AMERICANS: A Brief History to 1877

I

"... THIS NEW MAN"

In 1492 Christopher Columbus sailed from southern Spain and landed, after a trying voyage, on San Salvador. Most of the facts about that epic journey are clear, but their interpretation remains in question. Should Columbus be credited with discovering a new world? Or should the Norse sailors from centuries before? Or Indians before that? Does hoisting a flag and setting foot to sand complete the act of discovery? Or must one also be aware of what has been found, as Columbus was not?

Unresolved questions about the discovery of America are appropriate, because Americans have long argued, not about the facts of American history, but about their arrangement and interpretation. In 1765, for instance, England passed a Stamp Act to tax the American colonies. Some colonists at the time, and a great many of their later descendants, interpreted that statute as proof of England's tyranny and colonial exploitation. This explanation has the authority of patriotic tradition, but the Stamp Act did not necessarily demonstrate either tyranny or exploitation. And although all Americans would describe the period between 1861 and 1865 as abnormal, they do not universally refer to the events of those years as the Civil War, nor do they agree on the causes or results of that conflict.

Semantic confusion compounds interpretive difficulty. Even the word "American" is used imprecisely. Citizens of the United States typically rule out all other inhabitants of the Western Hemisphere, assume an exclusive right to be "Americans," and then argue with one another about what the word means. Most people who considered themselves Americans before 1900 would never have included Indians, whose claim to be one-hundred-percent Americans had merit. Various modifiers introduce a spurious precision: German-American, Afro-American, patriotic American, deprived American, and, to define who is left out, un-American.

Moreover, the word "American" sounds singular, but the phenomena it describes are plural. The American woman, the black American, the American student, or even the American tourist, are mythical creatures; there are women and blacks and students in America, and wandering tourists abroad, and all resist definitive categorization. Americans come in two sexes, several colors, and all ages, shapes, and sizes. They come from all sections of a country that stretches from Maine to mid-Pacific. They work at various occupations, for which they receive various incomes, which they spend in various ways. They watch ball games, television, girls, the stock market, and their neighbors. They worship various gods, not all of which are religious, and some worship no god at all. They raise children who differ from all the other children in their suburb, block, apartment house, town, or ghetto, and who surely differ from those of any other environment. And, since they raise their children differently from the way their parents did, generations also differ.

Yet, Americans know that there is "an American," that there is "an American way of life," that, within the diversity, there is a common bond that unites them. For the word "American" connotes more than citizenship, residence, rights, and identification with the nation or state; "American" also describes a state of mind. In spite of individual peculiarities, Americans differ less from one another than they do from Russians, Turks, Japanese, or even Englishmen. In the mind of every American is a set of values, attitudes, habits, customs, morals, traditions, prejudices, and manners that prescribes and limits his behavior. In short, American culture, derived in part from other cultures, is nevertheless unique. An American may reject some or even all of his cultural limitations, but in doing so, he risks ostracism. Even when an individual decides to discard part of his cultural legacy, he usually expects other Americans to be true to their heritage and to play by the old rules.

That heritage and those rules establish an American behavioral perimeter, a boundary that divides the legal from the illegal, the orthodox from the heretical, the normal from the abnormal, the acceptable from what "just isn't done." Some of those limits are described in books of statutes or canon law; others are internal inhibitions that curb the instincts of individuals and restrict the choices from which the nation selects policies. The lives of Americans are regulated by a bewildering variety of political agencies—nation, state, county, municipality, school board, draft board, and sewer district. In addition, most Americans are subject to family control and voluntarily accept the norms of a host of organizations, such as the

Rotary Club, the Knights of Columbus, the American Federation of Musicians, the Urban League, and Delta Kappa Epsilon.

These groups have different objectives and different behavorial limits. Yet, those differences seem details when compared with the important ideals and assumptions upon which most Americans agree. A business executive and his employees may disagree profoundly during the negotiation of their contract, but both accept most of the clichés that Americans use to describe free-enterprise capitalism. Liberty had one meaning for American revolutionaries, another for abolitionists in the 1840s, and yet another for civil rights advocates in the 1960s. And liberty was also the ideal claimed by Tories and those who defended slavery and segregation.

Each generation of Americans must define for itself free enterprise and liberty, as well as equality, patriotism, individualism, justice, and other ideals. Each generation of Americans must adapt for itself the ethical systems, ceremonies, attitudes, faiths, and values of its predecessors. Each decision means psychic conflict for the individual and social conflict for the nation. Yet these conflicts should not obscure the continuity in American history, the fact that most Americans in the twentieth century accept most of the aspirations and assumptions of their forebears. Americans today, troubled by racial injustice, share with their white ancestors both the equalitarian ideal and the prejudice that has postponed racial harmony. The contemporary movement to preserve the environment meets the same economic obstacles conservationists met decades ago; today's unyielding economic attitudes arrived on this continent with the first settlers. The imperialistic greed critics discern in contemporary American foreign policy also brought on the war with Mexico, fought by a restless, aggressive, enterprising, grasping generation of Americans.

Henry David Thoreau, who opposed the Mexican war and was something of a misfit in nineteenth-century Massachusetts, once protested that he did "not wish to be regarded as a member of any incorporated society" that he had not formally joined. Thoreau complained that he could not resign from all the societies he had not joined because he could never compile a complete list. He discovered that some of these organizations, such as the Commonwealth of Massachusetts, did not accept resignations. Contemporary American nonconformists will rediscover Thoreau's dilemma. One can renounce American citizenship and find refuge in Canada or Sweden; one can reject the trappings of an American upbringing; one can refuse to study the American past and scorn its relevance. But the burdens of nationality turn out to be deeper than one's accent or a craving for hamburger. And the American past lingers in the behavorial perimeter, which some present Americans reluctantly inherit and which will influence the American future.

THE LAW AND THE PROFITS

Modern America does not preserve the infinite variety of the American past. The fact that Swedes once settled along the mid-Atlantic shore, for instance, is now of less significance than the fact that Englishmen and English institutions prevailed along most of the rest of the coastline. Even those settlers who were not Englishmen by nationality or inclination became English subjects. English laws and political principles, English currency and economic theory, English Protestantism and its ethic, English customs and English prejudices shaped the society to which newcomers had to adapt. Americans are the cultural heirs of Englishmen, even if individual genealogies show Irish, Mexican, or African ancestors.

Since England governed the colonies for nearly two centuries, the political institutions of the nation and the political assumptions of its people derive from the British experience. A civil war, a bloodless revolution, and a great deal of constitutional debate in seventeenth-century England had curbed royal power. Three thousand miles of ocean diluted that power still further. Authorities in the colonies, representing the Crown, a proprietor, or a colonizing corporation, permitted delegates of the settlers to join in political decision-making. The House of Burgesses first met in Virginia in 1619; the Fundamental Orders of Connecticut established the representative General Court in 1639; in 1701 William Penn gave in to the demands of Pennsylvanians for a representative assembly. Although governors and representatives wrangled endlessly about prerogatives, the principle, imported from England, that some regulations require the consent of the governed was not disputed.

As the colonial assemblies were modeled on Parliament, so institutions of local government resembled those in England. Counties (in Virginia and Maryland) and towns (in New England) enforced local regulations, built roads, and licensed businesses. County clerks recorded wills and the contracts of indentured servants. Sheriffs collected taxes and carried out the decisions of justices of the peace and of the county courts. None of these officials behaved precisely like his counterpart in England, but every colonial bureaucrat drew upon the British experience.

And British experience was explicitly relevant in the courts. Legal questions tend to reflect the complexity of the society from which they arise. Early cases in the colonies, for instance, stemmed from relatively simple disagreements over wills and property lines. To such disputes colonial courts applied the English common law, which assured familiarity with local circumstance through a local jury and yet established common legal principles throughout the entire realm. Common law was traditional, not legislated, and it existed in the form of decisions, not statutes. Judges applied the wisdom of other judges or abstracted from earlier cases rules that seemed appropriate. The importance of precedent, the insistence upon a jury, and above all, the requirement that all citizens of whatever rank bow to the supremacy of law are among the legacies of English justice.

For all the similarities, Americans are not imitation Englishmen; parts of the heritage have been discarded. Unlike members of Parliament, for instance, American legislators must live in the regions they represent and renew their mandate frequently. American political parties—amorphous, inconsistent, undisciplined—are unlike the political parties of any other nation. American judges have abandoned some of the common-law precepts of their colonial predecessors. So the English heritage has only influenced, not determined, American political and legal assumptions.

Until very recently the respect of most Americans for their political institutions bordered on reverence. Before Washington became the destination of protesting demonstrators, it was the nation's secular shrine. However cynical Americans are now about the politician, they still express their aspirations in legislation, translate their needs into political programs, and believe that all problems are susceptible to political solutions. Americans respond to every injustice with the remark that "there ought to be a law."

Underlying the American faith in political institutions are several assumptions. Most Americans believe, for instance, that the ideal form of political organization is a stable government responsible to its electorate. Although the twentieth century has conclusively demonstrated that unrepresentative governments can achieve mass popular support, Americans nevertheless tend to regard these examples as temporary and somehow improper. Yet, for many people, even for many Americans, political stability is patently undesirable. Discontented people and ambitious nations want change, perhaps even chaos, rather than order. Stability, after all, is the maxim of those who are satisfied.

Argument, reason, and compromise—so runs the American political creed—will produce laws that will eliminate social friction. This article of faith conceals two optimistic notions: first, that all America's problems can be solved and, second, that man is rational. But in this century Americans are discovering that some problems are really dilemmas that mock the best intentions and the best efforts of the nation's best men. And the writings of Sigmund Freud, the career of Joseph Stalin, and the response of civilized Germans to Nazism have caused some Americans to wonder about man's innate rationality. Other peoples in other times have not thought reason the highest virtue, but rather have relied on religious faith.

The American impulse to use political action is not a universal method of solving problems. Instead of governments and politicians, many societies rely on a body of religious or secular doctrine to supply answers to social questions. Many of the peoples of Asia, including the Chinese, have no tradition of regular political procedure; philosophies and faiths furnish methods of meeting life's problems and provide punishments for those who err. Even before the Communist revolution, few Russians looked to politicians or legislators to achieve progress or justice. Those who opposed the Czars rejected parliaments as palliatives; they rejected present compromise and sought future perfection. Confronted with a challenge, a Communist refers to the theories of Karl Marx or Vladimir Lenin; an American telephones his lawyer or his congressman for action.

Laws and governments, Americans have always believed, should promote the welfare of the citizenry. Americans find baffling the idea that a state might have different interests from those of its citizens; the very distinction between state and citizens is strange. But for generations Europeans understood that "reasons of state," dynastic connections, or the whims of noblemen dictated policy that harmed the state's citizens. There is little evidence that today's Russian peasants want to overthrow the Communist regime, although in many ways it does not meet their needs. A Russian does not expect his government to be responsive while an American is unhappy if his is not.

So it has been since that November day in 1620 when the men of the *Mayflower* solemnly assembled "in the presence of God and one another," to form a "civil body politick, for our better ordering and preservation. . . ." Order was ever a concern of Englishmen and a "civil body politick" was the tested means to the end. English settlers brought their political prejudices, institutions, and ideals to the colonies. The settlers found it convenient first to claim the rights of Englishmen and then to add some that native Englishmen had yet to secure.

One of the undoubted rights of an Englishman was the right to enjoy his property. "The great end of men's entering into society," wrote John Locke in 1689, was "the enjoyment of their properties in peace and safety. . . ." Locke makes sense even to those Americans who know nothing of the English political philosopher. In the defense of property rights Americans have outdone their English forebears. Often, as was the case during more than two centuries of slavery, property rights have taken precedence over human rights. With the exception of the emancipation movement, the occasional assaults on property rights seem in retrospect rather feeble, partly because property has been so widely distributed that no challenge has had a popular base.

And those who at one moment have no property expect to get some the next. Americans have always been speculators, betting on the future. Sir Walter Raleigh, the stockholders of the London and Virginia companies, and every settler who came to the New World expected to turn a profit. Early immigrants staked whatever they had on their belief that the New World held more for them than the old. Some, with only their labor to pledge, shipped as indentured servants; others started with a plot of land and a few tools. Americans ever since have retained their appetite for profit and their faith in the American economy. If it falters, "Prosperity is just around the corner." Booms are a matter of course. "Don't sell America short" has been more than a slogan; it has been a secular creed.

Property in America has been the measure of accomplishment and the reward for effort. The accumulation of property, whether land or money, has always been a proper goal of life. America has been the land of opportunity, and Americans have come to think of economic growth as a permanent condition. We have assumed wealth to be unlimited; those who obtain it do so, not at the expense of other men, but from the earth or from some other natural source of riches. Thus, any addition to one man's fortune was a net gain for the whole society. Economic individualism —or, less tactfully, greed—was supposed to produce social progress as well as a personal fortune. Whether the example be the indentured servant who accumulated a sizeable estate, the immigrant who rose from bobbin boy to industrial magnate, or the personable businessman of Irish parentage who made a fortune in the stock market, Americans have been proud, not resentful, of those who succeeded.

The first immigrants, like those who came later, were simple people with simple tastes. Dukes, after all, do not usually emigrate, and paupers can rarely afford to. Most of the first arrivals were English yeomen—sturdy, hard-working farmers of the English countryside, whose agricultural skills and frugal habits were proverbial. The more prosperous settlers were gentry, men who in England had operated farms or occasionally businesses of moderate size, which brought them enough income for comfort but not enough for indolence. Although the companies and proprietors that established early settlements found their investments disappointing, the colonists themselves, whose expectations were more modest, discovered economic opportunity in land. And of land there was plenty. To own land in America became much more common than in England and carried fewer privileges. But the American landowner was as jealous of the rights of property as was the English squire.

The essential elements of what Americans call free-enterprise capitalism came with the earliest settlers. The terms are not precise, but Americans have always believed they knew what a "free market," "fair competition," "individual enterprise," and "equal opportunity" meant. And they have been equally sure that monopoly, socialism, and special privilege were beyond the bounds of acceptable economic behavior. The Puritans knew what was proper; central to their code of conduct was the notion that hard work was morally uplifting. Other Puritan virtues, such as thrift, perseverance, honesty, sobriety, punctuality, obedience, and, paradoxically, initiative, conveniently brought profits as well as clean consciences. Anyone can develop these virtues; capacity, aptitude, and genes are less important than character, which alone limits a man's horizon.

To be sure, Americans have not always practiced the economic theory they have preached. A monopoly, for example, even if unfair, has been enviously regarded as "good business." But while the economy has evolved from agricultural simplicity to the complexity of modern industry, the old economic vocabulary and many of the Puritan attitudes have endured.

A NATION OF PROTESTANT FARMERS

Behavior depends in part upon laws and the size of a man's bank balance. The way Americans behave, however, also results from the expectations of other Americans. The opinion of family, neighborhood, school, church, and clique can counteract the force of law and overcome financial handicaps. The assumptions and rituals that govern social contact, together with the natural impulse to associate with others, form cultural axioms, which serve as the base for probing American history.

One set of axioms derives from Protestant Christianity, especially in the form loosely called Puritanism. Usage has robbed the term of precision, and Puritans, in consequence, have been blamed for creating social traumas they did not cause and for encouraging traits they did not esteem. Both critics and admirers of the piety of the first settlers have attributed too much to the people and their faith. The Puritan ethic and Protestant Christianity are responsible neither for every virtue that ornamented American life after 1620 nor for every sin that stained it.

The Puritan, so the stereotype goes, was a gloomy, ascetic sort who felt guilty if music, sex, art, games, color, or alcohol made his life interesting. His fatalistic belief in predestination led to obsession with the state of his soul. He burned witches. His ministers preached of damnation in such vivid terms that congregations felt the flames and smelled the brimstone. Dour, driven, humorless, pious, penny-pinching, fanatical, and probably neurotic, the Puritan was plagued, as one iconoclast has written, by his "haunting fear that someone, somewhere, may be happy."

The picture will not do. The Puritan was no more concerned with his soul than some of his descendants are with their psyches. His life was no bleak succession of prayer meetings unrelieved by beauty or pleasure. Sobriety did not preclude the moderate use of spirits; a ban on music within the meeting house did not forbid it outside; Puritan pewter was gracefully designed to please the eye.

If not entirely humorless, the Puritan was serious. He believed his task on earth was to secure salvation; when he contemplated the magnitude of that undertaking, he was not likely to be much amused. For, Puritans held, men were sinful and could be redeemed only through the sovereign grace of God. The God of the Puritans was eternal, omnipotent, and omniscient, so of course He knew who would be saved and who condemned. Yet, predestination was not unjust, for man could not define justice for God. And, after all, life was full of inequities: as some were saved and some condemned, so some were rich and others poor, some fortunate and others not; the grace of God was beyond human understanding. Whatever his predestined fate, the Puritan worked. Even if he could not earn divine grace, he could at least earn the respect of man, which might in turn be a sign of God's pleasure with His servant.

For the Puritan, the school was second only to the church; education was essential to discover God's will through His book. In 1647 Massachusetts first attempted to establish schools to foil "ye oulde deluder, Satan," and teachers ever since have been expected to do more than train minds. Not only is the school now supposed to make students more productive, happier, richer, and incidentally wiser; it is also supposed to solve racial problems, reduce traffic accidents, entertain the community on Saturday afternoon, and toughen the national muscle and moral fiber.

Schools perform some of these varied functions because other social institutions have stopped doing so. Not many generations ago, education for living took place at home, in church, or on the job. Father, pastor, and foreman taught youngsters the important lessons; teachers taught Latin, rhetoric, and geometry—marks of culture, but hardly essential. The whole fabric of social life was learned at work, in the congregation, or in the family circle. Those who failed these lessons, American children were told, went to jail and, doubtless, to Hell.

Hard work, thrift, and perseverance, or else damnation—the Puritan's ethic was that of most of his countrymen of whatever religious persuasion, and it was an eminently sensible creed for an underdeveloped country. Generations of Americans who never heard of predestination learned early in life that leisure was an evil temptation, that thrift was the surest route to wealth, and that success came to those who kept trying. In that form, Puritanism persists.

Experience on the farm reinforced the message from the Puritan pulpit. Sloth and gluttony were not only sinful but also self-defeating, because hard work and temperance were required to produce and preserve the harvest. Life on the farm was the virtuous life; the independent farmer, who with God's help brought wealth from the earth, was the virtuous man. The independent, self-reliant family farm has provided the example for the family business, and agrarian aspirations, values, and habits persist. Americans still go to school by the agrarian calendar, give farmers a disproportionate share in legislation, protect them from a competitive market, and subsidize them through crop supports and in a host of more subtle ways. The nation's agrarian past has provided a model of virtue and a vision of utopia.

The city, by contrast, has seemed to be a center of sin, where thieves, gamblers, "slickers," and whores have waited impatiently to corrupt hardy sons of the soil. This image of the city as the tempting serpent belies the urban roots of the republic. The first settlers lived in towns as well as on remote, self-sufficient farms. A few mavericks sought the woods; most colonists preferred to cut them down. The frontier was something to be endured, not a sylvan utopia. Most settlers wanted to move with other people; they preferred an inhabited frontier. Neither the Pilgrims, nor the Puritans of Massachusetts Bay, nor the first families of Virginia were backwoods hicks.

Yet the dream of Americans, since the beginning, has been a dream of land. Open land lured Europeans across the Atlantic and their grandchildren across the Alleghenies. A man raised his family on the land, produced his bread and made his fortune from the land, and buried his dead in it. The dream lingers in modern America, few generations removed from the farm. Urban man's longing for that house in the country, for a suburban lawn and garden, and for the preservation of parks and open space testifies to his continuing love for the land.

MOVING

Restlessness has been a national trait since the first Americans left Europe and discovered that Jamestown was not just right either. Americans today lament their lack of roots even as they pack and fill out change-of-address forms; the mobile home symbolizes American rootlessness. This refusal to stay in one place means that large American communities are full of people who were born and educated elsewhere. "Where are you from?" is a standard conversational opening, because all Americans, it is assumed, are from someplace else. So a suburb of Spokane is quite like a suburb of Cincinnati; both are inhabited by people from Illinois.

Social mobility, Americans think, is as much a national characteristic as geographic mobility. Except for the black man, American society does have less rigid class lines than those of most other nations. But social mobility has been easier to believe than to achieve. For every Benjamin Franklin or Andrew Carnegie, there have been millions of Americans who began in rags and were buried in them. Yet, there have also been enough who progressed in skill, status, and property to keep the faith alive.

Geographic and social mobility—like the English political heritage, free enterprise, the Puritan ethic, and the agrarian past—tends to reduce regional and ethnic differences among Americans. To become a united, homogeneous society has long been an American ideal. As an article of national faith, Americans believe that "the melting pot," the frontier, and the schools have fused diverse nationalities (but not different races) into one unique people. Evidence of the inaccuracy of this faith is as near as the closest urban neighborhood. Italian, Jewish, and Polish areas still exist in American cities, to say nothing of black, Puerto Rican, and Mexican enclaves. Many immigrants never reached the frontier; some who did preserved their European culture and language in the isolated wilderness. American schools have always mirrored the community that provided them; local control has reinforced local values.

Yet the myth of the melting pot, however demonstrably inaccurate, is not wholly self-delusion. The goal—one people—is a worthy goal, even if it is not completely achieved. Many ashamed Americans are striving to remove geographic, racial, and religious distinctions that still divide the United States. Regardless of local peculiarities, schools teach the same skills, and for most Americans, education is still the ladder to success. All churches reprove immorality, which they define in almost the same way. Most lodges and clubs begin their meetings by saluting the American flag. Whatever the differences between Forth Worth and Fort Lauderdale, both have a chamber of commerce that exaggerates the city's virtues and solicits settlement. *E pluribus unum* is probably an unattainable ideal, but the United States has progressed in its self-imposed task of making one people from many.

SLAVERY

Since the day in August, 1619, when a Dutch trader unloaded twenty Africans in Jamestown, the black man has been the unacknowledged exception to most generalizations about Americans. In America, we know, all men are created equal, except black men. In America, we know, everyone has an equal chance to get rich, but blacks have substantially less chance than whites. America, we know, has a fluid society, where status depends upon ability, but it also depends upon the color of one's skin. Not all these distinctions were apparent before independence, and not all of them would have developed in quite the same way had slavery not persisted into the nineteenth century. But legal discrimination began early, for seventeenth-century legislation distinguished between white indentured servants, who served a stated term, and black ones, whose permanent bondage passed to their descendants. White Americans grew accustomed early to thinking of blacks as slaves, and the habit has never been completely broken.

The connotations of the word "black" suggest that the prejudice is as old as the language. Neither "black" nor "white" is a neutral word; both have symbolic and emotional overtones. When used together, the two words stand for contrast and suggest irreconcilable opposites. Americans are in some sense the captives of their vocabulary.

The prejudice against Africans went beyond England and far beyond words. Spanish and Portuguese plantations in Latin America also used enslaved black labor. Racial lines in Latin America were less clearly drawn than in the British colonies, and the Roman Catholic Church insisted that baptism and instruction in the faith made blacks the spiritual equals of their masters. Spanish and Portuguese law seemed to make slavery less harsh than British slavery, and less a badge of racial inferiority. But caste lines often replaced racial ones, and Latin American masters, although officially more tolerant, did not in practice treat their slaves more justly than slave-owners in the British colonies.

Slavery in those British colonies was not exclusively a southern phenomenon, although most of the black population lived south of Maryland. As late as 1671 slaves constituted only a small portion of Virginia's population, but the Southern black population grew rapidly, while it declined in the North. Northern involvement extended past the few visible black servants to the white ship captain who traded in slaves without noticeably impairing his Puritan convictions. For too long—for more than two centuries—most white Americans repressed any nagging fear that the mere existence of slavery mocked their lofty moral pretensions.

WHAT IS AN AMERICAN?

"What then," asked Hector St. John de Crèvecoeur in 1782, "is the American, this new man?" Well might Crèvecoeur have asked, for he had guessed wrong on the American Revolution and wound up an exile. But his writing glowed with admiration for Americans, whose uniqueness he believed lay in their expanse of unsettled land, their mixture of nationalities, and their unparalleled chance to improve themselves. Every subsequent foreign visitor has repeated Crèvecoeur's question, and if so inclined, published his answer, as did Alexis de Tocqueville, James Bryce, and a host of less perceptive tourists. Americans, too, continue their search for national identity. In their continuing effort to discover the precise dimension of their behavioral perimeter, Americans are polled, prodded, and poked, and their psyche is bared in countless books and articles each month.

This is one of those books.

CHRONOLOGY

24,000 B.C.   Man first arrives in the New World

1000 A.D.   Viking visitors

1492   Columbus discovers "an Other World"

1517   Luther initiates the Protestant Reformation

1585   Raleigh's Roanoke Island settlement

1607   Jamestown settlement

1620   Plymouth settlement

1732   Georgia granted a charter

II

NEW WORLD ORIGINS

Thomas Jefferson once reminded John Adams, "Before the establishment of the American states nothing was known to History but the Man of the Old World." Jefferson's "Man of the Old World" in several senses was "Man of the New World" as well. Man was not indigenous to the Western Hemisphere. The first arrivals were the Mongoloids, erroneously named Indians by Christopher Columbus. Perhaps 26,000 years ago they crossed over a narrow land strip, now submerged below the Bering Strait, connecting Siberia to Alaska. Slowly they fanned out southward, into the plains of the Southwest, down into Mexico and Peru. They may have been joined in about 3,000 B.C. by Asian voyagers who scattered along the western coasts of the Americas.

These first American settlers developed varied cultures: the Stone Age Mayans in Guatemala and Honduras built monumental palaces and temples; the Aztecs in Mexico and the Incas in Peru developed remarkably sophisticated civilizations. In North America perhaps a million Indians of diverse cultural development, from the Basket-Weavers on the western coast to the politically sophisticated Algonquians along the Atlantic seaboard, subsisted as hunters, farmers, and fishermen. America before Columbus was something more than "a game preserve for squalid savages" (as Theodore Roosevelt once asserted). But when Europeans finally came to the New World in strength, they encountered limited and generally uncoordinated opposition, and they absorbed relatively little of the Indian culture they displaced.

The physical geography of the Americas had a much greater impact upon European colonization. The indented coastline made for widely dispersed settlements—and considerable separatism. The Appalachians slowed westward expansion and forced a concentration of population in the East during the seventeenth and eighteenth centuries; eventually the trans-Appalachian West emerged with its own identity, its own special interest. The arid climate and lack of good harbors slowed settlement on the Pacific coast; the first significant Spanish settlements in California were not established until the 1770s. And the flow of America's rivers proved particularly influential: in the East the rivers provided highways westward as far as the mountains; but in the trans-Appalachian West the rivers ran from north to south, drastically affecting the pattern of migration. The Midwest was linked more closely to the South than to the Northeast until the railroads appeared; then sectional sympathies began to shift.

Pre-Columbian settlements by Europeans did not last. The first European visitors to the New World were probably the Vikings, who established settlements on Iceland, then Greenland, and perhaps Labrador and Newfoundland by 1000 A.D. None were on hand to welcome Columbus or John Smith. The Old World of the Middle Ages had to undergo changes before it could conquer the New.

THE EUROPEAN CONTEXT

But those changes began to occur. The feudal manor, for instance, with its static agricultural economy, had been supplanted by commercial capitalism, with its reliance upon money, rather than service. Nation-states emerged from the alliance of merchants with erstwhile feudal monarchs. Merchants helped finance the standing armies that the Crown used to suppress its rebellious feudal vassals; as a reward the King granted new chartered privileges to his friendly creditors. Order and security were the desire of both merchant and monarch. They worked together for new secular laws, applicable on a countrywide basis. And they cooperated in de-emphasizing canon law and the international (and supranational) influence of the Roman Catholic Church.

The Church, centered in Rome and long supreme in Western Europe, found its religious assumptions and temporal influence increasingly challenged. The apparent inconsistency of the Church's ascetic ideals and secular practices aroused widespread criticism. This criticism had reached a climax in 1517, when Martin Luther nailed on the Wittenberg church door ninety-five theses denouncing papal abuses and deceptions. Essentially a conservative reformer, Luther insisted upon salvation through faith (rather than through the sale of "indulgences") and argued for direct communion with God through the Bible (rather than through the Pope).

In 1536, some fifteen years after Luther was excommunicated, John
Calvin published his famed *Institutes of the Christian Religion* and presented a radically different theology. Calvin saw man as a sinner always
tempted; the death of Christ redeemed but a select few, who were predestined for salvation. Even though a life of good works might not redeem him,
each man had a duty to live piously in the hope of being one of the elect.
Calvin believed that government should glorify God; thus, the state had an
obligation to educate the people in the true faith. His theology sanctified
productive labor and rejected the ascetic practices advocated by the Roman
Catholic Church. Indeed, Calvin saw the production of wealth and its enjoyment as part of the Godly life; God would only reward the pious: poverty
was a badge of sin and often the result of it. Merchants naturally found the
Calvinist ideology more hospitable to commercial activity than the Catholic
doctrine, which considered trade a necessary evil at best.

The precise origin and timing of commercial capitalism is difficult to
identify. It made great gains during the Crusades in the twelfth and
thirteenth centuries. Although the Crusades had a genuine religious basis—
to wrest the Holy Land from the infidel—their side effects were secular.
Ships built to transport the crusaders to the East were later used for trade;
profits were to be made from furnishing supplies to the armies, and the
European invaders discovered eastern luxuries, particularly spices, silks,
drugs, and perfumes, which the crusaders determined to continue to enjoy
after they went home. (Spices were especially appreciated for their value in
preserving foodstuffs.) Thus arose a demand for new commodities that were
conveniently compact and easily shipped long distances; and the demand
was largely matched by an increasing capacity to supply and distribute,
especially to the profit and satisfaction of the strategically placed Italian
merchants. Merchants and consumers along the Atlantic coasts of Europe
were less pleased; they gave serious thought to alternative trade routes to
the oriental sources of the spices and silks in such demand.

But mercantile ambition was not enough. Logistical and technical
support was vital. With the fourteenth century came the Renaissance, a
rebirth of learning and a fresh enthusiasm for scholarship. Out of the
Renaissance came a reacquaintance with man and his past, his achievements in ancient Greece and Rome. And from this reaffirmation of man's
potential came a new view of his abilities to fashion his own earthly fate,
in part with the aid of recent scientific knowledge. The magnifying lens,
gunpowder, the printing press with movable type (1450), clocks, new navi-
gational aids, such as the compass and the astrolabe, all contributed to the
Renaissance man's sense of capability and opportunity and reduced both his
ignorance and his superstitions.

EARLY EXPLORATION

Western Europeans resented the cost of importing eastern goods
through the Mediterranean merchants. The new nation states found their

dependence upon Italian merchants humiliating. The unfavorable trade balance lead to a serious currency shortage, followed in some instances by efforts to prohibit the outflow of gold and silver. The solution seemed simple: the Western European nations must deploy national resources to seek another sea route to the East, a route that the new science and ancient geography suggested must exist.

The first in the national procession was Portugal, unified under King John I in 1383. Unable to expand eastward against the Castilians, the Portuguese looked to the sea for opportunity. John's son, the famed Prince Henry the Navigator, who ruled from 1415 to 1460, never went to sea himself but he did promote exploration of the African coast, first in a search for black slaves, then in quest of Asia and the Indies. Success came in 1488, when Bartholomeu Dias rounded the Cape of Good Hope, pointing the way for Vasco da Gama's voyage to India in 1498. Portugal thus broke the mercantile supremacy of the Italian commercial cities, and the Atlantic ports of Lisbon and Antwerp became new trade centers for Western Europe. Portugal subsequently laid claim to Brazil when, in 1550, trade winds carried Pedro Cabral to the eastern shores of South America.

Spain was also a newly unified nation (Ferdinand of Aragon married Isabella of Castile in 1469). Ironically, it was a Genoese seaman in an unsuccessful search for another route to Asia who gave Spain its early leadership in the New World. Christopher Columbus (1451–1506) was hardly original in his conviction that the earth was round, that sailing due west would bring him to the Indies. His distinction was his comforting underestimate of the distance from Spain to Asia, along with his tenacity in seeking Isabella's support. His success in reaching the Bahamas after a scant six weeks at sea, on October 12, 1492, has obscured his own sense of failure. As a colonizer and administrator Columbus probably deserved his self-criticism. His three subsequent voyages were anticlimactic, futile attempts to reach the Asian mainland. Columbus died a deeply disappointed man. He never fully realized his accomplishment: he never understood that an entire continent barred his way to the East. His monarchs, however, saw the immediate wealth available to them in what Columbus vaguely termed "an Other World," and in 1494, with the aid of a Spanish-born Pope, they divided the New World with their rival nation, Portugal, in the Treaty of Tordesillas. Neither nation knew yet the extent of its pretension. Nor were others ready to offer effective challenge.

France, for instance, found too many domestic distractions at that time to allow serious attention to overseas adventures: until the mid-fifteenth century France was engrossed in expelling the tenacious English from French soil; France then spent nearly a century squabbling with the Pope and dissipating resources in fruitless wars with the Hapsburgs in Italy. Nor were the British in a much better position: Henry VII, who ruled from 1485 to 1509, was naturally parsimonious and in any case preferred to secure his dynasty at home rather than engage in expensive undertakings abroad; his son, the much-married Henry VIII, who ruled from 1509 to 1547, was less close-fisted but no less involved with domestic difficulties, which were due partly to his extravagance and partly to his dedicated quest for a legiti-

Columbus at the royal court of Spain

mate male heir. Thus, for more than fifteen years after Columbus' first voyage the Spanish settlement on Hispaniola, or Haiti, was the only European colony in America. But from this affluent base Spanish explorers soon embarked on an extraordinary sequence of conquests.

The achievements of the conquistadors, the Spanish military adventurers and explorers of the sixteenth century, are as astonishing as they are controversial. By 1508 Alonzo de Ojeda had established a settlement in the region of Panama; five years later Vasco Núñez de Balboa reached the Pacific, and Ponce de León discovered Florida (which he thought an island); between 1540 and 1542 Francisco Coronado clanked his way in heavy armor through Arizona and New Mexico into Kansas; in the same period Hernando de Soto moved westward through Florida to discover the Mississippi River; and Juan Cabrillo sailed up the California coast beyond Monterey to San Diego Bay. More spectacular were the conquest of the Aztecs by Hernando Cortés in 1521 and Francisco Pizarro's subjugation of the Peruvian Incas a decade later.

The ruthlessness of the conquistadors has shadowed the extraordinary achievement. These Spanish conquerors lived in an age of cruelty and intolerance, and their actions reflected the temper of their times. They enslaved and in the process virtually annihilated some native populations, which were then replaced with black slaves from Africa. Still, there was more to Spanish empire than a brutalizing quest for wealth. In less than a

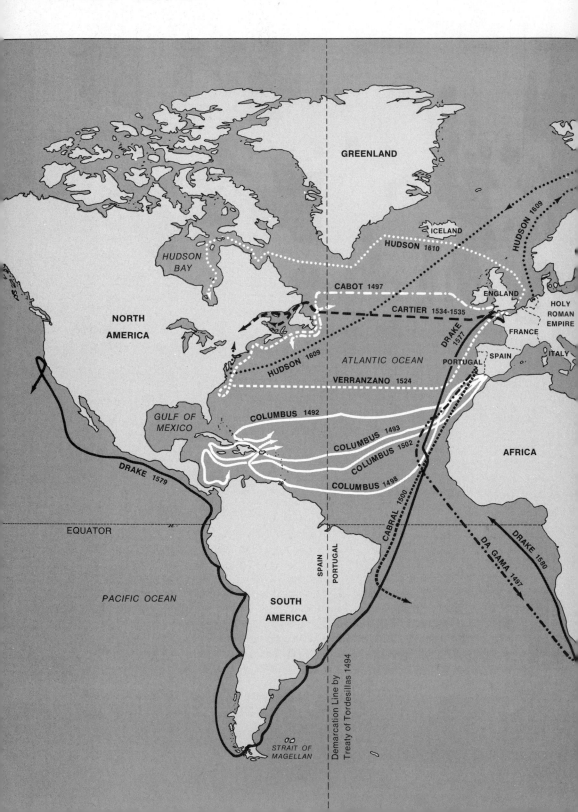

VOYAGES OF DISCOVERY

GREENLAND

HUDSON BAY

ICELAND

HUDSON 1610

CABOT 1497

HUDSON 1609

ENGLAND

HOLY ROMAN EMPIRE

CARTIER 1534-1535

NORTH AMERICA

DRAKE 1577

FRANCE

SPAIN

PORTUGAL

ITALY

ATLANTIC OCEAN

HUDSON 1609

VERRANZANO 1524

GULF OF MEXICO

COLUMBUS 1492

COLUMBUS 1493

COLUMBUS 1502

AFRICA

COLUMBUS 1498

DRAKE 1579

CABRAL 1500

EQUATOR

DRAKE 1580

DA GAMA 1497

PACIFIC OCEAN

SPAIN

PORTUGAL

SOUTH AMERICA

Demarcation Line by Treaty of Tordesillas 1494

STRAIT OF MAGELLAN

century, more than 160,000 settlers scattered over vast territories, governing some 5 million natives and introducing Spanish language, learning, and agriculture. With the sword of the conquistadors came the cross of the Spanish priests. Cathedrals and universities testified to a new civilization in the New World, an empire that, for all the inflexibility of its commercial policy and its centralized government, outlasted the dominions of the British and French.

Both England and France approached the challenge of the New World with much initial hesitation. England advanced its first tenuous claim to North America on the basis of John Cabot's voyage along the Atlantic coast between Newfoundland and the Chesapeake Bay (1497-98). Modestly funded by Henry VII, Cabot sought the western sea route to the Asian mainland. Twenty-six years later Francis I of France sponsored the voyage of Giovanni da Verrazano, who had no more luck than Cabot in the same quest. But unlike Henry VII, Francis I did not give up. In 1534 he supported further voyages by Jacques Cartier, who sailed up the St. Lawrence River to the future sites of Quebec and Montreal. Not until the reign of Elizabeth I (1558–1603) did the English again take up their interest in North America. The first effort came under the leadership of Sir Humphrey Gilbert, whose settlement in Newfoundland in 1583 failed. This was followed closely by Sir Walter Raleigh's unsuccessful colony on North Carolina's Roanoke Island, which disappeared without a trace before 1591. For all England's envy and hostility to Spain, no English colony remained in the New World when the Elizabethan age concluded. And yet, a few years later there were major new settlements planned, and a new age of English colonization began.

ORIGINS OF ENGLISH COLONIZATION

Although English colonization was essentially a seventeenth-century phenomenon, its origins derive partly from the theological controversies of the preceding century. The ideas of Luther and Calvin bitterly divided Western Europe. In England the Protestant revolt gained unexpected encouragement from Henry VIII. Although he himself held no powerful religious convictions, Henry separated from Rome and made himself head of the Church of England, primarily to secure a divorce from Catherine of Aragon. His sickly son and heir, Edward, who ruled between 1547 and 1553, embraced a more serious form of Protestantism, but Mary, who succeeded her half-brother Edward, tried to restore Roman Catholicism. When Elizabeth I, Mary's half-sister, ascended the throne in 1558 she knew she depended upon her Protestant subjects for survival. The Pope regarded Elizabeth as illegitimate and formally excommunicated her in 1570. An astute politician, Elizabeth embraced a theological compromise—a Protestant creed with many Roman Catholic forms. But her Anglican Church was unacceptable to Roman Catholics and Calvinists alike, and she persecuted both impartially.

Elizabeth's Anglicanism probably made conflict with Catholic Spain unavoidable, and she did little to reduce its likelihood. Elizabeth aided the Protestant Dutch in their rebellion against Spain; she quietly encouraged such "sea dogges" as Francis Drake in raids upon Spanish treasure fleets in the New World. Elizabeth even knighted Drake in 1580 after he circumnavigated the world and returned with £600,000 in Spanish bullion—the Queen's share was £263,000. Philip II of Spain sought revenge with his Armada in 1558, but the combination of poor Spanish strategy, miserable English weather, and superior English seamanship allowed Elizabeth's survival. English sea power, an essential ingredient in colonization, was confirmed and available.

There were other vital ingredients for colonization besides religion and sea power. The sixteenth century was a period of rapid economic growth for England. The middle class grew in size and wealth and perfected its business structure and organization. Joint-stock companies, such as the Muscovy Company, the Levant Company, and, the most famous, the British East India Company, reduced risks and increased resources. The English population grew from 3 million in 1485 to 4 million by the end of the sixteenth century. The wool trade flourished, aided by refugees from European wars and religious persecution. Profits from sheep-raising stimulated the enclosure movement, which saw common lands fenced off by private acts of Parliament for the benefit of the sheep-owners. The consequence was a reduction of land for cultivation, a form of technological unemployment, and a sharp increase in the numbers of the landless poor. Food prices rose far beyond the reach of the lower classes, partly because of a decline in food-production, partly as a result of the European price revolution, brought on by the great flow of gold and silver from Spanish America.* By 1600 one in every three Englishmen was on poor relief, not assisted as before by the charitable endeavor of the monasteries, which Henry VIII had dissolved. Nor did the conditions improve rapidly. The early seventeenth century saw disastrous harvests, which drove food prices still higher, and the Thirty Years' War closed off England's European markets, contributing to a severe depression. There was, in short, no lack of incentive for Englishmen to consider leaving home.

ENGLISH COLONIZATION: THE SOUTH

The death of Elizabeth I in 1603 brought to the throne the inept and unpopular Stuart dynasty. Elizabeth's death also precipitated new religious and political dissension that provided the impetus for England's colonization of North America. In 1606, less than two years after making peace with Spain, James I granted two charters, one to the Virginia Com-

*Prices rose 250 percent between 1500 and 1650. Most affected were workingmen, whose real income declined nearly 50 percent, and the old aristocracy, dependent upon a fixed income.

pany of London, which authorized settlement in America between the thirty-fourth and forty-first latitudes, and the other to the west-country investors in the Virginia Company of Plymouth, for settlement between the thirty-eighth and forty-fifth latitudes. Although the grants clearly over-lapped, the companies were warned to keep at least 100 miles apart in their actual settlements. The Plymouth Company made the first move, establish-ing a short-lived colony on the lower Kennebec, but it was the London Com-pany that established the first successful English settlement at Jamestown, Virginia, in April, 1607.

Both Virginia companies had similar motives: a quest for gold, a hope for the long-sought passage to Asia, and a pious interest in converting pagan Indians to Christianity. Such aspirations induced the London Com-pany stockholders to fund three ships, the *Susan Constant*, the *Godspeed*, and the *Discovery*, which sailed from England in December, 1606, with over 100 would-be settlers and considerable optimism. Captain Christopher New-port selected the island of Jamestown as his base, in spite of its malarial nature; his main concern was defense, not physical comfort.

Weak initial leadership and the futility of efforts to find gold pro-duced disaster in the colony's early years; fewer than half the original colonizers survived the first year. But John Smith provided leadership, and John Rolfe found in tobacco an economic base for future growth and pros-perity. In 1616, 2,500 pounds of tobacco were exported; by 1618 the total climbed to 30,000 pounds, and by 1627, it reached 500,000 pounds. A tobacco rush supplanted the hunger for gold: the settlers neglected food cultivation as they planted tobacco seeds everywhere—in graveyards and even in Jamestown streets. In 1619 a Dutch trader stopped by and sold some twenty black slaves, and the future of the Virginia economy seemed assured.

Actually relatively few slaves made their appearance until the end of the century. The London Company resolved to add to the labor supply by establishing the "head right" system, whereby settlers arranged their own transportation and that of dependents in return for 50 acres per "head" transported. Once established, settlers favored the use of white indentured servants, who sold their labor for a period of years to pay for their passage. But black slaves appeared in larger numbers in the 1680s, when the British Royal African Company made its efficient presence known; slave prices declined just as British restrictions were making bondservants more diffi-cult to acquire.

Politically, Virginia afforded an unsteady example for later colonies to follow. After John Smith's early departure, little leadership was forth-coming until Sir Edwin Sandys arrived in 1618; Sandys introduced the head-right system. In 1619 he convened the first representative assembly in the New World, announcing that Virginians would live "by those free lawes" that prevailed in the mother country. Three years later an Indian onslaught reduced the colony's population by some 250, furnishing James I with a handy excuse to revoke the London Company's charter in 1624.

Bankruptcy actually preceded revocation. In its eighteen years the Company invested—and lost—some £250,000 and sent over some 6,000 set-tlers, of whom only 1,200 survived. The Company's leadership sometimes

THE INCONVENIENCIES

THAT HAVE HAPPENED TO SOME PER-
SONS WHICH HAVE TRANSPORTED THEMSELVES

from *England* to *Virginia*, vvithout prouisions necessary to suftaine themselues, hath
greatly hindred the *Progreſſe of that noble Plantation*: For preuention of the like diforders
heereafter, that no man fuffer, either through ignorance or misinformation, it is thought re-
quifite to publish this fhort declaration: wherein is contained a particular of fuch necef-
faries, as either private families or fingle perfons fhall haue caufe to furnifh themfelues with, for their better
fupport at their firft landing in Virginia; whereby alfo greater numbers may receiue in part,
directions how to prouide themfelues.

(Table of provisions: Apparell, Tooles, Victuall, Houshold Implements, Armes — with prices in li. s. d.)

Whofoeuer tranfports himfelfe or any other at his owne charge vnto *Virginia*, fhall for each perfon fo tranfported before Midfummer 1625.
haue to him and his heires for euer fifty Acres of Land vpon a firft, and fifty Acres vpon a fecond diuifion.

The requirements of a properly equipped emigrant to Virginia in 1622. Note confirmation of the "head right" system at bottom of page.

demonstrated a capacity for business sagacity and sometimes for administrative wisdom, but it failed to combine such essential virtues. A succession
of Crown-appointed governors administered Virginia as a royal colony
with infrequent recourse to the representative assembly until 1639, when
the King finally appointed a governor with instructions to convene at least
once a year the house of burgesses Sandys had established.

Maryland was Virginia's first neighbor and the second "plantation
colony" to be founded. The brainchild and possession of a former stock-
holder in the London Company, Maryland was the first proprietary colony.
Sir George Calvert, later made Lord Baltimore, wanted his own colony for
the personal advantage of his family and for the benefit of fellow Roman
Catholics who were encouraged to settle there. His son inherited the royal
charter granted by Charles I in 1632 and began settlement on the northern
bank of the Potomac in 1634. Maryland had several advantages over
its uneasy neighbor: the Calverts pursued a conciliatory policy with the
Indians, selected a healthy settlement site at St. Mary's, and enjoyed provisions imported from Virginia and New England. Like Virginia, Maryland had a form of representative government, subject in this case to the
approval of the proprietor and the governor he appointed.

The Calverts were less successful in realizing their hope for a Catholic
refuge. From the outset Protestants were in the majority, which explains in

22

part Maryland's famous "Act Concerning Toleration" (1649) that granted religious freedom to all Christians who believed in the Trinity.* Five years later the Protestant majority in a rebellious assembly briefly repealed the measure. Political and religious conditions in the mother country affected the Calvert control. In 1691 William and Mary took control of the colony and established the Church of England there. Not until the fourth Lord Baltimore renounced his Catholic faith in 1715 did the Calverts regain proprietary rights, which they exercised until the American Revolution.

Just as Maryland owed much to the benevolence of Charles I, the Carolinas derived their proprietary status from Charles II's sense of obligation to eight court favorites who helped him regain his throne in 1660. He conferred on these gentlemen title to all land between the thirty-first and thirty-sixth latitudes. The 1663 charter gave the Lords Proprietors essentially the same rights enjoyed by the Calverts in Maryland, with the stipulation that Carolina laws were to be agreeable "to the laws and customs of England." In a bid for settlers the Proprietors promised a representative assembly and some religious toleration (for Protestants only). In practice the owners did little for their province beyond outfitting a modest expedition in 1670 that located at Charleston. Huguenot refugees from Catholic repression in France and a constant influx of West Indian planters swelled the settlement; the latter group was primarily responsible for the swift popularity of slavery in the southern portion of the province. By 1700 the population totaled some 5,000 persons, half of whom were slaves working on rice plantations.

To the north, in the Albemarle Sound area, a very different and less pretentious society emerged. Scattered settlers, many from Virginia, pursued diversified agriculture and earned for their region the label of "a vale of humility between two mountains of conceit." But nowhere was proprietary rule particularly effective or rewarding. By 1712 North Carolina had its own governor, and seventeen years later the Crown bought out the surviving Lords Proprietors and the Carolinas became two separate royal colonies.

The last of the southern settlements, Georgia, was established 125 years after the first. The philanthropy, paternalism, and imperialism that produced Georgia illustrated the changing attitudes of England toward colonization and even suggested problems that would contribute to the American quest for independence. The philanthropists were the twenty-one paternalistic proprietors of Georgia: best-known was General James Edward Oglethorpe, a tough-minded military man who looked upon Georgia as a vital buffer between the Spanish in Florida and the English in South Carolina and also as an alternative to debtors' prison for England's poor. But Parliament's grants of some £130,000 to Georgia during its trusteeship went for imperial defense, not to aid debtors. The 1732 charter guaranteed religious freedom to Protestants and fifty acres to each settler. There was no immediate provision for a representative assembly. Few debtors ever

---

*Nonbelief in the Trinity was declared a capital offense, a fact that placed Jews and atheists in some danger.

reached Georgia; they rarely passed the careful scrutiny of the trustees, who also sought to embargo slavery and "Rum, Brandies, Spirits or Strong Waters." Settlers' resentment of such restrictions matched the trustees' rapid disillusionment with their noble experiment. By 1752 the trustees were ready to surrender their colonial ward to the English state, and Georgia joined the ranks of royal colonies, complete with a Crown-appointed governor and an elected general assembly.

ENGLISH COLONIZATION: NEW ENGLAND

Men like Sir John Popham and Sir Ferdinando Gorges, leading figures in the Virginia Company of Plymouth, shared at least some of the humane and expansionist impulses later exemplified by Oglethorpe in Georgia. But the Plymouth Company's Sagadahoc settlement on the lower Kennebec foundered barely a year after its establishment in 1607. When the company reorganized as the Council for New England in 1620, it functioned largely as a landholding group with sea-to-sea title between the fortieth and forty-eighth latitudes. John Mason, an associate of Gorges, joined with him in taking a grant in 1622 from the Council for the area between the Merrimac and Kennebec Rivers, a grant they later divided but did little to develop. Mason eventually gained formal title to New Hampshire and Gorges secured Maine, both confirmed by royal charter in 1629.* But the Council had lapsed into inactivity by 1623 and surrendered its charter to Charles I in 1635, partly to aid the Crown in its conflict with the Puritans who settled in Massachusetts Bay.

One of the more successful New England settlements was that established at Plymouth, the first of the religious commonwealths that came to dominate New England. Plymouth had its origins in the sustained discontent of radical English Protestants with the moderation and compromise within the Elizabethan Church of England. The Puritans wanted to "purify" the Church of much of its ritual (which they saw as Popish); they wished to abolish the Anglican Book of Common Prayer, elevate the Bible as a source of divine truth, and preach the Calvinist doctrines of predestination, original sin, and salvation through grace. Central to their faith was their "covenant theology," whereby God pledged salvation in return for the faith of His chosen few. They extended this covenant concept to the secular realm, arguing for contractual obligations between government and the governed. The Puritans believed that James I and his son Charles were increasingly ignoring those obligations. The "good community" would be one that combined church and state; it would be, ideally, a theocracy.

Puritans found it hard to agree on the best way to achieve their goals—or even to agree on the precise form of their objectives. Most sup-

---

*Migration from Massachusetts Bay led to the annexation of New Hampshire in 1643; in 1679 Charles II separated New Hampshire from the Bay Colony. Massachusetts purchased Maine from Gorges' heirs in 1677.

ported a Presbyterian form of church governance, as in Scotland, Holland and parts of Germany. Others favored independent parishes in which each congregation would choose its minister and church officials. Within this faction there was further division: there were those who wanted to maintain independent churches within the Church of England and those who wanted to separate. Separatists founded their own congregational church in Nottinghamshire in 1606. Faced with mounting persecution, they migrated and finally settled in Holland at Leyden three years later. But the economic and political disadvantages there induced some Separatists, led by William Bradford, to migrate to Virginia.

The emigrants, as an unincorporated joint-stock company, first secured permission and then money from the London Company, and then chartered the *Mayflower* late in the summer of 1620. But the Pilgrims did not of course reach Virginia. After a stormy voyage they sighted Cape Cod and finally disembarked at Plymouth on December 26, 1620. Before landing they drafted the Mayflower Compact, a preliminary form of government based on majority rule.

Lacking supplies and unprepared for the rigors of the New England climate, the Plymouth settlers suffered severely in the first year: less than half their original number lived through the winter, and at one time only seven were well enough to bury the dead. Without Indian assistance, the

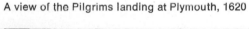

A view of the Pilgrims landing at Plymouth, 1620

leadership of William Bradford, and religious dedication, the Pilgrims might not have survived. The colony was never especially prosperous or populous. The settlers had pledged to work for seven years and to put the fruits of their labor into a common store and assign all profits to the London investors. But this exercise in economic cooperation failed: no profits appeared, and the London merchants withdrew their support. The Pilgrims negotiated a financial settlement, whereby they paid £1,800 in modest install-ments and thus secured title to their land. By 1630, the colony numbered only 300 settlers; in 1691, when William and Mary incorporated the settle-ment into Massachusetts Bay Colony, Plymouth could count a population of only 7,000.

Many substantive differences divided Plymouth from its northern neighbor, Massachusetts Bay. To be sure, Calvinists settled both. But unlike Plymouth, Massachusetts was not an ill-planned, under-financed, meagerly populated Separatist settlement. Rather, Massachusetts Bay must be counted among the most coherent of colonization ventures, well-funded, well-conceived, and well-executed. The Bay Colony began in 1623 as a small fishing post at Cape Ann, financed by Dorchester businessmen. That venture failed and some settlers returned to England, while others moved south to Salem. The Salem settlement attracted the attention of John White, an Anglican minister with Puritan sympathies, who saw a chance for mission-ary work among the Indians. Accordingly, he helped organize the New England Company and secured a patent from the Council for New England. When in 1629 Gorges attempted to revoke the grant, the Company success-fully appealed to Charles I and gained a new royal charter as the Massa-chusetts Bay Company.

The Crown authorized a conventional trading company but failed to stipulate that the colony should be administered from the mother country. This oversight gave the Company its unique opportunity: when economic depression and religious persecution increased in England, John Winthrop and eleven other Puritans joined in the Cambridge Agreement in 1629 and pledged to take themselves and the Company to Massachusetts. Thus began the so-called Great Migration, a flood tide of English emigration. Seventeen ships and some 2,000 settlers crossed to the Bay Colony in 1630; by 1642 about 25,000 had migrated and founded a score of towns radiating from the principal settlement at Boston. Since Puritans numbered only one-fourth of the original expedition, it would seem that economic motives may have outweighed religious reasons in the initial impulse to migrate.

The economic and religious origins of Massachusetts Bay affected its political history. The Cambridge Agreement transformed what began as a trading venture into a corporate act of colonization. When the Company moved to Boston it lost its profit-making identity; the only subsequent fiscal effort of note was an issue of new common stock secured by land in Massachusetts, but this amounted to little more than an act of small-scale philanthropy. Most of the later capitalization of the Bay Colony came from the wealthy Puritans who sold their English property and funded their own migration to Massachusetts. The corporate origin of the colony had an important and unique political consequence when the Company Governor, Deputy Governor, and council of assistants (voted by stockholders) became the first governmental structure of the province itself. In effect, the colony was self-governing, but only by about a fifth of the community. For this was a Bible Commonwealth, in which only good Puritans qualified to become freemen; the freemen constituted perhaps as little as 20 percent of the total number of settlers.

Predictably, the Bay Colony's form of self-government and its preoccupation with its own version of the true religion did not satisfy everyone. Charles I thought he had been tricked and instituted legal action to nullify the 1629 charter, but the English Civil War erupted before he could complete his design. It was not until 1691 that Massachusetts Bay became a royal colony.

Independent spirits, such as Anne Hutchinson and Roger Williams, also issued an early challenge to the religious oligarchy. Anne Hutchinson had arrived with her husband and children (eventually fourteen in number) in 1634; she joined the Boston church but soon questioned its teachings. She suggested others were gifted with deeper spiritual insight than Pastor John Wilson and contended that Christianity was less a matter of good works than of the spirit within, which led to communion with the Lord. She and her assistants were denounced as Antinomians (a label assigned to any who attacked Puritanism). A lengthy controversy concluded with their banishment from the colony in 1638. With her family and friends Anne left for Rhode Island and settled in Portsmouth; later they moved to what is now New York State, where they were butchered by Indians, an atrocity John Winthrop thought clear evidence of the hand of God.

Roger Williams was more fortunate. A Cambridge scholar who championed the rights of Indians, he questioned the land title of the Bay Colony and insisted the power of civil magistrates did not extend to matters of conscience or religion. Williams too was banished. He fled to Narragansett Bay, where he founded Providence in 1636. Other dissenters settled in Rhode Island, or "Rogues' Island," as stalwart Puritans termed the predominantly Baptist settlements. Williams secured a Parliamentary patent for the colony in 1644 and a royal charter from Charles II in 1663.

Never really reconciled to the Rhode Island "latrina of New England," Massachusetts Bay entertained more cordial views toward other neighbors. The Connecticut settlements largely derived from Puritan migration from Massachusetts Bay, such as that led by the Reverend Thomas Hooker in 1636 into the Connecticut River Valley. In 1639 the newly established towns of Hartford, Wethersfield, and Windsor united in the Fundamental Orders of Connecticut, which, keeping an eye on the struggle between Charles I and Parliament, carefully recognized neither but copied faithfully the governmental arrangements of the Bay Colony. In an effort to establish religious uniformity, Connecticut provided a death penalty for atheists and persecuted dissenters from congregational Puritanism. Other Connecticut settlements, such as Saybrook and New Haven, were joined to the main colony under the royal charter of 1662.

THE MIDDLE COLONIES

English expansion into the Connecticut River Valley preempted a Dutch claim to the territory between Maryland and Massachusetts. For Holland the seventeenth century was a golden age when, liberated from Spain, it achieved preeminence as a commercial and maritime nation and collided with England in three major naval wars. Dutch interest in the New World stemmed from Henry Hudson's voyages of exploration—in 1609 he looked for the Northwest Passage along the river now bearing his name. Holland established a trading post on Manhattan Island as early as 1612 and chartered the Dutch West India Company in 1621. The first major settlement came in 1623, soon followed by the famous purchase of Manhattan from Indians for twenty-four dollars. The Dutch built a fort and founded New Amsterdam as capital of their colony of New Netherland. But the settlement grew grudgingly and British, not Dutch, settlers soon moved in. Holland was less crowded than England, and the Dutch lacked the incentives that drove Englishmen to migration. By 1638 the population in New Netherland was actually declining, so Governor Peter Stuyvesant welcomed New England migrants. By 1645 the Dutch West India Company was bankrupt, and its colony became prey to English ambition.

England's resentment of the Dutch presence reached its climax when Charles II found that New Netherland stood in the way of his policy of commercial regulation in the colonies. In 1664 the King granted the territory between the Connecticut and Delaware rivers to his brother and heir, James, Duke of York. When James dispatched an expedition to New Amsterdam, Stuyvesant promptly surrendered, and New Netherland became the proprietary colony of New York. James was virtually absolute monarch of his province. He ruled—from England—until 1686 with moderation but without a representative assembly, and he established English law and the Anglican Church.

James did not exercise his authority over the entire area granted him:* Massachusetts and Connecticut successfully withstood his claims, and the Duke assigned the region from the Hudson to the Delaware to Sir George Carteret and John, Lord Berkeley. Berkeley sold west New Jersey to a Quaker group in 1674; Carteret's heir followed suit with the eastern part in 1680. For a time New Jersey was united as a part of New York, but in 1738 the Crown constituted New Jersey a separate royal colony. Delaware, which had been the scene of the only Swedish settlement (1638–55), was granted to William Penn to be part of his proprietary province in 1682; the three "lower counties" of Delaware were allowed their own

---

*Charles II granted his brother all of Maine between the St. Croix and Kennebec rivers and from the coast to the St. Lawrence, all islands between Cape Cod and the Narrows, and all land from the western boundary of Connecticut to the eastern shore of Delaware Bay.

COLONIZATION: Sequence of settlement[1]

1585 Roanoke Island (Sir Walter Raleigh)
1607 Sagadahoc (Plymouth Company)
1607 Jamestown (London Company)
1620 Plymouth (Pilgrims)
1623 New Netherland (Dutch West India Company)
1630 Massachusetts Bay
1634 Maryland (Cecilius Calvert, 2nd Lord Baltimore)
1636 Connecticut (Thomas Hooker)
        Rhode Island (Roger Williams)
1637 New Haven (John Davenport and Theophilus Eaton)
1638 Swedish Delaware
1663 Carolinas
1681 Pennsylvania (William Penn)
1732 Georgia

[1]Omitted are scattered piecemeal settlements (Maine, New Hampshire) and colonies that changed ownership or shared government (New Jersey, New York).

assembly in 1704 but remained under the Pennsylvania governor until independence.

Pennsylvania itself was not part of James's original grant, but owed its separate existence to Charles II and William Penn, after whose father, Sir William Penn, the colony was named. Penn's father had been a distinguished admiral to whom the Crown owed some $80,000. But the debt alone does not explain Charles II's agreement to grant Sir William's son the area between the fortieth and the forty-second latitudes. Penn's proprietary charter was also testimony to his ability to win royal support in spite of his notorious Quaker faith.

The Quaker sect was established by George Fox, who preached that true Christianity was being subverted by worldly ways. Success had even corrupted the Reformation. Quakers believed in the innate divinity of man, who achieved his salvation by true repentance and faith; they rejected ritual, oaths, war, and a tax-supported church. Many fled persecution in England only to find worse treatment in America. In Massachusetts, for being a Quaker preacher, Christopher Holder was sentenced to thirty lashes with a three-corded whip, three days and nights in a bare cell without bedding or food and drink, and nine wintry weeks in jail without a fire but with a whipping twice a week. (Holder recuperated in Barbados, then returned to Dedham and was brought to Boston to have an ear lopped off.)

Many early fanatical Quakers sought and found martyrdom, but Penn preferred to establish a colony in which the Quaker views on religious and political toleration might be practically applied. He made his request to Charles II in 1680; the King responded, after much deliberation, the next

William Penn

year. The result was a proprietary colony under royal surveillance: Penn was required to maintain an agent in London; he was enjoined to comply with English mercantile regulations and to submit Pennsylvania's legislative actions to the Crown's Privy Council for review. Penn undertook a tremendous publicity campaign, distributing pamphlets in Dutch, French, and German. He proclaimed his commitment to a liberal land policy and to freedom of worship (for all except Catholics and Jews). The Indians posed no threat, thanks to the Iroquois domination of the weak Delawares and Penn's careful negotiations for their land. Philadelphia was founded in 1682; in 1683 some three thousand settlers arrived in the province. Pennsylvania grew more in three years than New Netherland had in forty.

But for Penn the cost was high. He had constant boundary controversies with New York and Maryland, and he was always embroiled with contentious settlers. Because Penn was identified with the exiled James II, whose professed enthusiasm for religious toleration Penn took seriously, William and Mary deprived Penn of both charter and colony for two years, from 1692 to 1694. Frequently in debt, Penn found his proprietary revenues hard to collect; at one time he unsuccessfully attempted to sell his province back to the Crown for £12,000. But Penn's heirs eventually found economic as well as spiritual rewards in this last but most successful of England's proprietary colonies.

Over the span of about 125 years England established its sovereignty in an uneven fashion—along the length of North America, from Maine to Georgia. The exceptions to the English monopoly of North America's Atlantic seaboard were significant: the Spanish presence in Florida and the French thrust into the St. Lawrence were to create major problems in the eighteenth century as well as occasional difficulties in the seventeenth. But the extent of England's influence in North America was impressive, especially to European rivals. It remains a source of astonishment that so small an island should exert such influence and should command so vast a continental domain.

That empire was diverse. Its economy shifted sharply from colony to colony. Religious purpose and identity were no less varied. There were divisions within colonies as well as between colonies. Settlers came from many nations and spoke many languages. Some came in search of a better life, a farm of their own; some sought, and infrequently found, religious toleration; some looked for, and often did discover, religious freedom; and some came involuntarily, to discharge an obligation to an Old World society in the New World. There were royal colonies, proprietary colonies, corporate colonies. But for all there was a measure of self-government, a measure of economic, religious, and political opportunity. And for all there was an association with a small island 3,000 miles distant, a mother country whose concept of their purpose and role proved increasingly at variance with their own.

Suggested Reading

The best treatment of the European context for discovery and colonization is furnished by J. H. Parry, *The Age of Reconnaissance* (1963); for the English scene, see Wallace Notestein, *The English People on the Eve of Colonization** (1954) and, for a more recent account of social conditions, Carl Bridenbaugh, *Vexed and Troubled Englishmen, 1590–1642* (1969).

Samuel Eliot Morison is still probably best known for his *Cristopher Columbus, Mariner** (1955), which first appeared in a two-volume version, *Admiral of the Ocean Sea* (1942); his most recent book, *The European Discovery of America: The Northern Voyages* (1971), is a thoroughly engaging and superbly illustrated treatment of all known voyages across the North Atlantic to the New World prior to 1600. Early Spanish colonization is admirably presented in Charles Gibson, *Spain in America** (1966), and Paul Horgan, *The Spanish Conquistadores* (1963). Of the several excellent studies of the first Americans, the best are Harold E. Driver, *Indians of North America** (1961), and Alvin M. Josephy, Jr., *The Indian Heritage of America* (1968). C. W. Ceram's *The First Americans* (1971) is an unusually readable review of archeological discovery in the New World. For British colonization, see Wesley Frank Craven, *The Southern Colonies in the Seventeenth Century* (1949), Samuel Eliot Morison's very readable *Builders of the Bay Colony** (1930), and Richard S. Dunn, *Puritans and Yankees, The Winthrop Dynasty of New England 1630–1717* (1962).

For an excellent introduction to New England Puritanism, see Alan Simpson, *Puritanism in Old and New England** (1955), and Darrett B. Rutman, *American Puritanism: Faith and Practice** (1970).

*Available in paperback edition

CHRONOLOGY

1636 Harvard College founded

1637 Pequot Indian War

1643–84 Confederation of New England

1650–96 Navigation Acts

1662 Half-Way Covenant passed by Congregationalists

1675–76 King Philip's War

1676 Bacon's Rebellion

1685–88 Dominion of New England

1689–91 Leisler's Rebellion

1692 Salem witchcraft delusion

1704 *Boston Newsletter,* first colonial newspaper, appears

1726–56 Great Awakening

1735 *Zenger* Case

1754 Albany Congress proposes Plan of Union

1768–71 North Carolina Regulator War

III

COLONIAL AMERICA

The British as empire-builders were more noted for their proclivity for migration than for a capacity for imperial planning and organization. The British as colonists revealed a comparable lack of foresight and comprehension. They did of course bring with them social and political traditions that influenced colonial institutions. But such intellectual and cultural baggage proved less helpful when the colonists confronted problems of intercolonial and imperial relations. Here was political terrain as uncharted as the New World before Columbus.

THE COLONIAL ECONOMY

Although the colonists might have arrived unprepared for some political battles, they were well equipped to pursue their professions and develop a healthy economy. About 90 percent of American colonists engaged in agriculture. They adopted some Indian crops—maize, or Indian corn, tobacco, sweet potatoes, pumpkin, squash, wild rice, potatoes—and brought others from the Old World—small grains, clover, forage grass, citrus fruit, farm animals (except turkeys). Draft animals enabled the European immigrants to improve significantly upon Indian cultivation techniques, but the very abundance of land argued against scientific agriculture. Colonists rarely rotated or fertilized their crops; after they ruined the soil in one area, they cleared another and ruined that, too. Equipment was primitive, and abandoned farms were commonplace.

Throughout the colonial period Americans clustered along the Atlantic seaboard, where they found the greatest opportunities and the fewest obstacles. The coastal plain, which varied in breadth and soil quality, was not a primeval forest; Indians had been clearing land for their own farms for generations. The Narragansetts, for instance, had cleared land up to ten miles inland; just a few miles upriver from the starving Jamestown settlers were hundreds of acres of cleared land ready for colonists' crops.

The southern "plantation" colonies were properly known for the cash crops they raised for export. The wide coastal plain, with its rich soil and long growing season, favored the cultivation of tobacco in the northern tier and of rice and indigo in the two southernmost colonies. Tobacco cultivation depleted the soil especially rapidly and tied its producers to a one-crop economy that was highly vulnerable to price fluctuations. Initially, the market price was extremely attractive—three shillings a pound in 1619 —but within a decade it had dropped to one-twelfth of that sum. Over the next century and a half the price hovered around two pence a pound and sometimes dropped to as low as one penny—occasioning plant-cutting riots in Virginia in the 1680s. By 1690 production had risen to 20 million pounds per year and proceeded to increase fivefold by the eve of the Revolution. Declining prices forced tobacco farmers into large-scale, plantation-style production and into heavy dependence upon slave labor. Much the same was true for the South Carolina rice-growers, whose production rose from 90,000 barrels in 1740 to 155,724 barrels in 1771. Indigo, a vital textile dye, was introduced to the southern mainland in the 1740s and encouraged by British subsidies of six pence a pound; by the 1770s over 1 million pounds of indigo were raised annually. The Revolution wiped out the subsidies and ended production of this cash crop.

Grain was the basis of colonial agriculture. In the South, Indian corn, raised primarily for livestock, was probably more valuable than tobacco. The back country grew wheat, oats, barley, and rye. From the Potomac to the Connecticut rivers, with some exceptions in New York, small farms raised wheat and other cereal crops, as well as fruits and vegetables. With ample wheat for export, milling became an important industry in New York.

Subsistence farming was a part of the economic life of all the mainland colonies, but it increased in importance northward from the middle colonies to New England. New England's farms were mainly devoted to Indian corn, followed by oats, rye, barley, and flax. Dairy farming was popular in Connecticut and Rhode Island, where a few slave traders practiced a plantation-style agriculture, and there was some sheep raising, particularly on the offshore islands where the threat of wolves could be controlled.

Throughout the British colonies the agricultural economy and landholding opportunities interacted. Although many settlers came to America to escape surviving vestiges of feudalism, a feudal farm system did endure in isolated instances. In Maryland and New York, for example, large landowners (called patroons by the Dutch) had authority to hold their own manorial courts; such courts sustained the Lord's feudal privileges and regulated his tenants' lives. South Carolina's Lords Proprietors attempted to establish a feudal class structure. More significant was the quitrent, first a feudal payment to the local Lord for protection and then a form of annual land tax. It was rarely invoked in New England but was commonplace elsewhere. Local forms of feudal tribute varied: usually the quitrent was paid at a rate of two to four shillings per hundred acres; in New York one landowner paid one beaver skin annually for a million-acre tract; in Pennsylvania another magnate contributed one red rose annually. In the royal colonies the income went to the Crown; in the proprietary provinces a few patient and conscientious proprietors collected a sizable revenue from quitrents.

These feudal practices were not alone responsible for the genuine economic inequalities that prevailed in colonial America. There was ample opportunity for landed wealth. In the middle and southern colonies protected estates inherited only by the first-born son nourished the growth of large landholdings and encouraged a new aristocracy. The head-right system introduced in early Virginia was widely copied. It enabled the wealthy to become wealthier by funding additional immigrants. In the eighteenth century the head-right system fell into disfavor, but it was still easy to have a county surveyor (particularly in the southern colonies) lay aside an unappropriated area to which title might be secured from the Governor.

Land hunger was real, and it was gratified: William Byrd II inherited 26,000 acres and left 180,000 to his profligate heir in 1744; Robert Carter, also of Virginia, left an estate of 300,000 acres, 1,000 slaves, and £10,000 in cash; Benjamin Fletcher, Governor of New York from 1692 to 1698, is estimated to have given his friends about 75 percent of the land then available in the colony. Landholding arrangements were usually different in New England, where geography combined with tradition to favor villages in which each family received a small lot in the township and perhaps a hundred acres in surrounding tracts. Frequently ministers and magistrates acquired the best land. The result was provincialism and clannishness. Newcomers were unwelcome; denied a free share in communal land, they were often forced to attempt a purchase or, more likely, move to the frontier.

But for all the inequality of its distribution, land was available, and as a partial consequence, labor was not. Colonists attempted to meet the persistent shortage by producing large families and using servants, both white and black. The white bondsmen, or indentured servants, were often free immigrants who pledged their labor for three to seven years in return for their trans-Atlantic passage. Yet a significant number—possibly 50,000 or more—came involuntarily in discharge of court sentences for major crimes. British courts equated fourteen years of servitude in America with capital punishment in the mother country; seven-year terms were assigned for less serious crimes. Benjamin Franklin once suggested that, at the very least, Americans should return England's favor by shipping rattle-

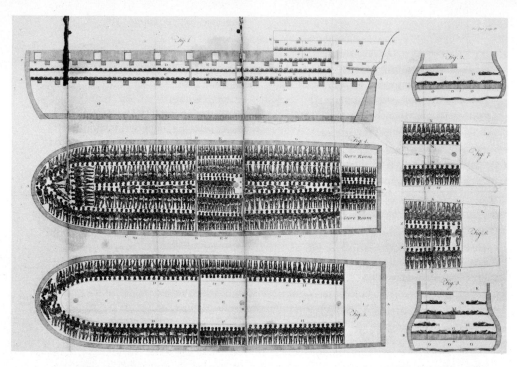

Conditions on the slave ships. The sketch at the bottom is the only known live drawing executed on a slave vessel.

snakes to the mother country. Yet there never seemed enough white bondsmen; they were costly, and their servitude was temporary. For many Americans the answer was the black slave.

The eighteenth century was the true age of colonial slavery: Virginia had 16,400 slaves in 1700; by 1760, with 140,600 slaves, almost half the Virginia population was black; by 1776 one-fifth of the total colonial population were slaves and could be found in all the British colonies. Few expressed concern, other than owners who feared that unrestricted importation of blacks would drive prices down, thus depreciating their investment. Even Philadelphia's Quakers owned blacks and supported savagely repressive legislation designed to sustain slavery. There were a few instances of private manumission of slaves, but some of those seem to have been prompted by a desire to avoid the cost of keeping a slave in his old age. Protest, while grudging and slow, did come: in Pennsylvania in 1765 the Society of Friends disowned Quakers who imported slaves; three years later the Quakers' Yearly Meeting urged general manumission—but with limited results. There were only a few critics, like John Woolman, who seriously addressed the moral issue of slavery before the Revolution.

The scarcity of labor inhibited the colonies' capacity to industrialize, as did the lack of capital and difficulties with transportation. But there was never a lack of colonial incentive to overcome such obstacles: British goods cost about twice as much in America as in Britain, and the colonial trade imbalance created a serious shortage of currency for exchange with the mother country.

These facts of colonial economic life led virtually every farmer and planter to undertake small-scale manufacturing to produce cloth, soap, candles, furniture, and crudely fashioned tools and utensils. Iron smelteries, some subsidized by colonial legislatures, sprang up throughout the colonies. Domestic bounties also encouraged distilleries and cloth mills. But the strongest encouragement came from England itself. Beginning in 1705 the mother country launched a program designed to foster the production of needed naval stores—tar, pitch, turpentine. The British also purchased colonial ships and ship timber. (Perhaps 75 percent of American commerce was carried in colonial-built ships by 1775.) But the English viewed other colonial manufacturing activity less favorably. The Hat Act of 1732 tolerated the colonial hat industry to the extent that no hats could be exported from the colony of manufacture; the Iron Act of 1750 encouraged the colonial iron industry only in its production of bar and pig iron, which had then to be manufactured into finished goods in England.

By the mid-eighteenth century Americans were able to meet an astonishing number of their own economic needs. Massachusetts produced shoes; Pennsylvania manufactured wool stockings; paper production and publishing were widespread, and breweries and distilleries even more so. Timber and furs contributed to the economy of all the colonies. The fishing industry was a mainstay of New England's economy from the beginning. A major whaling industry, with a fleet of 360 ships, produced some 45,000 barrels of sperm oil by the 1770s. This growing sophistication of the colonial economy brought America into increasing commercial conflict with the mother country.

COLONIAL COMMERCE

By the seventeenth century, England, in company with most European nation-states, had come to believe that its power (and possibly survival) depended upon its wealth. Since the acquisition of riches meant prosperity and national security, England took steps to promote and regulate this aspect of its economic life. This view of national economic purpose, known as mercantilism, powerfully affected the English perception of the American colonies. The English considered the colonies to be vital sources of raw materials and important markets for English manufactures. The possession of colonies enhanced national self-sufficiency, security, and power. A favorable trade balance and the husbanding of bullion were the mercantilist goals of English statesmen throughout the history of the first British empire.

In this context England began to regulate colonial commerce as early as the 1620s, when the Crown decreed that Virginia's tobacco had to be shipped exclusively to the mother country in British vessels. At the same time tobacco was forbidden to be grown in Great Britain, and very high import duties were imposed upon foreign-grown tobacco. While England was caught up in its Civil War in the 1640s, the Dutch threatened to monopolize colonial trade. But once Cromwell had triumphed over Charles I, England was able to address the Dutch commercial threat. The result was the interregnum navigation laws that required (1) foreign ships trading with the English colonies be licensed; (2) goods from Asia, Africa, or America be shipped in English ships; and (3) intercolonial trade be conducted in English ships. (English ships included colonial vessels.)

But this was merely a beginning. In 1660 Charles II catered to English mercantile interests with the Navigation Act that restated the earlier interregnum legislation and added an enumerated list of items—initially, sugar, tobacco, and cotton—that the colonies could send only to England or to another English colony. Three years later the Staple Act required most European goods destined for America to be shipped via England. And a decade later Charles supported the Plantation Duty Act, which imposed duties on enumerated articles to be paid by colonial shippers at the port of export. New England's infractions of the Navigation Acts system provoked this legislation, which in turn occasioned the dispatch of British customs officials to the colonies. William and Mary codified earlier legislation in 1696, adding new enforcement provisions through vice-admiralty courts, which did not require a jury trial. Colonial laws contrary to these Navigation Acts were declared automatically void.

In the eighteenth century England progressively lengthened the enumerated list to the point that most colonial exportations were covered. Forced to sell to—and to buy from—England, even tobacco-planters and rice-planters found themselves earning less and paying more in a noncompetitive market. The major beneficiaries seemed to be English middlemen whose charges for freight, handling, insurance, and distribution cut deeply into plantation profits. Northern colonies, lacking staples welcome in England,

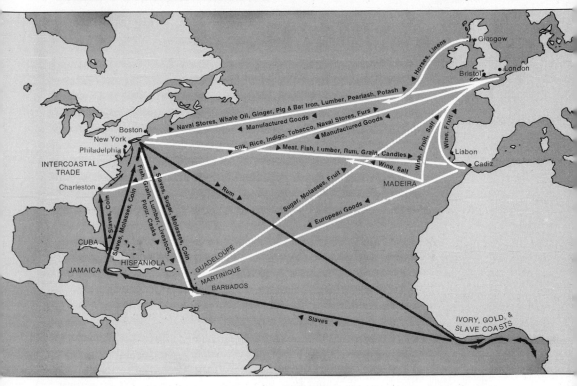

were driven to complex trade patterns to earn currency with which to buy English goods. New Englanders shipped fish and lumber to Spain and Portugal in return for wines, fruits, and coin, which they then took to the mother country for English goods. Or they shipped northern wheat, fish, and other provisions to the Caribbean in return for currency, sugar, molasses, and rum, much of which in turn was again exchanged for English goods.

Perhaps the best known of the triangular trade patterns involved the export of Boston rum to Africa, where it was exchanged for black slaves, who were in turn shipped to the British West Indies for coin and molasses, which was used to manufacture more rum. Molasses also attracted British attention in the form of the Molasses Act of 1733, a measure that imposed a duty of sixpence per gallon on colonial imports of foreign molasses. Since the British West Indies could not meet mainland colonists' needs, this could have been particularly burdensome. But the measure went unenforced, and the British Treasury never budgeted income from its duties.

The northern colonies probably fared better than those to the south; English support of New England shipbuilding fostered a major currency-earning industry, one that enabled Boston to emerge as an important distributor of goods to other colonies.

But currency was still hard to come by. The colonists invariably needed more gold and silver to conduct domestic and foreign trade. They attempted various expedients, such as commodity money: tobacco was designated legal tender in Virginia and Maryland, as were beaver and

COMMERCIAL REGULATION

1650-51   Interregnum navigation laws (Cromwell)
1660   Navigation Act: enumerated list (Charles II)
1663   Staple Act
1673   Plantation Duty Act
1696   Navigation Act: vice-admiralty courts (William and Mary)
1732   Hat Act
1733   Molasses Act
1750   Iron Act

wampum in New York. But this currency was cumbersome and subject to debasement by spoilage. Promissory notes and bills of exchange helped, but the favored devices were illegal mints and printing presses. Massachusetts set up a mint in 1652 and issued coins until 1684, when Charles II stepped in. Between 1730 and 1750 there was widespread colonial resort to paper money, usually unsecured and rapid in its depreciation. Even some New England merchants welcomed the British act of 1751 prohibiting legal tender bills of credit in that region.

British regulation of the colonial economy occasioned inconvenience and irritation, but it was hardly tyrannical or exploitative. Some colonists' difficulties reflected their own improvidence and the easy credit given them by English merchants. England was the natural financial and distribution center for colonial commerce and a logical source of capital funds. Colonial shipping benefited from protective features of the navigation laws, as did colonial recipients of British subsidies for indigo and naval stores. In any case British enforcement of those measures to which colonists objected was remarkably lax. Smuggling was commonplace, and customs officials were easily bribed. Although the mother country placed its own interests above those of the colonies, England did practice an early form of imperial preference that gave Americans a well-protected marketplace, often at the cost of the English consumer.

COLONIAL SOCIETY

Obviously, any reference to the "English" colonies must be qualified. Large numbers of non-English immigrants made their contributions to what Hector St. John Crèvecoeur called "this promiscuous breed, that race now called Americans. . . ." The largest non-English group was the Scotch-Irish, who settled in western Pennsylvania in large numbers; some of them were refugees from the unsuccessful uprisings against the first two Hanoverian monarchs (in 1715 and 1745), others came from the ill-fated settlement in northern Ireland. Germans, many of whom were refugees from the Thirty Years War (1618–48) and its bitter aftermath, received a warm welcome from William Penn. They kept to themselves and retained their own language and customs. (The Amish, still abundant in Lancaster county, are the best-known Pietist survivors.) In addition, there were numbers of Dutch (in New York), Huguenot refugees from France (prominent in South Carolina), some Jews (first admitted to New Amsterdam), and Welsh, Swedes, Irish, and Swiss. All could acquire British citizenship after 1740, when Parliament stipulated a seven-year residence prerequisite. Of the fifty-six signers of the Declaration of Independence eighteen were of non-English ancestry and another eight were born outside the colonies.

This diverse population almost doubled every twenty-five years after 1700: there were some 200,000 people in 1688, about 1.8 million by 1750, and 2.5 million by 1775. Early marriage was common, and large families were the rule: the average family increased by one child every two years. The largest concentration of population was in the southern colonies—in 1763 some 700,000 people, of whom over a third were black slaves.

The colonial population remained predominantly Protestant, with the majority belonging to Calvinist denominations, such as the New England Congregational, the Presbyterian, and the Dutch and German Reformed churches. The balance were Baptists, Quakers, Lutherans, Pietists, Methodists, Roman Catholics, and Jews. The Church of England did not prosper in America, in spite of support from the mother country, except in Maryland and Virginia. Local autonomy was a common colonial objective of various religious groups, among them the evangelical Baptists, Pietistic German sects, such as the Mennonites, Moravians, and Dunkers (Baptists who believed in triple immersion), and the Congregationalists.

The Congregationalists emerged as a bulwark of oligarchic and theocratic conservatism in New England. In seventeenth-century Massachusetts, attendance of the Congregational Church was required by law, and Sunday, with its two sermons, was the emotional and intellectual climax of the Puritan week. According to Calvinist doctrine, man's instincts were naturally evil, to be suppressed for the good of his soul. On Sunday Congregationalists were forbidden to "make mince pies, dance, play cards, or any musical instrument, save the drum, trumpet and Jew's harp." But with the passage of time came concessions; in 1662 the Half-Way Covenant permitted baptism to children of "half-way" members—persons in good standing with the church but who had not testified to their experience of God's grace. By the end of the century it was possible to take communion without a prior public confession to faith.

Even so, there were resurgences of religious fanaticism, of which the best known and most lamentable was the witchcraft delusion in Salem. In 1692 the two young daughters of the local minister began to behave eccentrically, and they blamed their conduct on neighbors whom they identified as witches. A special court soon found its hands filled as the witchcraft mania infected the entire community. By the time Governor Phips was persuaded to abolish the court it had legally murdered 20 persons, including 14 women and a Congregational minister. Fifty who had confessed to being witches survived—the prosecution contended the Devil would not permit his genuine servants to admit their identity—and another 150 still awaited trial as the panic passed. But events of the times—the bloody King Philip's War (1675–76), which cost the lives of one in every twenty New Englanders and

Drama at Salem: the trial of George Jacobs for witchcraft

was viewed as God's judgment upon his errant children, a smallpox epidemic, outbreaks of major fires, Cotton Mather's books on witchcraft—all fed the climate of hysteria and superstition that made the tragedy possible.

In the 1720s a broad new wave of evangelism threatened the Puritan oligarchy, as well as the unity of other sects. The Great Awakening was a spontaneous interdenominational revival movement, which began with the vigorous preaching of Theodore Frelinghusen and Gilbert Tennent, followed in the 1730s by Jonathan Edwards and George Whitefield. In Northampton, Massachusetts, Edwards sought to communicate to his congregation the intensity of his own religious convictions, to demonstrate anew the omnipotence and splendor of Calvin's God. Whitefield, a traveling English evangelist and the herald of American Methodism, made seven trips to the American colonies to urge the spiritual regeneration of his vast audiences and to argue for a return to Christ and an end to sectarianism. But a reaction against such emotional fervor followed. Edwards' relentless exhortation led to his dismissal from the Northampton parish in 1750. Whitefield's crowds diminished in size. Schisms appeared among many sects: some conservative Puritans preferred the quiet comfort of Anglicanism; revivalist "New Side" Presbyterians separated from the "Old Side" conservatives until 1758. The outcome of the Great Awakening was greater religious diversity, significant weakening of ministerial authority, more religious toleration, and a greater emphasis upon the importance of the individual.

Although America's Old World heritage favored formal education only for the aristocratic few, many Protestants who settled in the colonies sought to make all society at least literate. The Puritans in particular argued that

42

all should be able to read the Bible in order to study the source of divine truth, and that ministers should be scholars of Greek and Latin in order to read the original records of the Christian faith. The concept of public education was imperfectly grasped and infrequently practiced, but Massachusetts provided some leadership with a law in 1647 requiring a schoolmaster in a town of 50 families and a Latin grammar school for communities with more than 100 families. The fine for noncompliance was only £5, however. Other New England colonies passed similar legislation, with the exception of Rhode Island, where there was concern that public schools might lead to coercion in matters of private conscience.

Religious division unquestionably inhibited the growth of public education. Anglicans in New York opposed the school system established by the Dutch; Roman Catholics in Maryland resented Anglican efforts on behalf of public education in that colony; Quakers quoted George Fox, who said, "God stood in no need of human learning" and who termed Greek and Latin "the unsanctified work of pagans." And in the South planters grouped together to hire a schoolmaster for the private tutoring of their children: generally southerners saw public education as a badge of poverty and an act of charity, although this view did not allow education for slaves.

Higher education fared better. A majority of the colonies had colleges by 1770, usually supported by the locally dominant church. Harvard was founded in 1636, but no degrees were conferred until 1642, and no charter was granted until 1650 (by the General Court, wtih doubtful authority). The College of William and Mary was founded in 1693 and Yale in 1701. "The College Enthusiasm," as Ezra Stiles of Yale termed the wave of new colleges

George Whitefield, a Great Awakener

after 1746, was a consequence of the Great Awakening and the renewed colonial concern for denominational education. Twice as many colleges were founded between 1746 and 1769 as in the preceding century, and the number of new colleges doubled again between 1769 and 1789. Many of the new colleges sought to reduce costly denominational conflicts: King's College (Columbia) included representatives from four denominations in addition to the Anglican members; Rhode Island College (Brown) tolerantly named Baptists, Quakers, Congregationalists, and Anglicans as trustees. "There is so much defect in all [of us]," commented Stiles, "that we all need forbearance and mutual condescension."

The curriculums of these institutions, open only to men, were generally similar. Logic, rhetoric, philosophy, grammar, ancient history, Greek, Latin, and Hebrew were common course requirements. Some interest in science and modern languages developed at King's College and Benjamin Franklin's Philadelphia Academy. Complaints about the relevance of college programs were common, as were charges of lax academic standards. "Ignorance wanders unmolested," and "after four years dozing there, no one is ever refused the honours of a degree." One real test was financial, for the fees were only within reach of the wealthy.

If the American colonists had depended exclusively upon formal educational institutions for their learning and wisdom they might well have remained ill-informed and untutored. Fortunately, this was far from the case. The colonists were an astonishingly bookish people. John Adams spoke for many when he asked in his diary, "How can any man judge, unless his mind has been opened and enlarged by reading?" Book collecting was popular, and collections ranged from the 40 volumes Peter Jefferson left his son Thomas to the 3,500 volumes amassed by William Byrd II. Even a Baltimore County ironmaster, Joseph Smith, left a modest estate comprising clothing, a pen knife, two razors, an ink pot, and Rapin's *History of England*. For those less fortunate there were subscription libraries; Franklin founded the first in 1731 in Philadelphia,* and others quickly followed in Charleston, Newport, New York, and Lancaster. By 1766 there was a total of sixty such libraries. The book shelves were crowded with volumes on theology, geography, law, and particularly on history and politics. Most were imported from the mother country, but many were printed in America, often as a sideline to newspaper publishing.

The first colonial newspaper, the *Boston Newsletter*, had appeared in 1704; between 1713 and 1745 some twenty-two newspapers were launched, and by 1765 every colony could boast of its own paper. At first the press, modest in size and ambition, focused upon advertisements, shipping news, and local items of interest. Soon attention extended to the larger world of colonial and international politics.

Historians have exaggerated the degree to which the famous case of John Peter Zenger's *New-York Weekly Journal* provided freedom of the colonial press. Zenger's acquittal after his indictment for seditious libel meant freedom for Zenger, not for the press; as late as 1804 New York

*The Library Company of Philadelphia still survives; in 1773 it was located in Carpenter's Hall and served effectively as the first Library of Congress.

The first colonial newspaper

courts were rejecting truth as a defense against charges of criminal libel, and throughout the period of the Revolution Patriot intimidation of the press was rampant.

To some extent, the proliferation of American colleges, libraries, and newspapers was a reflection of the growing urbanization of the colonies. Such cultural amenities prospered in the towns and cities. With the growth of commerce and the increasing sophistication of the economy, primitive trade centers became urban centers. Philadelphia, the largest colonial city, had a population of some 30,000 by 1770; Boston was close behind, followed by New York, Newport, Charleston, Salem, New Haven, Baltimore, Norfolk, and Wilmington. Annapolis and Williamsburg were political centers with seasonal social importance. The towns and cities might have contained only 10 percent of the total population, but they exerted a cultural and political influence far beyond mere numbers. The colonial cities were commercial centers, not industrial sites. Even so, their polluted surface wells, open sewers (until the 1740s), and uncollected garbage would have disturbed any thoughtful ecologist. Urban problems were not unknown in colonial America.

COLONIAL POLITICS

From the outset of English colonization settlers made known their concern for representative self-government patterned after that of the mother country. Companies, proprietors, and the Crown alike found themselves obliged to broaden the base of colonists' political involvement in the affairs of their province. Significant and steadily increasing assumptions of self-regulation were common to all English colonies in North America. Politics soon became an avenue to power, wealth, and reputation in the New World as well as in the Old. Although the British Crown was also the colonists', Englishmen in America soon sought to define legislative power so that its center of gravity would be in the colonies.

The titular head of government in all colonies was the Governor. In Connecticut and Rhode Island he was elected by the legislature, and in Maryland, Delaware, and Pennsylvania, he was named by the proprietor. In the eight royal colonies the Crown appointed the Governor. These royal Governors were representative of the British governing class: there were those such as Queen Anne's cousin, Lord Cornbury, a drunkard and an embezzler given to wearing women's clothes; there were others like Alexander Spotswood of Virginia or William Shirley of Massachusetts, men of distinct ability who governed with skill and intelligence. The Governor of a royal colony held office at the King's pleasure; sometimes that pleasure was of brief duration, but tenure averaged five years. Each Governor's authority was more apparent than real: his approval of colonial legislation was essential but could be overridden by the Crown; he could summon and dissolve the colonial Assembly, and sometimes he could control his Council, the upper house, but his influence over the lower house steadily diminished.

Colonial legislatures were generally bicameral; the Council was usually selected by the Governor, sometimes from a listing furnished by the lower house. Initially prestigious, the Council was a colonial version of England's Privy Council with combined judicial, executive, and legislative functions. Although gubernatorial acts required the approval of Council members, their independence was restrained by the fact that they held office at the Governor's pleasure. The lower house clearly had greater independence: elected by qualified property owners and usually weighted in favor of the tidewater gentry, the colonial Assembly saw itself as an equivalent to England's House of Commons, particularly in regard to personal privilege, freedom of debate, and control over appropriations, including the Governor's salary. If the Governor ran counter to the wishes of his colony's Assembly he could anticipate financial harassment: as New Yorkers noted in 1741, they would "starve him into compliance." Just as in England Parliament used its power of the purse to bring the Stuarts to heel so did the colonial Assembly extend its power at the Governor's expense.

Throughout the colonial experience there was division and dissension, particularism and separatism, both within and among the colonies. The

causes of internal division—and the open insurrection they sometimes produced—varied from colony to colony. Frequently, economic and political
frustration were factors; as the earliest settlers grew in prosperity and
power, they came to dominate provincial political life, provoking the resentment and anger of recent immigrants, who were excluded from the charmed
inner circle of influence. Constant infusions of immigrants and continuous
expansion of the economy aggravated social, class, and political friction.
Bacon's Rebellion in Virginia, the Leisler Rebellion in New York, and the
Regulator movements in the Carolinas were manifestations of this discontent.

Indian attacks on the Virginia frontier occasioned Bacon's Rebellion,
but charges of political privilege and discriminatory taxes aroused public
support for the intemperate demagogue Nathaniel Bacon. The precise
motives for Bacon's angry march against the Governor, Sir William Berkeley, in 1676 are unclear, owing to Bacon's sudden death from dysentery ("the
flux") and the vigorous retribution taken by Berkeley against the rebels. In
the Leisler revolt (1689–91) Jacob Leisler, a contentious German merchant
in Manhattan, led a city mob against the entrenched oligarchy; he subsequently summoned a representative assembly that moved against the trade
monopoly of New York merchants and gave more power to local communities. Leisler's was a class struggle, one that the honest but hot-tempered
German mismanaged; charged with treason by governor Henry Sloughter,
Leisler and his brother-in-law were hanged in May, 1691.* The Carolina
Regulators are less easily categorized. In South Carolina in the 1760s and
1770s there was relatively little hostility among the tidewater, frontier, and
back-country sections; here the Regulation movement took the form of a
vigilante group acting against lawlessness on the frontier, an effort toward
more, not less, government. In North Carolina, however, the Regulators
were western debtors protesting extortion and corruption on the part of the
eastern establishment headed by Governor William Tryon. Government
forces triumphed over the Regulators in a comic-opera battle in 1771, and
Tryon promptly executed seven rebel leaders. Many Regulators subsequently
sided with the Loyalists in the Revolution, because they identified patriot
leadership with the ruling aristocracy.

If Americans had difficulty discovering unity in a single colony, they
found greater challenge in their periodic experiments with intercolonial
union. Of all such efforts before 1774, the Confederation of New England
was most nearly autonomous. Created in 1643 when the mother country was
diverted by domestic divisions between Crown and Parliament, the Confederation was a conscious colonial effort to meet common dangers from the
Dutch, French, and Indians. Massachusetts Bay, Plymouth, Connecticut, and
New Haven constituted the membership of this Puritan confederacy and
appointed eight commissioners to deal with Indian problems, foreign
threats, and internal differences. The so-called United Colonies had limited

---

*In 1695 Parliament reversed the verdict and returned Leisler's property to his
family; Leisler's personal resurrection was clearly more difficult.

effectiveness: the commissioners had only an advisory role, and member colonies were overawed by the preponderant power of Massachusetts. The commissioners did assist with several boundary disputes and brought some coordination to the New England effort against King Philip of the Wampanoags and his allies in the bloody Indian war of 1675–76.

By 1680 the British government—which never recognized the Confederation of New England—had developed its own reasons for intercolonial union. Charles II established the Lords of Trade and Plantations (a new committee of his Privy Council) and sent Edward Randolph to investigate New England's notorious noncompliance with the new Navigation laws. Randolph's reports led directly to the revocation of the Massachusetts Bay Charter in 1684 and the decision to establish the Dominion of New England. In 1685 James II appointed Sir Edmund Andros as Governor-General of the Dominion, which was made up of New York, New Jersey, and the New England colonies. Colonial legislatures were abolished, their power transferred to Andros and a Council named by the Crown. Andros' efforts to levy new quitrents, impose Anglicanism, and challenge earlier land titles brought an immediate outcry. The occasion for the downfall of the Dominion was soon forthcoming: in England Protestant alarm over the birth of a Roman Catholic heir to James II brought about the Glorious Revolution in 1688 and the invitation to William and Mary to assume the throne; news of the overthrow of James reached New England in March, 1689, and stimulated a spontaneous and successful uprising against Andros. In 1691 William and Mary granted Massachusetts a new charter, which substituted a property qualification for the earlier religious test for suffrage. The new royal province incorporated Plymouth and Maine; other colonies resumed their former style of government.

Interest in intercolonial union did not end with the ill-fated Dominion. English enthusiasm for more efficient imperial administration persisted, as did colonists' concern for an enhanced defensive capacity in the face of the growing French and Indian menace. The British Board of Trade gave serious consideration to a defensive union of the colonies in 1754 but rejected the proposal for domestic political reasons. At the same time, England called for a meeting of representatives from the northern colonies to improve American relations with the Iroquois. The result was the Congress that opened in Albany in June, 1754. Colonial delegates made modest progress with their Indian diplomacy, then turned to discuss the need for some form of confederation for "general Safety and Interest." The result was a Plan of Union comprising a President-General appointed (and paid) by the Crown, and a Grand Council, elected by the colonial assemblies. This new intercolonial legislature would administer western lands and Indian affairs, levy taxes, and direct general defense, subject to the approval of the President-General. Despite mounting fear of the French, not one colony approved the Albany Plan. Some feared it would open the door to stricter British rule; others resented the reduction of their sovereignty. In any case, colonial approval was irrelevant since the British government had already decided colonial union was neither timely nor wise; the arrival of copies of the Albany Plan in London did not provoke action or comment.

THE CONTEST FOR EMPIRE

The defense needs of the English colonies reflected the international crisis that marked the mid-eighteenth century. Although this crisis was largely one of major European dimensions, North America was now part of the Old World's difficulty in living peacefully with itself. Anglo-French rivalry in the New World occasioned the outbreak of the French and Indian War, or Great War for Empire, which lasted from 1754 to 1763.

French power in North America began with Samuel de Champlain. This soldier-explorer led a trading expedition up the St. Lawrence to the falls above Montreal in 1603, later explored the coast northward from Cape Cod, reached the lake that bears his name, and founded a settlement in Quebec in 1608. Perhaps his most serious error was his alliance with the Algonquin Indians against their Iroquois enemies; the Iroquois never quite forgot or forgave. Quebec grew almost grudgingly, partly because Champlain saw it only as a Jesuit missionary outpost, partly because of its checkered history of company rule before the absolutist Louis XIV, who ruled from 1643 to 1715, took over. Royal rule took the form of Crown-appointed governors, backed—and sometimes undermined—by an Intendant (a fiscal and judicial overseer for the king), and a bishop who governed as a Superior Council.

The First Intendant, Jean Talon, brought a thousand troops and the stability needed for colonization. Talon's objective was the extension of French influence to the west and south. Accordingly he sponsored the expeditions of Louis Joliet and Father Marquette, who in 1673 descended the Wisconsin River to the Mississippi. In 1682, Sieur de La Salle explored the Mississippi down to the Gulf of Mexico, naming the region Louisiana for his sovereign, the Sun King. A decade later France sponsored an agricultural settlement in the Illinois area, which was later assigned to Louisiana for administration. The major population growth on the lower Mississippi took place early in the eighteenth century: by 1730 Mobile and New Orleans were firmly established, with a total settlement of some 5000 whites and 2000 slaves. Yet, by 1750 the combined population of New France and Louisiana reached only 60,000.

The French settlements were widely scattered, exclusively Roman Catholic in religion, autocratic in government, and feudal in design. The French experiment in feudalism discouraged independent settlement. French colonists were much more victimized by their mercantilist mother country and were much less agrarian in their economy than the English colonists. This absence of a firm agricultural base and the lack of diversified industry combined to render New France economically vulnerable.

French emphasis upon the fur trade and fishing industry aroused the jealousy and resentment of their English competitors. And neither politics nor religion endeared the French colonists to their English neighbors. But conflict did not surface immediately, partly because the nature of colonization was so different. The English colonial presence was open and conspicuous, from Maine's rock-bound coast to Georgia's low-lying shores. French colonization was slow, feebly supported, and handicapped by the physical geography and feudalism of New France. It required events in Europe to set conflict in motion.

Colonial America was never an entity separate from its European source. Nowhere is this fact more evident than in the Anglo-French wars of the colonial period. Between 1620 and 1680 the Stuarts were (with Cromwell's interruption) on the English throne; the Stuarts tended to ally with their Catholic friends in France. But the arrival of William and Mary altered this cozy relationship overnight: Louis XIV recognized James II as the legitimate ruler of England and thus precipitated King William's War (1689–97, known in Europe as the War of the League of Augsburg). This was followed by Queen Anne's War (1702–13). In both instances England and France were heavily committed in Europe and gave little attention to the American theater.

The occasion for Queen Anne's War, called the War of the Spanish Succession in Europe, was Louis XIV's support for his grandson to succeed to the Spanish throne, coupled with French insistence on recognizing the son of the deceased James II as rightful monarch of England. Significantly, the new (French) King of Spain, Philip V, assigned the valued *Asiento*—the exclusive right to supply slaves to Spanish colonies—to a French company, which infuriated the envious English. Spanish involvement led to a futile military minuet of South Carolina and Spanish Florida. English plans for major attacks on the French in Canada collapsed and were succeeded by a successful Anglo-American operation against Port Royal, Acadia; the French were outnumbered by at least eight to one. In the ensuing peace settlement at Utrecht in 1713 British gains reflected the scale of the Franco-Spanish defeats: France ceded Newfoundland, the Hudson Bay area, and all of Acadia except Cape Breton Island and acknowledged British suzerainty over the Iroquois; the British finally accepted Philip V as King of Spain and received a thirty-year grant of the coveted *Asiento*.

Anglo-French relations did not improve in the twenty-six years of peace that followed Utrecht. Each power prepared for the next encounter in colonial America: the French strengthened Fort Louisburg on Cape Breton Island, making it an invaluable base from which privateers preyed on New England fishing and shipping; border disputes abounded; rivalry for the fur trade persisted as both sides constructed forts on Lake Ontario. There were growing commercial difficulties with Spain. It was in this context that an English sea captain, Robert Jenkins, claimed that his ear was sliced off by a Spanish naval officer; his tale, along with the news that Spain had revoked the *Asiento*, aroused sufficient emotion in England to bring about the War of Jenkins' Ear in 1739. What began as a colonial war with Spain enlarged into a war in Europe (the War of the Austrian Succession) aimed at France. In America (where it was known as King George's War) Georgia managed a stalemate with Florida, but the big event was an Anglo-American attack on Fort Louisburg, which fell after a forty-nine-day siege. As with Queen Anne's War, the peace settlement was dictated by developments elsewhere: under the Treaty of Aix-la-Chapelle (1748) a new six-year truce was declared, wherein England returned Fort Louisburg to France, to

ANGLO-FRENCH WARS, 1689–1763

1689–97 King William's War (War of the League of Augsburg)[1]
1702–13 Queen Anne's War (War of the Spanish Succession)
1739–42 War of Jenkins' Ear
1744–48 King George's War (War of the Austrian Succession)
1754–63 French and Indian War, or Great War for the Empire (Seven Years' War, 1756–63)

[1]Names in parentheses refer to how the wars were known in Europe.

the lasting disgust of New England, in order to regain Madras in India. But nothing—in Europe or America—was really settled.

Both sides used the brief period of peace to prepare for the next reckoning. The British strengthened their hold upon Nova Scotia while the French expanded their influence above Lake George and Lake Champlain. But the newest and most crucial area of conflict was the Ohio Valley, where the French linked their Louisiana settlements with New France to the north; a strong link would undermine the English capability to expand into the trans-Appalachian west. It was near the Monongahela River that young George Washington met his first defeat when he had to surrender at Fort Necessity on July 4, 1754.

The undeclared French and Indian War had been thus underway for two years before it became the Seven Years' War in Europe (1756–63). A long struggle between Prussia, allied with England, and Austria, allied with France and Russia, for control of Central Europe drained France, distracted England, and served neither nation. Spain at first remained neutral but eventually was persuaded by France to enter the war—just in time to lose Florida to Britain.

In America the British confirmed their tendency toward incompetent leadership. Defeat followed defeat: the French took Fort Oswego in 1756, repulsed a British attack on Fort Louisburg in 1757, and even captured Fort William Henry, on Lake George, that August; the West was visited with fire and pillage, the French seeming to do what they pleased. Not until William Pitt came to power did the direction of England's fortunes improve. A superb orator, incredible egotist ("I am sure I can save this country and that no one else can"), and excellent strategist, Pitt put new vigor into the national war effort and new leaders in command of its forces. In 1758 Jeffrey Amherst and James Wolfe captured Fort Louisburg, and later that year, John Forbes (with Washington on his staff) reached the smoldering ruins of Fort Duquesne in the Ohio Valley. Deserted by their Indian allies, the French were in retreat. The next year was conclusive: Wolfe landed nearly five thousand men on the Plains of Abraham outside Quebec; both Wolfe and the French commander, the Marquis de Montcalm, fell in the ensuing battle, but Quebec was taken. A year later the remaining French army surrendered Montreal, and the war was essentially over in America.

But making the peace was almost as difficult as winning the war. Pitt was maneuvered out of office as too eager to widen the war rather than end

General James Wolfe lands on the Plains of Abraham above Quebec.

it. A new king, the young George III, wanted his former tutor, Lord Bute, in the government and had his way. Eager to end the costly conflict, Bute made major concessions to France. The resultant Treaty of Paris (1763) was so unpopular that it gained Parliamentary approval only through ruthless use of patronage. By the Treaty, England acquired New France and all of North America east of the Mississippi; Spain, in return for the restoration of Cuba, assigned Florida to England, and as a compensation, France ceded to Spain the Louisiana territory west of the Mississippi by a separate secret treaty; England returned to France the captured West Indian islands of Guadeloupe and Martinique, and France retained fishing rights on the Newfoundland banks.

Perhaps the most difficult problem for England had been the decision to retain Canada rather than the islands of Guadeloupe and Martinique. France had made clear its determination to resume the war rather than part with all three possessions. It was noted that the islands' exports to England in 1761 were forty times those of Canada, that as islands they were more easily controlled, and that they would meet New England's economic need. Those advocating Canada argued that control of the North American fur trade was vital, that Canadian markets would expand and be receptive to British trade, that only the expulsion of the French would bring stability and peace to British America. Of course the acquisition of Canada made for a tidier map and happier planters in the British West Indies, who did not care to compete with Guadeloupe and Martinique.

Of course, there were English cynics who predicted that the removal of the French threat to the English mainland colonies could well lead them into independence; after all, the colonies would no longer need their mother country. Benjamin Franklin, for one, could not take this prospect seriously: the colonies had been unable to support union against the hated French in 1754, so what chance could there be for union against the mother country?

Suggested Reading

One of the most readable and illuminating surveys of Colonial America is Clarence L. Ver Steeg's *The Formative Years, 1607–1763** (1963), which can be most profitably accompanied by Daniel J. Boorstin, *The Americans: The Colonial Experience** (1958), and Louis B. Wright, *The Cultural Life of the American Colonies** (1957).

Carl Bridenbaugh has made vast contributions to our understanding of the American as colonist; his studies of colonial cities—*Cities in the Wilderness** (1938) and *Cities in Revolt** (1955)—are remarkably informative. Bridenbaugh's *Myths and Realities: Societies of the Colonial South** (1952) is readable and provocative.

Richard B. Morris' *Government and Labor in Early America** (1946), retains its value, particularly when read with Jack P. Greene, *The Quest for Power* (1963), and Charles Sydnor's charming study of *Gentlemen Freeholders** (1952). Michael Kammen's *Empire and Interest: The American Colonies and the Politics of Mercantilism** (1969) includes a useful introduction to Anglo-American commercial and economic difficulties. Lawrence A. Harper's *The English Navigation Laws* (1939) remains the reference volume on that subject.

In *White over Black* (1968) Winthrop D. Jordan has furnished an outstanding study of the black experience in early America. For further reading on colonial religion, see Edwin S. Gaustad, *The Great Awakening in New England** (1957), and Alan Heimert, *Religion and the American Mind from the Great Awakening to the Revolution* (1966); Marion L. Starkey's *The Devil in Massachusetts** (1952) is less demanding but very good reading. Colonial education is admirably treated in Bernard Bailyn's brief essay, *Education in the Forming of American Society** (1960), and in Robert Middlekauff, *Ancients and Axioms* (1963).

The history of France in America is still poorly recorded, but Lawrence Henry Gipson gave a fine summation in the fifth volume of his massive *The British Empire before the American Revolution* (1942); G. M. Wrong's *The Rise and Fall of New France* (1928) is still a good survey, and Howard H. Peckham supplies a fine military history in *The Colonial Wars, 1689–1782** (1964).

*Available in paperback edition

CHRONOLOGY

1760   George III ascends throne

1761   Britain invokes writs of assistance; challenged by James Otis

1763   Pontiac uprising
Proclamation of 1763 grants western lands to Indians

1764   Currency Act
Sugar Act

1765   Stamp Act

1766   Stamp Act repealed
Declaratory Act

1767   Townshend Acts
John Dickinson's *Letters from a Farmer in Pennsylvania* published

1770   Townshend Acts repealed
Boston Massacre

1773   Tea Act
Boston Tea Party

1774   Coercive Acts; Quebec Act
Thomas Jefferson's *Summary View*
First Continental Congress meets in Philadelphia

1775   Battles at Lexington and Concord
Second Continental Congress meets

1776   Thomas Paine's *Common Sense* issued
July 2: Lee's resolution on independence approved 12-0
July 4: Jefferson's Declaration of Independence approved 12-0
July 9: New York endorses Declaration

IV

THE REAL REVOLUTION,

1763–1776

Thirty-five years after the official conclusion of the American War for Independence John Adams was still pondering, "What do we mean by the revolution?" It was not the war—"That was not part of the revolution. It was only an Effect and consequence of it." He was convinced that "the real American Revolution" was the "radical change in the principles, opinions, sentiments, and affections of the people." Adams, significantly, did not contend that the change extended to religious, economic, or social assumptions. But he did identify the American proclivity to respond to problems with political resolution. Although not all the causes of his "radical change" are clear, change did in fact take place, much of it between the conclusion of the war for empire in 1763 and the proclamation of independence in 1776.

At first glance Anglo-American relations appear to have been unusually harmonious in the early 1760s. British arms and British ships, with some colonial support, had destroyed French power on the North American mainland. The acquisition of Canada opened up vast new economic opportunities. Americans basked in the reflected glory of their membership in the greatest empire ever known. As Benjamin Franklin remarked, the colonies felt closer to their mother country than to one another.

George III (1760-1820)

But gratitude is poor political currency, and the British soon discovered that their American colonists were conveniently forgetful of the blood and treasure that had brought them security. Self-interest no longer bound them to the mother country. Colonists rapidly realized that their safety and welfare no longer depended upon Britain; indeed, they soon found their interests threatened and frustrated by their mother country. The young King who ascended to the throne in 1760 was mentally and emotionally unstable, but George III was deadly serious about politics. His blindly complacent conservatism led him to view American disaffection as a wanton attack on an ideal and perfect kingdom. As the collision course between England and America became increasingly apparent Americans were increasingly persuaded that it was British policy to deny them the fruits of the victory of 1763.

In a decade and a half American colonists found unity in war with the very nation that had made them secure. Few American revolutionaries either calculated or anticipated the consequences of their seemingly foolhardy insistence upon their rights and privileges. War with their mother country was unsought; independence was announced with a widespread misgiving and hesitation, and not a few patriots declined this ultimate step and joined the ranks of those loyal to Britain.

CONFLICTING INTERESTS IN THE WEST

Anglo-American misunderstanding was first exposed by conflicting interests in Western lands so recently wrested from French control. Before 1760 Britain and the colonies had worked together in developing the West. They had then a common objective—to encourage population growth in order to frustrate French expansion. But after 1763 settlement could no longer be considered a defensive measure. Southern planters, discouraged by diminishing profits, and northern merchants, dismayed by British commercial restrictions, looked westward for new speculative opportunities and profits. Britain feared that rapid expansion westward would reduce the value of British investment in the eastern section of America. Moreover, the fur trade looked lucrative to British merchants, and they did not want hordes of settlers destroying the fur-bearing animals and disturbing the Indians. After 1760 the British and the Americans differed sharply on the appropriate treatment of Indians: the British preferred to leave them alone and thus avoid Indian problems, but the Americans began a systematic occupation of Indian lands, driving the Indians away and thereby stirring up trouble.

When, in 1760, Lord Jeffrey Amherst, the British Commander in Chief, stopped distributing gifts to the Indians as a measure of economy, unscrupulous colonial traders moved in, debauching the Indians with liquor, swindling them with ease. Indian resentment and alarm mounted, fed in part by French agents, who falsely promised national support. But the occasion for a major Indian uprising was the news that France had indeed ceded their lands to Britain in the Treaty of Paris. Ably led by Pontiac, an Ottawa chief, Indians swept over seven of the nine British garrisons in the Upper Ohio Valley by June, 1763. Pontiac's brief success owed something to the poor judgment of General Amherst, who discounted the threat and left his forts undermanned, but it owed more to surprise. Smallpox-infected blankets and two major military expeditions in 1764 eroded Indian power; Pontiac held out until 1765.

The British government did not wait to subdue Pontiac before addressing the problems in the West. Lord Shelburne had considered the question of the Indian policy even before news reached London of Pontiac's attacks. Shelburne planned to close to settlement lands west of the headwaters of the rivers flowing into the Atlantic (and not yet secured by purchase or Indian grant). In October, 1763, Shelburne's plan, known as the Proclamation of 1763, was approved and issued without the provisional character Shelburne had intended. George Washington, an avid speculator in Western lands, spoke for many when he remarked "I can never look upon that proclamation in any other light . . . than as a temporary expedient to quiet the minds of the Indians." Most colonists saw the Proclamation as arrogantly restrictive; their anger abated only slightly when Britain proceeded to negotiate Indian treaties that opened more land to settlement.

COMMERCE AND CURRENCY

Commerce and currency had long been sources of American difficulties with the mother country, and the war with France merely added another dimension to their complexities. Many colonial merchants were not able to resist the enormous profits to be made from selling provisions to the enemy. The British government reasserted its complete authority to regulate colonial commerce. To enforce that control Britain invoked writs of assistance, or general search warrants, in the quest for smuggled goods in colonists' private homes and shipping. Long in use in the mother country, such writs were not customary in America. When the writs came up for renewal on the occasion of the coronation of George III, Boston merchants retained James Otis to challenge the legality of the writs in 1761. The writs, Otis charged, violated the fundamental rights of British subjects as confirmed by the Magna Carta. "An act against the Constitution," Otis insisted, "is void." John Adams, present in court, was enthralled: "Otis was a flame of fire," Adams recalled later, "American independence was then and there born." The judge, who found Otis less persuasive, referred the question to London, where the government promptly declared the writs constitutional.

The currency impasse provoked similar rhetoric based on similar constitutional concepts. Always faced with a currency shortage, the colonists has compiled a history of monetary experimentation, to which the war with France added another chapter. For many colonists, especially in the South, the only way to respond to the war's fiscal demands was to issue paper money or to establish commodities as currency. They used paper currency to finance local military efforts and pay off British creditors. And even before the war Virginians had used tobacco to meet local commitments.

The Anglican clergy in Virginia might have benefited from this arrangement when tobacco prices rose sharply in 1755 and 1758, but the Virginia Assembly passed a law pegging clerical salaries at a third of the going market price. The outraged clergy persuaded the British Privy Council to disallow the Virginia legislation and then brought suit for the balance due. But Patrick Henry, defending the vestrymen, attacked the clergy as parasites and the royal disallowance as unconstitutional. Virginia's charters, thundered Henry, guaranteed Virginians their rights, "as if they had been abiding and born within the Realm of England." As a result of young Henry's oratory the plaintiff in the case, the Reverend James Maury, received the most nominal compensation, precisely one penny in damages. The impunity with which Henry could attack the King (he had "degenerated into a tyrant," Henry claimed, and should forfeit "all rights to his subjects' obedience") and the attention colonists gave such remarks suggest that the costs for Britain were far greater.

Virginia's creditors were strong supporters of the British postwar drive against colonial paper money. Their campaign reached a successful conclusion in 1764, when Britain passed a new Currency Act extending to all colonies the prohibition applied to New England in 1751. A postwar depression made such legislation disastrous for Americans: the British action denied the colonists their most convenient and available medium of exchange. Most modern economists argue that currency in circulation should be expanded, not reduced, in time of depression. Britain, however innocently and justifiably, did contribute to the economic difficulties of its American colonies—and was readily blamed by them.

TAXATION

The friction provoked by British commercial and currency regulations was minor compared with the colonists' reaction to Britain's revenue-raising efforts. A staggering national debt and heavy domestic taxes convinced Chancellor of the Exchequer George Grenville that the colonists should contribute to the cost of the new military establishment needed to protect them. Grenville hoped to raise from the colonies one-third to one-half of the £350,000 needed for 10,000 troops. To this end he tightened the administration of the customs service and then, in 1764, introduced the American Revenue Act (more popularly known as the Sugar Act). The Sugar Act was the first serious effort to tax for revenue rather than for purposes of imperial regulation. In order to defray "the expenses of defending, protecting and securing the said colonies" the new measure reduced the duty on foreign molasses from sixpence to threepence per gallon, increased the duty on sugar, prohibited the importation of foreign rum (which was negligible), imposed high duties on wines, and then made provisions for rigorous enforcement.

Since the anticipated net income was only £20,000, the economic advantage was hardly worth the substantial political price. The Massachusetts General Court protested the infringement of "the most essential rights of Britons"; New York's Assembly flatly opposed Parliamentary taxation; and John Dickinson warned fellow Pennsylvanians against efforts "to tax them into obedience."

The Sugar Act sensitized Americans to taxation as an issue. They were more immediately hostile to Grenville's next revenue effort, the Stamp Act of 1765, which proposed to raise between £60,000 and £100,000. The Act levied internal taxes upon the colonies through duties on a wide range of colonial legal and commercial documents, including customs papers, playing cards, newspapers (and advertisements therein), pamphlets, and almanacs; rates could reach 200 percent. The stamp agents would be American, and the revenue was to be spent in the colonies. But offenders were to be tried without a jury, which was a breach of the rights of Englishmen in the colonists' view.

Colonial hostility to the Stamp Act was swift and widespread, for Grenville had now alienated three powerful political groups: lawyers, publishers, and merchants. A Virginia attorney courted treason when he reminded the

Assembly that "Tarquin and Julius [Caesar] had their Brutus, Charles his Cromwell. . . ." Patrick Henry insisted that only the House of Burgesses had the right to lay taxes and warned that anyone who disagreed would "be deemed an enemy to his Majesty's Colony." By August, 1765, riots had erupted in Boston, followed swiftly by others in Newport, New York, Annapolis, and Charleston. Patriots, often in organizations called Sons of Liberty, persuaded most stamp collectors to resign their posts. Rioters all but destroyed Chief Justice Thomas Hutchinson's home in Boston.* In October nine colonies sent delegates to a Stamp Act Congress in New York; walking a constitutional tightrope, the Congress acknowledged Parliament's imperial authority but denied it any right to levy internal or external taxes upon the colonies.

The Stamp Act was enforced only in Quebec, Nova Scotia, the Floridas, and the British West Indies. American newspapers appeared without stamps (sometimes omitting the publisher's name from the masthead); cargoes, lacking stamped papers, gained clearance without duties; college presidents awarded degrees by letter rather than by stamped diplomas; many courts suspended proceedings, to the general pleasure of debtors, and merchants formed agreements not to buy British goods until the law was repealed.

Domestic politics in Britain eased repeal of the hated Stamp Act. In June, 1765, George III dismissed Grenville because of what the King imagined to be an insult to his mother (Grenville had omitted her from the Regency Commission). Grenville's successor, Lord Rockingham, lacked enthusiasm for such controversial legislation. When Pitt, in a major parliamentary speech, urged outright repeal of the Stamp Act, British merchants, who were inconvenienced by the disruption of their American trade, supported him. During the debate Franklin warned Parliament that any distinction between internal and external taxation (if, in fact, it existed) would soon disappear if the Stamp Act did not.† And so, largely for reasons of expediency, Parliament voted repeal in March, 1766. But simultaneously Parliament passed the Declaratory Act, which boldly asserted Parliament's authority over the colonies "in all cases whatsoever." Anti-American feeling was high in Britain, and as long as fiscal problems remained there would be further efforts to raise revenue through taxes.

The Rockingham ministry did not long survive the demise of the Stamp Act. By the summer of 1766 an oddly assorted coalition, led nominally by an ailing Pitt, now in the House of Lords as Lord Chatham, and his friend the unimpressive Duke of Grafton, had taken office. The Chancellor of the Exchequer, Charles ("Champagne Charlie") Townshend was by default the effective head of government. If the colonists had failed to read the storm signal in the Declaratory Act, they could not long ignore the significance of Townshend's new role. Long interested in colonial affairs, Townshend had for years urged effective revenue taxes to defray the costs

*Ironically, Hutchinson opposed the Stamp Act; but because he believed in the sovereignty of Parliament, he was identified with the hated tax measure.
†Colonists generally accepted Parliament's right to impose external (regulatory) taxes at this time.

of imperial administration and defense. His hand was only somewhat forced by a British taxpayers' revolt that cut the land tax by £500,000 a year. New colonial taxes were both necessary and just in Townshend's view.

In November of 1766 Townshend modified the Sugar Act in a realistic fashion by imposing a penny tax on all molasses entering colonial ports— a profitable measure that brought £12,000 in revenue by 1768 and £20,000 by 1772. More substantial, and therefore controversial, were the Townshend Acts passed in 1767. A new enforcement program reaffirmed the legality of writs of assistance, set up four more Vice-Admiralty Courts to try breaches of the Navigation laws, and established a new Board of Customs in Boston to supervise collection of duties more closely. The Townshend duties were external taxes to appease those Americans whose case against the stamp duties rested on opposition to internal taxes; these new duties, expected to produce some £40,000 a year, were levied on glass, painter's colors, paper, and tea. The revenue was to defray customs-administration costs and pay the salaries of colonial governors and judges, who might thereby achieve a degree of fiscal and political independence they had rarely experienced when the colonial legislatures voted such funds. Finally, Townshend proposed the suspension of the New York Assembly until it complied with the Quartering Act passed two years earlier; under that measure colonies had been obliged to supply provisions and barracks for troops based within their borders. New York, as a major colonial highway, found the Quartering Act an onerous as well as a devious taxing device, but finally bought relief from the threatened suspension of its legislature by voting an unrestricted sum for the troops.

The Townshend Acts passed with large majorities; such Parliamentary opposition as surfaced dwelt mainly upon the impolitic nature of the taxes rather than on the question of authority. An untimely death robbed Townshend of the opportunity to view the results of his legislation, but his ministerial associates watched with dismay as the anger of the colonists steadily mounted. Bostonians urged a selective boycott of imports. In Philadelphia John Dickinson began the publication of his famous *Letters from a Farmer in Pennsylvania,* the first carefully dated November 5, to commemorate the anniversary of the day William III had landed in England to rescue England's liberties in 1688. Dickinson's tone was one of sweet, patient reason, reflecting a lawyer's concern for history, custom, precedent, and justice. He found evidence of an advancing Parliamentary program of tyranny aimed at the destruction of the constitutional liberties of Englishmen in America. Parliament was, he charged, practicing a dubious double standard by attempting to deny American legislatures the very rights for which Parliament had long fought in England. The Townshend duties, Dickinson concluded, were only superficially regulatory; in reality they were a form of taxation as unconstitutional as the Stamp Act they were meant to replace. Nearly every colonial newspaper reprinted Dickinson's *Letters,* and by 1769 seven editions had appeared in book form.

As the *Pennsylvania Chronicle* went to press in February, 1768, with Dickinson's final installment, Sam Adams voiced the political opposition to Townshend's legislation that was stirring in Massachusetts. In a circular letter to the other colonies, Massachusetts urged unity against taxation without representation. Although the language was moderate, the newly appointed Secretary of State for Colonial Affairs, Lord Hillsborough, denounced Massachusetts for attempting to disturb "the public peace." When the Massachusetts legislature refused to rescind the circular letter, Hillsborough had Governor Bernard dissolve the Assembly. Meanwhile Boston merchants moved forward with their proposals for trade reprisals against the mother country. By August, 1769, New Yorkers also had joined in a nonimportation agreement, followed by Philadelphians the next spring. Even conservative Virginians were passing vigorous resolutions that spring, insisting upon their exclusive right to tax themselves. When Governor Botetourt responded to the Virginia Resolves by dissolving the Assembly, its members moved down the street to the Raleigh Tavern and voted their own nonimportation agreement.

These actions were not yet completely effective because many colonists found it profitable to ignore boycott efforts; others subscribed in part because economic difficulties made a patriotic virtue of harsh necessity. The vigor with which patriot vigilante groups, such as the Sons of Liberty, terrorized violators of nonimportation and nonconsumption agreements suggested that colonial unity of action would be hard won. Unruly mobs probably alarmed and alienated as many as they intimidated.

Sam Adams' effective direction of the Boston mob provoked Hillsborough into sending several regiments of troops in June, 1768. Their presence brought only an uneasy peace, increasingly ruptured by clashes between soldiers and mocking citizens. On March 5, 1770 a mob attacked a customhouse sentry. Alarmed, Captain Thomas Preston mustered a small detachment to protect the customs treasury; an unidentified voice shouted "Fire!" and the troops did just that.* Five Bostonians lay dead or dying in the snow, including Crispus Attucks, an itinerant seaman and the first black casualty of the Revolutionary War. Momentarily stunned, the mob angrily prepared to attack the troops, who discreetly retired to the nearby guardhouse. Lieutenant Governor Thomas Hutchinson brought peace by moving the troops out of the city. When Captain Preston and his troops were brought to trial for murder, John Adams and Josiah Quincy, Jr., skillfully and courageously defended them. All were acquitted except two who, allowed the medieval custom of pleading "benefit of clergy," were branded on the hand and freed.† A form of justice may have been served, but so was patriot propaganda: Massachusetts had its martyrs, and the memory was kept fresh by annual public orations, such as Joseph Warren's eloquent injunction in 1775 to "take heed, ye orphan babes, lest, whilst your streaming eyes are fixed upon the ghastly corpse, *your feet slide on the stones bespattered with your father's brains.*" The British were already losing the propaganda war.

*Preston was accused of murder, but it is unlikely that he ordered the fatal volley: he was directly in the line of fire.
†"Benefit of clergy" derived from the Middle Ages, when the Church claimed clerical transgressors for its ecclesiastical courts; the vital qualification was literacy, demonstrated by a recital of the twenty-third (or "hanging") psalm.

The BLOODY MASSACRE perpetrated in King—Street BOSTON on March 5th 1770 by a party of the 29th REGT

Unhappy Boston! see thy Sons deplore,
Thy hallow'd Walks besmear'd with guiltless Gore:
While faithless P—n and his savage Bands,
With murd'rous Rancour stretch their bloody Hands;
Like fierce Barbarians grinning o'er their Prey,
Approve the Carnage and enjoy the Day.

If scalding drops from Rage from Anguish Wrung,
If speechless Sorrows lab'ring for a Tongue,
Or if a weeping World can ought appease
The plaintive Ghosts of Victims such as these;
The Patriot's copious Tears for each are shed,
A glorious Tribute which embalms the Dead.

But know, Fate summons to that awful Goal,
Where Justice strips the Murd'rer of his Soul:
Should venal C—ts the scandal of the Land,
Snatch the relentless Villain from her Hand,
Keen Execrations on this Plate inscrib'd,
Shall reach a Judge who never can be brib'd.

The unhappy Sufferers were Mess.rs Sam.l Gray, Sam.l Maverick, Jam.s Caldwell, Crispus Attucks & Pat.k Carr
Killed. Six wounded; two of them (Christ.r Monk & John Clark) Mortally

Paul Revere's view of the Boston Massacre

Ironically, on the very day of the "Boston Massacre" Townshend's successor was presiding over the repeal of the duties that had indirectly occasioned these tragic events. Actually, Pitt and Grafton had been ready to urge repeal as early as 1768, so alarmed were they over the economic and political portents; but Lord North, the new Chancellor of the Exchequer, objected. In 1769 he grudgingly agreed to repeal, largely because British

63

merchants were restive; business losses were mounting, and only nominal revenues could be discovered. And so, on March 5, 1770, Parliament voted to repeal all the controversial duties except that on tea; since tea was not grown in England, English producers would not be injured and at the same time Parliament's authority would once again be confirmed.

North's concessions were grudging, and the colonists knew it. But the urge for peace and prosperity was powerful. Trade with Britain had declined to £1.6 million in 1769; by 1771 it was up to £4.2 million. The ensuing three years were superficially tranquil and encouraging; in reality, fundamental questions survived, and patriot agitation continued. Sam Adams helped organize committees of correspondence that spread as far as South Carolina to keep one another informed about British transgressions. Friction between merchants and customs officials persisted. In 1772 Rhode Islanders successfully attacked and burned the British revenue cutter *Gaspée*. A Boston mob tarred and feathered a customs official and then carted him through the streets as a public spectacle. Peace often seemed possible only so long as royal officials declined to enforce Parliament's wishes.

Even so, radicals despaired of maintaining any colonial unity of purpose and resolve without further British provocation. Parliament, however, came to their rescue. In 1773 Lord North rushed through the Tea Act in a desperate effort to keep afloat the sinking British East India Company. The company had over 17 million pounds of tea in its British warehouses, but colonial smuggling provided inferior Dutch tea at a lower price made even more attractive by nonpayment of the threepenny tea tax. The Tea Act permitted the company to export up to 7 million pounds of tea free of the tax usually paid on its entry into Britain; further, such exports, while still subject to the Townshend duty, could be sold directly in the colonies through the company's own agents. Thus the company would enjoy a comfortable monopoly of the American market, bypassing both English and colonial middlemen in the process. Colonial tea merchants and smugglers were equally outraged as they calculated the lower price at which the superior British tea could now be sold. Some, more altruistic, attacked the measure as an insidious device to raise revenue by making a hated external duty more tolerable. Still others suddenly discovered in tea the source of all sorts of threats to American health; allegations circulated that tea caused cancer, impotence, and premature senility. Presumably, smuggled Dutch tea held no such terrors.

Colonial tempers rose as charges of monopoly and unfair taxation were made. Radicals determined no British tea would be landed; those merchants selected by the company to handle its tea were intimidated and persuaded to resign; ship captains were warned of their personal peril. In Boston, Governor Hutchinson forced a confrontation by refusing permission for three tea ships to leave port without unloading their cargoes. Patriots feared the tea might be seized for nonpayment of duties, then landed and auctioned—thus gaining the market they wished to deny it. So, in December, 1773, radicals, poorly disguised as Indians, boarded the vessels and dumped forty-five tons of prime tea into the harbor. In Charleston the tea was in fact landed and seized for nonpayment of duties, but it remained in a warehouse for three years before being auctioned for the treasury of the newly sovereign state of South Carolina. New Yorkers preferred to emulate the Boston example. The other tea ships turned around and sailed back to England, their cargoes intact. The Boston Tea Party was for John Adams "an Epoch in History," for Lord North, the work of "New England fanatics." But John Adams was correct in one respect: it did have, as he said, "important consequences."

COERCIVE ACTS

The alarming destruction of property in Boston Harbor dismayed many Americans. But England's immediate and vigorous response drove hesitant colonials toward the radical camp. When such pro-Americans as Pitt—now Lord Chatham—found Boston's action "criminal," Lord North knew he had plenty of support. In March, 1774, he summoned Parliament to discuss the American disturbances and determine appropriate punitive measures.

As author of both the Tea Act and the coercive legislation that followed the Tea Party, Lord North has long been blamed almost personally for the Revolution that ensued. This view oversimplifies both the Revolution and the men who fought it. Frederick North, second Earl of Guilford, was no simple anti-American puppet of George III. An able debater and shrewd politician, he had no thought of becoming a colonial tyrant. To be sure, North was fiercely loyal to his monarch, but North had another loyalty as well. He was moved by profound constitutional convictions that Parliament was the supreme legislature in the British empire; he would make necessary concessions for the sake of peace, but he would allow little questioning of Parliament's authority. North had dominated the Pitt-Grafton ministry upon the death of Townshend in September, 1767; in January, 1770, he headed a new government that held power until the total collapse of its American policies in 1782. He had the unreserved support of his King; without it neither North nor his policies could have survived for those twelve critical years. The King and his first minister were complementary forces; they understood each other, and politically they thought alike. They particularly agreed on the wisdom of the Coercive Acts of 1774.

Lord North's first response to the Tea Party was the Boston Port Act in March 1774; it called for closing Boston to all shipping until the East India Company was recompensed for the destroyed tea. In May and June additional measures fed the fires of controversy: under the Massachusetts Government Act the royal Governor, rather than the Assembly, would select the membership of the Council; the Governor would also select most judges and other officials; town meetings were to require the Governor's consent. The Administration of Justice Act provided that a royal official charged with a capital offense committed in the course of his duties could be tried in another colonial court or in Britain if the Governor doubted the likelihood of a fair trial in the local court. A new Quartering Act made local authorities responsible for finding billets for troops in troublesome areas.

Finally, in 1774, came the Quebec Act, not a punitive measure but one visited with bad timing and an unfortunate association in the colonists' minds: this measure filled a decade-old promise of autonomy and religious privileges for French residents of the province. Specifically the act extended Quebec's borders to the Mississippi in the west, the Ohio in the south, and Hudson Bay in the north. French residents were permitted French civil law (which did not include trial by jury) and "the free Exercise of the Religion of the [Roman Catholic] Church, subject to the King's supremacy"; government would be continued with a royal Governor and appointed Council, but with no representative legislature.

For many Americans the Quebec Act was the worst, the most intolerable, of all North's measures: the land-hungry—particularly the Virginians —felt shut out of their Northwest; fur-traders felt victimized by British traders operating from Montreal; and many Protestants felt encircled by the popery they had fled the Old World to escape. Quebec, in short, seemed to illustrate everything that was so desperately wrong with British rule: it offered precedents for an alien religion and legal system and for government without the consent of the governed. The news that General Thomas Gage was not only to continue in command of the troops in Massachusetts but was also to replace Hutchinson as Governor confirmed the colonists' worst fears. Resistance was essential.

THE IDEOLOGY OF REVOLUTION

The Boston Port Act provoked the widespread criticism of parliamentary tyranny; many argued that, if Boston's economic life could be thus destroyed, so could that of New York or Philadelphia. From Boston, from New York, from Williamsburg came calls for an intercolonial congress to discuss a common program for resistance. Philadelphia was to be the meeting place; early September, 1774, was the date; during the summer the colonies named their delegates, discussed their instructions, debated their ideas.

Ideology shaped the cause and course of the American Revolution as much as did the economic and political developments of the 1760s and 1770s. Americans saw themselves as transplanted Englishmen, with the rights of Englishmen but also with their reluctance to take precipitate and violent action. The colonists reached for their pens, not only to clarify their political thinking but also to persuade their readers (and themselves) of the logic and justice of their position. Revolution was hardly an American reflex; certainly if it was to take place, if it was to succeed, it needed the widest support, the most general agreement.

The philosophical justification for revolutionary action was familiar enough to most Americans. As offspring of the Age of the Enlightenment, they were aware of the natural-rights arguments of John Locke in his *Second Treatise of Government* (1690). Locke argued that government should not deprive a man of his property without his consent and contended that a people could overthrow a government that had clearly betrayed its obligations to the governed. Many were familiar with Algernon Sidney's

English Colonies, 1776

Discourses on Government (1698), which furnished many of the same arguments in a more vigorous style. Sidney insisted that tyranny should be blocked at the first opportunity, lest despotism fasten too tight a yoke upon the people.

But Americans sought and found additional support for their stand. As expatriate Englishmen, they were well informed on the history of their mother country and frequently refreshed themselves on its lessons. Thomas Jefferson furnished the ablest brief for the colonial case when he drafted his *Summary View of the Rights of British America* to instruct the Virginia delegates to the first Continental Congress.* In this eighteen-page pamphlet Jefferson politely addressed the King as "chief magistrate of the British Empire" and reminded his monarch of the ancestral rights of all Englishmen, rights he traced back to the noble Saxons who had migrated from their German forests without retaining allegiance to the land of their origin. He noted the long struggle for freedom in England, its near success in the

---

*Illness prevented Jefferson from attending the special Virginia convention, which met in August, 1774; he sent two copies of his resolutions to Williamsburg, where they were received enthusiastically. The reputation earned by the *Summary View* unquestionably led to Jefferson's later assignment to draft the Declaration of Independence.

seventeenth century, and its seeming eclipse in the eighteenth. William the Norman had brought feudal tyranny to Saxon England; George III should not permit the same experience for British America. Parliament, corrupt and unrepresentative, appeared to have adopted and extended the Stuart despotism of Charles I and James II; it was now up to the King to intervene, to end parliamentary usurpations in America. "Let not the name of George III be a blot on the page of history," was Jefferson's prayerful conclusion.

In this ideological context the first Continental Congress convened on September 5, 1774. Fifty-six delegates—representing all colonies except Georgia—packed into Philadelphia's Carpenter's Hall to discuss just what action they should take. The delegates were far from united: there were cautious moderates, anxious conservatives, and a few impatient radicals. They were predominantly men of social, intellectual, and political distinction. About one-third were college graduates; thirty were lawyers (twelve had studied in the mother country); nine were planters, joined by a like number of merchants.

Joseph Galloway of Pennsylvania argued for a new plan of union, replete with a legislative Council (elected by the colonial legislatures), presided over by a President General (named by the King) with veto authority. The core of his proposal was the provision that Parliamentary legislation affecting the colonies would require the Council's approval, and Council legislation would require Parliamentary concurrence. Thus further Coercive Acts would be effectively prevented. But Galloway's plan was defeated by one vote, perhaps because of the personal unpopularity of the author. In any case, it is unlikely that Lord North would have cared to share imperial sovereignty in such a fashion.

Instead of Galloway's plan, the Congress adopted the Massachusetts Suffolk Resolves, which denounced the Coercive Acts as unconstitutional, proposed a militia for defense, and demanded immediate economic sanctions against Britain. The Congress then voted a Declaration of Rights and Grievances, which conceded Britain's right to regulate external commerce— but little else. Finally, the Congress approved a Continental Association under which British imports and the slave trade would cease as of December 1, 1774, to be followed by an embargo on exports to Britain the following September. Delegates were cheerfully confident that such economic warfare would once again persuade British merchants to work for the rapid repeal of the detested Coercive Acts and thus rescue the empire. In this optimistic frame of mind the Congress concluded its lengthy sessions and adjourned on October 26, 1774, but the delegates agreed to reconvene the following May if Parliament had not responded appropriately.

THE ROAD TO REBELLION

Colonal hopes rested more upon the record of the past than upon the reality of the present. Britain had indeed retreated when faced with colonial resistance to the Stamp Act and then to the Townshend duties; but retreat was no longer likely. Anti-American sentiment had steadily risen in Parliament; Edmund Burke's voice had been almost alone in opposition to the Boston Port Bill in 1774. British mercantile interests had become less susceptible to American pressures, because they had found markets elsewhere. When North called a general election in 1774, the American question was largely ignored by the electorate in favor of more urgent local issues. Lord North had wide support for his American policies; it was his inability to execute them that eventually brought his political downfall.

"The dye is now cast," commented George III in September, 1774, "we must not retreat." And his new Parliament agreed. Chatham pleaded in vain for compromise; his proposal for the withdrawal of troops from Boston and a pledge against revenue measures without colonial consent was voted down nearly four to one. In February, 1775, Parliament declared Massachusetts in a state of rebellion, which the King should suppress with up to 10,000 troops if needed. Lord North then offered his own plan for reconciliation: Parliament would not tax a colony that itself raised the necessary revenues requested. He did not abandon his right to tax. Nor did he abandon his inclination to repression: in March he secured passage of the New England Restraining Act, which forbade fishing off the Grand Banks and restricted New England's international trade to Great Britain and the British West Indies. Before a nearly empty House of Commons Burke fruitlessly sought sanity and concessions, reminding his few listeners that the spirit of liberty was "stronger in the English colonies probably than in any other people of the earth." But the drift to war continued unimpeded.

Americans were even more divided, uneasy over the course of events, reluctant often to acknowledge just where the inexorable logic of their arguments had led them. Patrick Henry might wax emotional and paraphrase Addison's *Cato* with remarks on "liberty or death," but even John Adams found this fatal alternative "cold comfort." Action resolved thought: military

British troops return from Concord.

developments would help resolve the political. In April General Gage received orders from the Secretary of War to seize military stores that were reported in nearby Concord. His seven or eight hundred troops met seventy Americans on the Lexington village green and left eight dead and ten wounded.

Incredible though it seemed to many colonists, the Congress continued to make conciliatory gestures in spite of such events. John Dickinson's Olive Branch Petition blamed the North government for all Britain's difficulties in America, begged the Crown to prevent further parliamentary tyranny, pending efforts at reconciliation, and requested the repeal of the Coercive Acts and the Declaratory Act. John Adams denounced Dickinson's suppliant tone, but unjustly, for the Olive Branch was intended to show Americans —and the world—how patient and yet how wronged they were. It was now up to George III. Dickinson was much more belligerent in the Declaration of the Causes and Necessity of Taking Up Arms, voted by the Congress the next day, July 6, 1775. Here Americans announced their readiness to die to avoid slavery: "Our cause is just. Our union is perfect. Our internal resources are great, and if necessary, foreign assistance is undoubtedly attainable." The Congress raised armies not for independence but "for the preservation of our liberties." Two weeks later the Congress ordered a total of $3 million in paper money to finance its struggle, established a postal system, and then, on July 31, formally rejected North's plan for conciliation. The exhausted Congress adjourned for a month's rest on August 2.

After the Congress reconvened (this time joined by delegates from Georgia), it awaited Britain's response to its humble petition of July. The answer came early in November: the King refused to receive the Olive Branch; the House of Commons, less proud, formally rejected it as a basis for reconciliation by a vote of eighty-three to thirty-three. At the same time Congress learned of the royal proclamation of August 23, which declared the colonies in open rebellion. Even so, in December the delegates reaffirmed their allegiance to the Crown—while once more denying the authority of Parliament. Not that Parliament's feelings would be hurt; in the same month that esteemed body was passing the Prohibitory Act, which forbade all commerce with the rebellious colonies and proclaimed a blockade of their ports.

INDEPENDENCE DECLARED

Clearly the prospects for reconciliation had dimmed. By the end of 1775 the Crown was the sole surviving connection between the angry colonists and their mother country. The logic of that link was increasingly obscure for many. How could an American be loyal to a monarch who denounced his colonial subjects as traitors and rebels? How could an American delude himself that he was still a loyal subject when he was in fact at war with Britain and quietly negotiating for assistance from the French? Tom Paine, a recent arrival from the mother country, had no time for such sophistry, as he made plain in his widely read pamphlet *Common*

Sense, which was issued in January 1776. Paine's success stemmed from both his timing and his rhetoric. He said what many were finally thinking: Britain was corrupt, had forgotten its own legacy of liberty, and would soon corrupt America as well. It was not enough to oppose tyranny, one should oppose the tyrant too: "The blood of the slain, the weeping voice of nature cries, ' 'TIS TIME TO PART.' "

Common Sense contributed powerfully to the general colonial movement toward total separation from the mother country. By early April Congress was ready to open all colonial ports to all nations—except Britain. Within a week North Carolina had authorized its congressional delegation to vote for independence and foreign alliances. Rhode Island followed in a slightly more cautious fashion. Then came Massachusetts and Virginia. The stage was set for the final debates in Philadelphia when, on June 7, 1776, Richard Henry Lee of Virginia rose to move

> that these United Colonies are, and of right ought to be, free and independent states, that they are absolved from all allegiance to the British Crown, and that all political connection between them and the State of Great Britain is, and ought to be, totally dissolved. . . .

The opening speeches revealed strong reservations on the part of the middle colonies. As John Dickinson observed, while ripening rapidly they were not yet ripe for parting from Britain. Accordingly, further debate was postponed for three weeks while delegates consulted their constituents and congressional committees labored over the various sections of Lee's resolution. When discussions resumed on July 1, an initial ballot showed South Carolina and Pennsylvania opposed, Delaware divided, and New York still without instructions.* On July 2 South Carolina's delegation came out for independence; Caesar Rodney's arrival swung the Delaware vote; and Dickinson joined with Robert Morris in staying away, thereby creating a Pennsylvania majority for Lee's resolution.

Lee's resolution thus passed unanimously on July 2—the date that John Adams confidently predicted would hereafter be celebrated as the new nation's birthday. Actually, some thought the July 2nd vote something of an anticlimax: eight days earlier the Congress had passed resolutions defining treason as furnishing aid to Great Britain. This was unquestionably an explicit defiance of the sovereignty of George III, a formal act of revolution, and a *de facto* declaration of independence.

But the formal Declaration had yet to be approved. Jefferson believed his assignment to write it demanded no great originality of thought or scholarship. The object of the Declaration was to rally its colonial readers, to set down for all to see the justification for the momentous step the Congress was taking. For this purpose, the famous and felicitous opening paragraphs were perhaps the least important part of the document, although the proclamation of the identification of the rights of Englishmen with the rights of man was superbly, succinctly phrased. Whether the Declaration

---

*New York's delegates did not record their vote for independence until July 15.

Jefferson's rough draft of the Declaration of Independence

was a total commitment to freedom and equality for all Americans remains debatable: Jefferson did not insist that all men were equal—he thought otherwise—but he did claim equal legal and political rights for all free men. Not for black slaves. He did blame George III for forcing African slavery on the colonies, an indictment the Congress carefully deleted in the final version.

Most of the document was devoted to a summary of British iniquities, of violations of colonial charters, usurpations of the historic liberties that Englishmen brought with them to America. Jefferson and his colleagues had earlier attacked Parliament, but now they focused upon the King, a tyrant "unfit to be the ruler of a people who mean to be free." And yet George III was by no means the sole culprit. Jefferson pointed out that responsibility belonged also to the British people, who had constantly ignored colonial complaints about the tyranny visited on the colonies. Englishmen had been told "that submission to their Parliament was no part of our constitution, nor ever in idea, if history may be credited." And now came "the last stab to agonizing affection," the dispatch of "foreign mercenaries to invade and deluge us in blood." Jefferson's long, detailed list of causes for revolution demonstrated more than the colonists' clear right to rebel. He also showed the colonists' reluctant resort to the right of revolution and thereby reflected the intrinsic conservatism of many patriot leaders.

Independence emerged as a philosophical, legal, and historical imperative. On July 4, after a final two days' debate, Congress approved the Declaration. It was now the task of the American people to translate this moral mandate into political reality.

Suggested Reading

Among the many excellent studies of the origins of the American Revolution, Lawrence H. Gipson's *The Coming of the Revolution, 1763–1775** (1954) is one of the most succinct and attractive: also to be recommended are John R. Alden, *A History of the American Revolution* (1969), and John C. Miller, *The Origins of the American Revolution* (1943). The latter is not to be confused with Bernhard Knollenberg's *Origin of the American Revolution** (1960), which focuses on the period 1759 to 1766 and examines the British political context for American difficulties. Edmund and Helen Morgan's *The Stamp Act Crisis** (1953) establishes that crisis as the turning point in Anglo-American relations.

Clinton Rossiter supplied a pathfinding account of the colonists' concern for political liberty in *Seedtime of the Republic** (1953). Bernard Bailyn's *The Ideological Origins of the American Revolution* (1967) is the best and most coherent treatment of the political ideas of eighteenth-century colonists; Trevor Colbourn's *The Lamp of Experience* (1965) examines the colonists' sense and use of the past and suggests that their history enabled conservative colonists to take their revolutionary posture.

The decision for independence—and its form—is superbly treated by Carl L. Becker in *The Declaration of Independence** (1922) and, more recently, by David Hawke in *A Transaction of Free Men* (1964).

*Available in paperback edition

CHRONOLOGY

1776–81 Revolutionary War:
March, 1776: British evacuate Boston
September, 1776: Howe occupies New York
December, 1776: Washington surprises British at Trenton and Princeton (January, 1777)
September, 1777: Howe takes Philadelphia
October, 1777: Burgoyne surrenders at Saratoga
June, 1778: France enters war as ally of America
June, 1779: Spain enters war as ally of France
October, 1781: Cornwallis surrenders at Yorktown

1777 Congress votes Articles of Confederation

1781 Articles of Confederation ratified

1782 Preliminary treaty of peace (effective 1783)

1785 Land Ordinance

1785–86 Jay-Gardoqui negotiations

1786 Virginia disestablishes Anglican Church
Annapolis convention
Trevett v. *Weeden* case

1786–87 Shays' Rebellion

1787 Constitutional convention opens in Philadelphia
Northwest Ordinance

1787–88 State conventions ratify Constitution

V

THE NEW NATION,

1776–1789

"In establishing American independence," remarked David Ramsey in 1789, "the pen and press had merit equal to that of the sword." Ideas are indeed weapons, as Max Lerner noted one hundred fifty years later, but the merit of the sword was to be keenly tested by the new nation brought into being that hot, hopeful summer of 1776 by Jefferson and his colleagues. Their proclamation of independence drew open contempt on both sides of the Atlantic: they were, after all, calling for victory over the greatest empire known, over the nation that had recently humiliated France. Patriot and Loyalist alike wondered at American temerity and questioned prospects for military success. Muskets and artillery had to sustain Jefferson's provocative words.

Nor were military matters the only ones crowding the colonial mind in 1776. There were immediate political problems. How were erstwhile colonies to become self-governing states? What would be their new constitutional structure? How would they relate to one another? What internal change was called for? How would independence affect the American economy, the American society? Would there be, in fact, a real revolution, a change in the social order extending beyond a simple political separation from Great Britain? Could Americans indeed overcome the deep divisions created by the quest for independence itself? There was no lack of questions for thoughtful colonists who pondered their country's future. The thirteen years that followed the French and Indian War determined the verdict for independence; the succeeding thirteen years would decide how—and whether—America would emerge as a nation.

THE CONTEXT FOR CONFLICT

The immediate task facing Americans in 1776 was national survival. Their frequent self-doubts and sense of inferiority only compounded the discouraging odds. They remained a divided people, in spite of the patient, cautious approach toward independence. They lacked arms, armies, military traditions. They were without money and effective government. And the quality of their military leadership was as speculative as their prospects for the foreign alliance that many considered essential to victory.

The war for independence was also a civil war. Thousands of Americans professed their continued devotion to the mother country. Loyalists were not all rich property-owners fearful of losing their status and political power. Some just loved England. Others, convinced of British superiority, would not run the risks of supporting an unsuccessful rebellion. Still others were simply allergic to the label of rebel, which was one reason Patriots devoted so much time to arguing that theirs was not in fact a revolution, that *Britain* was rebelling against acknowledged *American* rights. Local politics often intruded: some New Yorkers supported the British out of distaste for the aristocratic Livingston family, which was firmly in the Patriot camp. For Samuel Seabury loyalty to the Crown was more a matter of style: "If I must be enslaved," he said, "let it be by a *King* at least, and not by a parcel of upstart lawless Committeemen. If I must be devoured, let me be devoured by the jaws of a lion, and not gnawed to death by rats and vermin."

There were Loyalists of every station, occupation, race, and religion. Possibly as many as 50,000 took up arms for Britain; about 8,000 appeared on British army rolls in 1780. Had the British made effective use of this support, the war might have taken a very different course. As it was, many Loyalists who came out openly for Britain found themselves ignored by British generals, deserted by British troops. The Patriots, on the other hand, sometimes practiced brutal intimidation: known Loyalists faced imprisonment and confiscation of estates; some were even tarred and feathered. But few were hanged. There was no genuine reign of terror in this revolution but rather a wide reverence for order, for law. And in any case, many Loyalists wisely removed themselves from Patriot reach; perhaps 80,000 ultimately fled to Canada, where they nurtured an enduring dislike for the United States.

The sad condition of the British forces more than compensated for internal American division. Britain's was a gentleman's army in many ways: officers bought their commissions; wives and mistresses of officers and men alike burdened logistics by traveling with the British troops. Some 2,000 women accompanied General "Gentleman Johnny" Burgoyne's 7,000-man army to its fateful rendezvous at Saratoga. Britain's main weapon was still

A British view of the American soldier (1776)

THE AMERICAN RIFLE MEN.

the 14-pound Brown Bess musket, inaccurate and limited in range. (There was no order to aim in the army manual.) Many saw the musket as merely a device to carry a bayonet. Britain had not abandoned its tradition for unpreparedness: in 1775 the army's total strength was less than 50,000, of which only 8,500 were in North America. American privateers and 3,000 miles of ocean intensified Britain's problems of supply and transportation; the nearly total lack of cooperation from the Royal Navy hardly reduced these difficulties. Finally, the British had a dangerous contempt for their American enemy. Since it was said that "the flower of Mr. Washington's army" was made up of "the Gleanings of British prisons," it seemed humiliating to risk death at the hands of riffraff—so demeaning that some disdained to fight in America. Still others refused from sympathy for the American cause. Faced with such limited enthusiasm, North's ministry looked to Europe for troops and hired some 30,000 Germans (of whom only 1,200 were the notorious Hessians).

In some ways, American military prospects seemed little better. Washington's greatest achievement as Commander in Chief may well have been keeping an army in the field, even if it rarely exceeded 8,000 in number. The heavy reliance upon militia reflected the American fear of standing armies and widespread unwillingness to enlist for the long term. Up to the rank of Captain, officers were elected, usually succeeding on grounds of popularity rather than competence. Few had significant military experience, which enhanced the value of such European volunteers as the Marquis de Lafayette, Baron von Steuben, and Count Pulaski. The amount of desertion provoked Washington to remark that he would "have to detach one half of the army to bring back the other." Poor clothing, equipment, and pay brought on mutinies in 1780, 1781, and 1783. No wonder Washington despaired, criticizing his troops as "an exceedingly dirty and nasty people."

Washington was, however, fighting on home ground. He knew his terrain and he could pick his battleground. He had short internal lines of communication and supply. And he had the inestimable assistance of British military and political mismanagement on a scale that dwarfed even the tribulations caused by Congress. In short, the War for Independence was like most wars: it produced much dissension, disaffection, and disorganization, a few heroes, and fewer effective leaders—on both sides. The ultimate American victory had some aspects of the miraculous.

THE WAR FOR INDEPENDENCE

Although Washington forced the British to withdraw from Boston in March, 1776, he failed dismally when he attempted to dislodge the British from New York later that summer. He even had the inadvertent help of the cautious and indolent General William Howe, whose ineffectiveness produced rumors that he was secretly in the American camp. Washington's winter forays at Trenton and Princeton helped raise American morale but had little military significance.

On the other hand, the grotesque miscarriage of General Burgoyne's plan to slice through New York and New England was of major military and political moment. Burgoyne had conceived of three British armies converging in New York, but one army, under St. Leger, was stopped at Fort Stanwix and the other, under Howe, moved south into Philadelphia instead of north up the Hudson River. Unaware of this lack of support, Burgoyne pushed southward from Canada, finally to be surrounded at Saratoga by a force three times the size of his own. On October 17, 1777, Burgoyne and his surviving 5,700 men surrendered their arms to General Horatio Gates.

The consequences were perhaps diplomatic rather than military (Burgoyne's men did not keep their parole and were to fight again in Virginia). Two months after Saratoga, France formally recognized American independence, while Lord North was again vainly seeking a settlement that might preclude a Franco-American alliance. Congress denounced the British overtures and in March, 1778, ratified the treaty concluded in Paris by Silas Deane and Benjamin Franklin. The American struggle became a theater in a new world war as first the French, then the Spanish and the Dutch entered the conflict.* In 1780, Russia headed a European coalition known as the League of Armed Neutrality to defy the British navy. By then, Britain's resources were seriously strained—and American opportunity increased.

---

*Spain did not enter as an American ally but in support of France, which promised Gibraltar and, later, Florida; Britain declared war upon Holland to close off commercial traffic with the Americans.

The strategic importance of Saratoga was not immediately apparent to Washington and his weakened forces as they wintered at their camp in Valley Forge while Howe enjoyed warm housing in Philadelphia. But Washington retained his command; Howe was replaced by Henry Clinton, who successfully withdrew to New York in June, 1778.

It became more and more apparent that the French alliance provided the opportunity for victory, not a guarantee. George Rogers Clark's victory at Vincennes in the West furnished the only notable American success in 1778. Washington was inactive, and his troops again suffered when they spent the winter of 1778–79 in New Jersey. The defection of the able but ill-used Benedict Arnold and agitation against Washington as Commander in Chief demonstrated a widespread domestic disaffection and uneasiness among American troops, which lasted into 1780.

But 1780 saw the beginning of the end for the British, who demonstrated their ability to snatch defeat from the jaws of victory. Clinton, in company with Lord Cornwallis and Admiral Peter Parker, seized Charleston in May, from which Cornwallis mounted a major victory over General Gates at Camden, South Carolina in August. But Cornwallis could not prevail against Daniel Morgan in North Carolina and so moved north into unprotected Virginia. Here Cornwallis fatally miscalculated: he marched his 7,000 men to Yorktown, expecting to be met by the British Navy. Instead, he discovered the French fleet of the Comte de Grasse and the combined armies of Washington and the Comte de Rochambeau (about 15,000 men), which had moved south from New York and Rhode Island. Clinton then miscalculated Cornwallis' ability to withstand a lengthy siege. As early as September 23, Cornwallis advised Clinton, "If you cannot relieve me very soon, you must be prepared to hear the worst." The worst occurred on October 17, when Cornwallis surrendered and so, in effect, ended the war.

PEACE

"Oh God! it is all over," cried Lord North when he heard of the humiliation of Yorktown. Actually the war was over only in America; elsewhere Britain was still a power to respect, as Admiral George Rodney's destruction of the French fleet in 1782 confirmed. Gibraltar survived the Franco-Spanish onslaught, and British armies remained in New York as well as in the Northwest. But Yorktown had a major impact upon the British political scene. North's parliamentary majority steadily shrank: his margin of 100 in 1780 was down to 19 early in 1782. Finally, on March 20, 1782, North resigned. George III contemplated abdication, but the prospect of his hated son becoming King led him to accept his new ministry reluctantly. Sir Guy Carleton, who replaced Clinton, had orders to conciliate, not fight. Meanwhile, Lord Shelburne initiated peace negotiations.

In spite of the British eagerness for an end to hostilities, accomplishing a peace was not a simple task. Neither France nor Spain cared to replace the British presence in North America with a powerful new United States of America; indeed, the Spanish regarded colonial rebellions with the natural distaste of a nation with colonies of its own in the New World.

Revolutionary War, 1775–1781

1775–1777

1777–1778

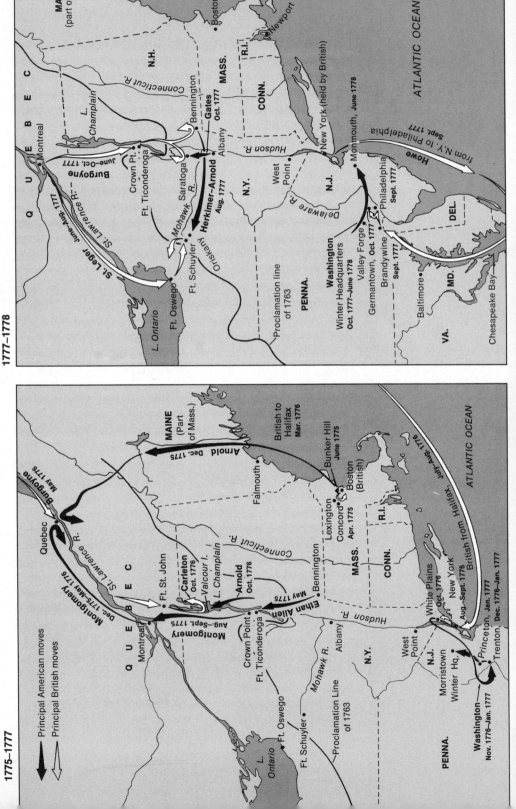

Principal American moves

Principal British moves

1778–1781

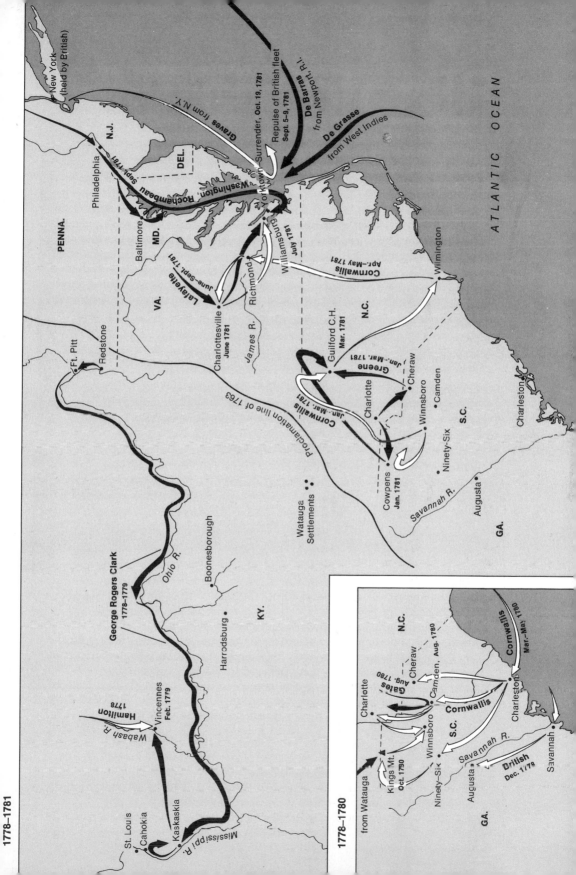

New York (held by British)

PENNA.

N.J.

Philadelphia

Baltimore

MD.

DEL.

Graves from N.Y.

Repulse of British fleet
Sept. 5–9, 1781

De Barras R.I.
from Newport

De Grasse
from West Indies

ATLANTIC OCEAN

Yorktown Surrender, Oct. 19, 1781

Washington, Rochambeau, Sept. 1781

Williamsburg
July 1781

VA.

Lafayette
June–Sept. 1781

Richmond

Charlottesville
June 1781

James R.

Cornwallis
Apr.–May 1781

Wilmington

Redstone

Ft. Pitt

Proclamation line of 1763

Guilford C.H.
Mar. 1781

N.C.

Cornwallis
Jan.–Mar. 1781

Greene
Jan.–Mar. 1781

Cheraw

Charlotte

Winnsboro

Camden

S.C.

Charleston

Cornwallis
Jan.–Mar. 1781

Cowpens
Jan. 1781

Ninety-Six

Augusta

Savannah R.

GA.

Ohio R.

George Rogers Clark
1778–1779

Boonesborough

KY.

Harrodsburg

Watauga
Settlements

Hamilton
1778

Vincennes
Feb. 1779

Wabash R.

St. Louis

Cahokia

Kaskaskia

Mississippi R.

1778–1780

N.C.

Charlotte

from Watauga

Kings Mt.
Oct. 1780

Winnsboro

Ninety-Six

S.C.

Augusta

Savannah R.

GA.

Cheraw

Camden, Aug. 1780

Gates
Aug. 1780

Cornwallis

Cornwallis
Mar.–May 1780

Charleston

Savannah

British
Dec. 1778

The British were no more eager to see a strong, independent United States but they were determined to cut their losses by wooing Americans away from the French embrace. The American peace commissioners, Benjamin Franklin, John Jay, and John Adams, made the most of such opportunities; they opened their negotiations with Britain with extravagant demands including the cession of Canada, and then settled for the boundaries of the Mississippi River on the west (which Spain opposed), the thirty-first parallel to the south, and the Great Lakes in the north. In return the Americans agreed to allow British creditors to sue for prewar debts and recommended that the states restore Loyalist property. The French Foreign Minister, Comte de Vergennes, was dismayed by Britain's generosity and the speed of the independent American diplomacy, but Franklin's tact not only overcame French alarm but won another large loan for the United States. Final agreement in the form of the Treaty of Paris, signed by Britain and the United States, took place on September 3, 1783.

Although the protracted peace negotiations brought formal acknowledgment of American independence many in Europe were skeptical of the future of the new United States. Cynics pointed to the vast divisions within the former British colonies and questioned the reality of the new nation. Certainly domestic developments during the war fed such doubts; the American future was anything but assured.

THE ARTICLES OF CONFEDERATION
AND STATE CONSTITUTIONS

The Revolution was much more than a war for independence. The underlying principles of Jefferson's Declaration seemed to confer a responsibility of demonstrating American capacity for freedom and for self-government. But it proved easier to identify such responsibility than to realize it. The thirteen colonies now had the task of shaping new governing structures to replace old British ones. The colonies also had to decide how much hard-won sovereignty to surrender to a federal government that had won the war. It is understandable that progress was unsteady and judgments sometimes flawed.

Many Americans soon questioned the judgments that produced the first federal government. Fully aware of the political risks in impairing the sovereignty of its member states, the Congress, unauthorized, undertook to create a form of national union adequate to the needs of national survival. In June, 1776, John Dickinson was named to head the committee charged with drafting the new national constitution. In spite of the bickering over slavery, the conflicting claims to western land, and the small states' nervousness over the power of their larger associates, in 1777 the Congress approved the plan and recommended its ratification by the states. Actually, congressional approval was unremarkable in view of the nature of Dickinson's proposed Articles of Confederation. He merely described on paper what was already practiced and conceded. It was, wrote Dickinson, "A firm league of friendship"; certainly it was not much more.

Dickinson had devised a league of sovereign states, which primarily assigned power to the Congress for external affairs. Each state, regardless of size or wealth, would have an equal voice, and the states would elect and pay their own delegates to the single-chamber national legislature. Lacking an executive, the Congress would operate through committees. Major questions would call for the support of nine of the thirteen states; constitutional amendments required unanimity. Congressional authority was confined to foreign policy (war and peace), the army, interstate and border disputes, the post office, Indian affairs, coinage, and loans. The authority to levy taxes or regulate interstate commerce was conspicuously absent.

But these limitations and omissions reflected political reality. Americans had declared their independence because they feared and resented the strong, centralized government of Great Britain. They were not about to replace one such administration with another—not even one of their own making. Even so, the new constitution waited four years for ratification. Those states with fixed western boundaries, such as Maryland, insisted that unsettled lands west of the mountains should be assigned to the new national government. But not until 1780 did New York finally promise to relinquish its western land claims to the Congress, a lead soon to be followed by Connecticut and Virginia. The way was then clear for ratification; Maryland formally accepted the Articles of Confederation in February, 1781, and the Congress proclaimed the new government of the United States of America in effect as of March 1.

The process of constitutional change in the states was relatively smooth, if less systematic than constitution-making on the national level. As early as 1774 all the colonies except Georgia had elected delegates to the First Continental Congress through extralegal conventions. These conventions provided the base from which the states moved to respond to the congressional recommendation in May, 1776, to "adopt such government as shall best conduce to the happiness and safety of their constituents."

Most of the constitution-making that ensued was more conservative than might have been expected in a revolutionary era. Often the new state constitution was merely a slightly revised version of the old colonial form of government, ordinarily with a major reduction in the power of the Governor. Most states denied the Governor the veto power and limited him to a one-year term; usually he was to be elected by the state legislature, which now wielded most constitutional power. The assemblies were bicameral from the outset (except those of Pennsylvania and New Hampshire), with the lower house frequently modeled after Britain's powerful House of Commons. Particularly significant was Virginia's precaution of incorporating George Mason's widely copied Bill of Rights, which was intended to protect citizens from even their own legislators. As Jefferson remarked in his *Notes on Virginia*, "An elective despotism was not the government we fought for"; he recalled that the time to guard "against corruption and tyranny is before they shall have gotten hold of us." The frequency of legislative elections was also significant: in careful contrast to Britain's septennial arrangement, most of the American states called for elections every one or two years, in the hope of keeping the legislators in close contact with the voters.

Historians have long debated the measure of democracy introduced by these new state constitutions. In fact, the constitution-makers were not consciously seeking democratic government; they were more concerned with stability and security. No state gave the vote to all white men; every state required some form of property-ownership for the suffrage, and in some instances (as in New York) the requirement increased, as did the frequently substantial property qualification for officeholding. Furthermore, the eastern sections of the states sometimes dominated both the constitution-making and the allocation of political representation that resulted. For example, the more populous western section of South Carolina received only half the number of legislators assigned the tidewater region. Although each state constitution cited the people as sovereign, Americans did not yet achieve the political democracy implied by the Revolution.

THE INTERNAL REVOLUTION

If there was not absolute democracy, there was reform. As increased economic and political opportunity brought new faces into the legislative halls, the influence and power of the aristocracy of wealth diminished. The war created its own opportunities for new entrepreneurs in trade and commerce. The confiscation and sale of Loyalist estates brought a considerable redistribution of landed wealth. In New York, for instance, Roger Morris' 5,000 acres went to 250 new landowners; James De Lancey's vast estate emerged as some 275 new farms. But in Somerset County, New Jersey, Patriots who had adjoining property divided the Loyalists' land and added to their existing propertied power.

Many saw the Revolution as an admirable opportunity to sweep aside the last remnants of New World feudalism. Quitrents, the annual feudal payments denoting obligations for ownership of land, were soon abolished, despite conservatives who thought to assign such revenues to the state governments. Entail, which prohibited the portioning of an inheritance, was ended by 1786. Primogeniture, which assured descent of property to the first-born male heir, lingered in some states until the turn of the century. Even the rights of women received some attention: most states gave daughters and sons equal inheritance rights. Although the democratizing effect may have been exaggerated, such reforms did facilitate the break-up of large estates. Jefferson, for one, was delighted: "Are we not the better," he asked a friend, "for what we have hitherto abolished of the feudal system?" For him such land reform was fully justified as a return to the pre-feudal, pre-Norman era of "our wise British ancestors."

Land reforms could advance equality of opportunity for whites, but they hardly helped black slaves. However, many Americans took seriously the philosophy underlying the Revolution. In fact, the founding of the Quaker Anti-Slavery Society took place a year before the Declaration of Independence was written. The implications of the natural rights of men were substantial. Did such rights know a color line? Could a struggle for freedom be waged for white men only? Crispus Attucks was one of the earliest casualties in the war, and he had company from the ranks of the

5,000 other blacks who joined in the revolutionary struggle. Beginning with Rhode Island and Pennsylvania, all states north of Maryland had provided for emancipation by 1804. And the number of free blacks increased sharply in Virginia between 1782 and 1810, although most blacks in southern states remained in slavery. In spite of improved opportunities for private manumission, even the most liberal Southerner rarely inconvenienced himself by freeing his slaves, except perhaps in his will. Even so, gradual emancipation seemed a possibility until the South discovered the cotton gin and a new reliance upon black servitude. Economic advantage obviously qualified concern for human rights. Slavery was generally unprofitable in the North, a fact that permitted greater altruism. Although most blacks secured their freedom in the northern states, they did not secure all the rights usually assumed to accompany freedom.

Religious and educational reform also accompanied the Revolution. Since the Anglican Church was most directly identified with Britain, those states south of Delaware in which Anglicanism was well established moved swiftly to terminate the Church's privileged position. Virginia's unusual religious arrangement—virtually a congregational organization for an Anglican denomination—along with the patriotism of its Anglican clergy led to a delay in disestablishment. But finally in 1786 Jefferson's Statute for Religious Liberty passed. The Congregational Church, well entrenched in the New England states, proved less vulnerable; not until 1833 did Massachusetts move toward the separation of church and state so earnestly advocated by James Madison and Thomas Jefferson. Other denominations moved more rapidly to organize independently; the Methodists found their own bishop in Francis Asbury, followed by the Roman Catholics with John Carroll. But disestablishment did not necessarily mean freedom of conscience: in Massachusetts and Maryland officeholders were required to swear an oath that they were Christians; in Pennsylvania one had to believe in the divine inspiration of the Scriptures; in Delaware belief in the Trinity was expected; and in New Jersey and the Carolinas Protestantism was demanded of officeholders. In short, the Revolution advanced freedom of worship, but Americans were still far from religious liberty.

The process of separation of church and state increased the number of academies and colleges throughout the nation. This renewed enthusiasm for higher education had both religious and political sources: religious sects continued to seek the promotion of their faith and its continuity, and states assigned some of their undeveloped landholdings for the support of colleges and "Seminaries of Learnings." The revived quest for knowledge advanced medicine, increased libraries, and gave new life to learned societies, such as the American Philosophical Society and the American Academy of Arts and Sciences.

In the difficult, unsteady process of addressing the tasks of independence, Americans slowly discovered their new identity and revealed the character and dimensions of their reluctant Revolution. There was no abrupt, sudden reversal of colonial customs and practices. But there was social, political, and religious change—and answers were earnestly being sought for new questions. Some four years after the war had ended,

Benjamin Rush recalled that, while the war was indeed over, the Revolution was not: "On the contrary, nothing but the first act of the great drama is closed. It remains yet to establish and perfect our new forms of government."

THE CRITICAL PERIOD, 1783–1787

Perfecting "new forms of government" proved an extended and difficult task. The Articles of Confederation, first debated in 1776 and finally ratified in 1781, furnished as much central government as the member states were then prepared to accept. Although the Articles provided a structure adequate to the needs of waging and winning the war, they appeared decreasingly responsive to national needs in the postwar years. The nineteenth-century historian John Fiske argued in *The Critical Period of American History* that the weaknesses and failures of the Confederation threatened the very survival of the nation. Modern historians have conceded the seriousness of the problems but have found the nation's condition less than perilous. In fact, Americans made genuine achievements under the Articles, but there were major problems which could only be resolved by the creation of a vastly stronger national government.

The most constructive work of the Congress of the Confederation lay in its legislation for the national domain. Since disputes over western land claims had delayed ratification of the Articles themselves, it was fitting that the Congress should successfully establish policy governing the future development of the west. Virginia furnished the occasion for action by finally surrendering western land claims to the Congress in 1784. The next year the Congress established a pattern for orderly settlement of the land north of the Ohio River, calling for townships of 6 square miles, subdivided into thirty-six sections of 640 acres, each to be sold by auction for at least one dollar an acre. The resulting revenue would help pay the vast national debt. Revenue from one section in each township was to support public education.

The Congress thus acknowledged both its responsibilities and its opportunities: it sought to bring order and government to the west and at the same time to secure desperately needed revenue. For well-organized speculators, such as the Ohio Company, this plan for settlement seemed a marvelous opportunity for quick wealth. The Ohio Company of Associates had acquired some 1.5 million acres for a dollar an acre in inflated colonial currency—or about eight or nine cents an acre in hard money. Having gained legal title, the speculators had to evict squatters and Indians, so law and order was an early political concern. The Congress responded with the Northwest Ordinance in 1787, providing for the evolution of territorial government: the territory would be under federal rule until the population reached 60,000, when statehood might be granted. New states were to enter without slavery but otherwise with privileges identical to those of the original thirteen.

Congressional success in legislating for the western domain was hardly matched in its conduct of postwar foreign policy. The Congress had authority

The Old Northwest

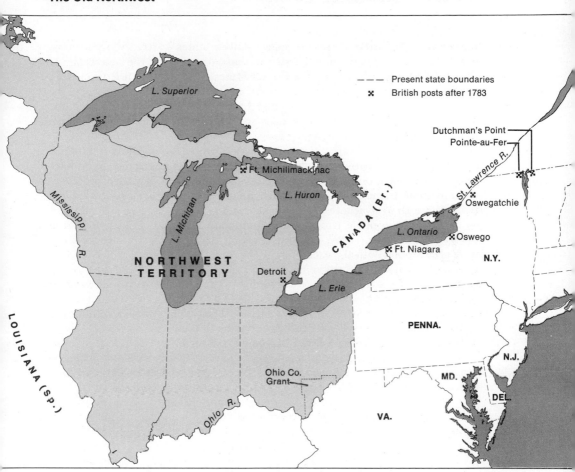

Township Survey under the Land Ordinance of 1785

A western township = 36 sq. miles
One section = 1 sq. mile (640 acres)

Half section (320 acres)

Quarter section (160 acres)

Half–quarter section (80 acres)

Quarter–quarter section (40 acres each)

6	5	4	3	2	1
7	8	9	10	11	12
Income reserved for school support →16	15	14	13
19	20	21	22	23	24
30	29	28	27	26	25
31	32	33	34	35	36

—1 mile—

Numbering system adopted 1796

Legend (map):
- - - Present state boundaries
✕ British posts after 1783

Dutchman's Point
Pointe-au-Fer
St. Lawrence R.
Oswegatchie
L. Superior
Ft. Michilimackinac
L. Huron
CANADA (Br.)
L. Ontario
Oswego
Ft. Niagara
N.Y.
NORTHWEST TERRITORY
L. Michigan
Detroit
L. Erie
PENNA.
N.J.
MD.
DEL
Mississippi R.
LOUISIANA (SP.)
Ohio Co. Grant
Ohio R.
VA.

to negotiate but little power to hold member states to treaty obligations. The lack of power gave foreigners little reason to respect the new republic that so hopefully called itself the United States. Relations with Britain were particularly uneasy. John Adams served as Minister in London, where he was usually snubbed. Britain declined to send a minister of its own for eight years, suggesting that one man would hardly suffice when thirteen were needed.

Certainly there were enough postwar disputes to engage any number of diplomats. The British complained that American states had enacted laws to obstruct collection of debts owed British merchants; they also protested continued harassment of Loyalists. On their part, Americans protested the British failure to evacuate military and trading outposts in the Northwest, as pledged in the peace treaty. These diplomatic difficulties did not disturb the flow of Anglo-American commerce, which British merchants encouraged with easy credit. With the exception of the West Indian ports, which Britain closed to Americans, postwar trade soon took on something of its prewar pattern, including a large trade imbalance that soon drained Americans of their specie.

Relations with Spain were difficult, complicated by Spanish resentment of the American presence in the trans-Allegheny West, by American resentment of Spanish control of the Mississippi, and by extravagant Spanish claims for its Florida border. Spain's decision to close the Mississippi to American shipping in 1784 led to negotiations between John Jay and Don Diego de Gardoqui in 1785–86. Jay asked the Congress to accept a settlement whereby the United States would give up use of the Mississippi for twenty-five years in return for trading concessions from Spain. The southern states would not agree and the proposal failed to secure the nine necessary votes for ratification. As Spanish intrigue continued in the West, there was a growing frontier suspicion that the northern states were ready to sacrifice the West in return for trade advantages. The futility of Jay's diplomatic exercise reminded others of the inadequacy of the Congress.

France was no more a friend than Spain. In fact, France persisted with a policy aimed at keeping the United States weak and dependent. France limited American commerce with the French West Indies, negotiated a treaty that allowed French consuls in the United States to try certain cases involving Frenchmen, and complained, with some reason, of the American failure to make payments on the huge debt still owed France. The Congress did succeed in negotiating two minor European trade treaties (with Sweden and Prussia) but met with rebuffs from other countries, which questioned the ability of the Congress to enforce its agreements at home.

Other aspects of Congressional authority were also vexing throughout the period of the Confederation. Debts not only remained unpaid but steadily increased. Initially the inability of the Congress to levy taxes was not very serious: during the war there was little hard money available for taxes. Both the Congress and the states resorted to lavish issue of paper money to finance the war; the depreciation of this currency—in fact a form of taxation—was so excessive that Congress abandoned its currency printing press in 1780. Instead, Congress resorted to loans, with rapidly diminishing returns at home but greater success abroad. The effort to raise revenues through a 5 percent import duty failed to secure the requisite Congressional unanimity. The postwar years saw Congress in dire fiscal straits, surviving largely on hope, Dutch loans, and the efforts of Robert Morris, who was Superintendant of Finance from 1781 to 1784.

The states themselves faced comparable fiscal difficulties, which contributed to the air of crisis that ultimately brought an end to the Confederation itself. The states had also resorted to paper money to finance the war, and despite rapid depreciation many were about to issue paper currency to finance the peace as well. The trade imbalance coincided with a deepening postwar depression and left debtors and taxpayers alike unable to meet their obligations. But creditors were not enthusiastic over a return to unsecured paper: they did not want to be repaid in money worth far less than the original loan.

In a majority of the states pressure for new issue of paper currency prevailed. But gloomy predictions of unrestrained inflation proved mistaken; most states controlled their currency carefully so that it gained ready acceptance. There were unfortunate and widely noted exceptions. Georgia's new currency declined in value by 75 percent within a year. New Jersey's well-secured paper was discredited by neighboring states, which practiced commercial warfare at New Jersey's expense. But the most alarming situation developed in Rhode Island, where a generous issue of paper money led to almost immediate depreciation. When merchants refused to accept the nearly worthless paper, the legislature enacted a law forcing them to accept it. Creditors fled the state to avoid meeting with their debtors. When, in December, 1786, the state's supreme court decided that the forcing act was unconstitutional,* the judges were brought before the legislature and roundly denounced.

The paper-money problem was often related to that of state indebtedness, much of which had been incurred during the recent struggle with England. The interest alone on such a debt created a heavy burden, leading some states to impose new and sometimes inequitable taxes. In Massachusetts, a conservative legislature placed the state on a hard-money base and then required redemption of outstanding debts at face value. Taxes ✓ skyrocketed, particularly for farmers, who found taxes (to be paid in specie) consuming one-third of their income. As a consequence, foreclosures and tax auctions became commonplace; in Worcester County 94 of 104 in jail were debtors. The failure of the state legislature to respond to the farmers' plea for relief led directly to Shays' Rebellion.•

The Rebellion began in the summer of 1786, when desperate farmers started to seize courthouses in an effort to halt foreclosure proceedings. Captain Daniel Shays, a veteran of Bunker Hill, led his fellow farmers to Springfield and forced the state Supreme Court to adjourn. Alarmed conservatives rallied to Governor James Bowdoin's call for volunteers to sup-

---

*The case of *Trevett* v. *Weeden* involved a Newport butcher (Weeden) who refused payment in the depreciated paper; although his case was dismissed on jurisdictional grounds, the judges established a precedent for a court test of the constitutionality of legislative action.

press this threat to property and order. At Petersham in February, 1787, General Benjamin Lincoln routed the rebels and Shays fled to Vermont. Shays was later pardoned, and the Massachusetts legislature modified its tax program. But the shock of the Rebellion endured. More than any other event, the Shays' Rebellion fed the growing conviction that only a stronger central government could assure law, order, and respect for property.

THE MAKING OF THE CONSTITUTION

"Something must be done or the fabric will fall," exclaimed George Washington on hearing of Shays' uprising. "We are fast verging to anarchy and confusion!" Jefferson was more sanguine—it was only "a *little* rebellion," fertilizer for the tree of liberty. But Jefferson was in France and separated from the American reality. Others had long contended that the Articles of Confederation were simply inadequate to their task, and as early as 1782, New Yorkers vainly urged a national convention to propose changes. Times were more favorable in 1786, when nine states accepted James Madison's suggestion of a meeting in Annapolis to discuss interstate commercial rivalry. Only five of the nine actually reached Annapolis; the delegates contented themselves with endorsing Alexander Hamilton's call for a convention to be held in Philadelphia to discuss ways in which they might "render the constitution of the Federal Government adequate to the exigencies of the Union." After some indecision, the Congress offered its own endorsement of the proposal and recommended a convention "for the sole and express purpose of revising the Articles of Confederation." By May 25, 1787, there were twenty-nine delegates on hand from nine states; they gathered in the Philadelphia State House and opened the discussions and debates that continued until September 17.

Eventually there would be fifty-five delegates participating in the Philadelphia convention. They represented every state but Rhode Island, which refused to attend because it did not want a stronger national government at the expense of state sovereignty. With the exception of Franklin and Washington, the delegates were not the heroes of the Revolution. Only eight of the delegates had signed the Declaration of Independence. Jefferson and John Adams were in Europe. Sam Adams, Richard Henry Lee, and Patrick Henry refused to come. But it was a brilliant, relatively youthful assembly. A majority were college graduates, in an age when few had the opportunity to attend college. Most had congressional experience, and all were chosen by their state legislatures. They saw themselves for what they were: practical politicians, pragmatic men seeking realistic solutions to national problems. Most were lawyers, and many, like James Madison, had helped draft their state constitutions. Instinctively, they consulted historical precedents; theoretical abstractions were not for them. "Experience must be our only guide," warned Dickinson. "Reason may mislead us."

Their motivations, like their purposes and achievements, have been much debated. Jefferson viewed the delegates as "demigods," while Charles Beard has suggested that the Founding Fathers operated mainly from personal economic interest. Most of the delegates were in fact from the propertied class, and some owned securities that would appreciate in value with a strong central government. But their political behavior did not necessarily coincide with their economic interest. The seven delegates who walked out of the convention or refused to approve its result were among the heaviest security-holders present. In practice the delegates rose above self-interest; their common interest was in providing a central government that could command respect at home and abroad.

Their debates and compromises illustrate that commitment. From the outset they held secret sessions to provide the freest of discussions; they even kept windows closed, in spite of the Philadelphia summer heat. Tempers rose with the temperature, sectional jealousies intruded with alarming frequency, and differences of opinion were both clear and sharp. But these disagreements have too often masked the delegates' larger measure of common purpose. No serious thought, for example, was given to merely patching up the government of the Confederation. There was general and continuing agreement that a strong national government should encompass defense, interstate commerce, taxation, law enforcement, protection of property, and the integrity of debt obligations.

Washington addresses the Constitutional Convention, September, 1787.

A major debate took place over the structure of the new Congress. The Virginia Plan and the New Jersey Plan assigned substantially similar authority to the new national Congress. The difference between the two drafts was one of method, not of objective: Virginia's Edmund Randolph sought a two-house national legislature with representation based upon population, while New Jersey's William Paterson favored a single-house legislature in which each state would have an equal voice. The deadlock was serious; Franklin, the religious skeptic, even went so far as to suggest prayers before each daily session. But Franklin also helped refine Roger Sherman's famed compromise, which established the bicameral system, with the Senate based upon an equal voice for all states and the House of Representatives based upon population.

Compromise determined the final details on most points. The Electoral College and the veto power of the President appeased those fearful of too much democracy; provisions for his impeachment contented those worried about potential dictators or monarchs; the three-fifths compromise allowed a partial counting of the slave as a base for computing representation in the House; another concession to the South, particularly South Carolina and Georgia, protected the slave trade at least until 1808 and further prohibited taxes on exports, upon which the South depended. The senators, with their six-year terms of office, were to be elected by the state legislatures, but the members of the House were to be elected every two years by popular vote. Age requirements for federal office reflected the delegates' quest for stability: the presidency called for a person at least thirty-five years old; the Senate demanded at least thirty years; only the House would tolerate a youth of twenty-five.

By September 17, the Constitution had been drafted. The surviving delegates, thirty-nine in all, signed the engrossed copy and virtuously adjourned for self-congratulation at the nearby City Tavern. They were not dissatisfied. Their compromises at once avoided the dangers of democracy and the hazards of despotism; they had provided a centralized national government, but one in which the states retained significant governmental authority. The conspicuous deficiencies of the Confederation were repaired: a simple majority could now enact legislation; a federal executive replaced the impotent committees of the Confederation; the power to regulate interstate commerce, to tax, and to raise an army were fundamental advances; a federal court system provided essential legal underpinning for the total structure; and it would not be unduly difficult to amend the Constitution. All that remained was to persuade the American people that it was in their interest to accept this new Constitution. That task would not be easy.

RATIFICATION

In Philadelphia the delegates had given the process of ratification considerable thought. They recalled the difficulty with which the Articles had gained unanimous approval and were well aware of the absence of Rhode Island from their deliberation. Accordingly, they decided that approval by nine states would be sufficient for the Constitution to take effect. The delegates also decided that ratification should be by special state conventions called for that express purpose, for the state legislatures were not likely to ratify a Constitution that would reduce their power; and further, if state legislatures could approve a Constitution, they could legally rescind their approval whenever they wished.

The delegates had calculated correctly. Only three states gave the Constitution their uncontested approval—Delaware, New Jersey, and Georgia. Connecticut was next to ratify by a comfortable 128 to 40 vote. Elsewhere, critics of the Constitution made known the strength of their objections. Anti-Federalists, such as Richard Henry Lee, cautioned lest "we kill ourselves for fear of dying." Patrick Henry claimed the proposed presidency "squints toward monarchy" and charged that the new Constitution would destroy the liberties secured in the Revolution. Many continued to fear that the Constitution would totally destroy the sovereignty of the states, that it would favor the propertied at the expense of the debtor class, that it was a conspiracy of the East against the aspirations of the West, that it represented a surrender to the South or, alternately, a devious victory for the mercantile North.

The best-known response to these objections came in the form of *The Federalist*, essays penned by Madison, Hamilton, and Jay between October, 1787, and April, 1788. In his famous tenth *Federalist* paper Madison called on his sense of constitutional adventure as he presented his view that the United States because of its vast size and variety of conflicting interests could indeed assure stability and justice. The influence of *The Federalist* was substantial. But even so, the fading Congress of the Confederation might not have transmitted the proposed Constitution to the states (which it did without recommendation) had it not been for the presence of ten congressmen who had recently served as delegates to the Philadelphia convention.

Federalist tactics varied from state to state. Pennsylvania, the first of the large states to ratify, did so in a questionable fashion. Federalists there rushed the call for a convention to reduce the opposition's chance to organize; Anti-Federalists boycotted the assembly so that there was no quorum for business, but the enterprising Federalists responded by forcibly dragging two Anti-Federalists into the State House. Federalists dominated the convention and on December 12, 1787, voted to ratify 46 to 23. In Massachusetts the divisions were particularly deep and the debates serious. John Hancock's final decision to support ratification proved helpful, as did the decision to recommend enactment of a federal bill of rights. The final vote was still close: 187 to 168. In Rhode Island the state legislature declined to call a convention but instead invoked a dubious referendum that resulted in overwhelming opposition to ratification. In Maryland the real debate took place during the election of convention delegates; Federalist dominance brought the 63 to 11 vote to ratify. South Carolina's tidewater gentry were satisfied with the Constitution and by a vote of 149 to 73 made the state the eighth to enter the new union. Federalist debaters in New Hampshire proved sufficiently persuasive for many delegates to change their position and vote to ratify; the final 57 to 47 vote for ratification was cast on June 21, 1788, the delegates unaware that theirs was the vital ninth state that would bring the new national government into existence.

The decision in New Hampshire was less conclusive than that in Virginia and New York. Virginia was the largest of the states, with one-fifth of the United States's population. A majority of Virginians probably opposed ratification at the outset, but the Federalists proved politically adroit and argued their case with care and skill. Washington's influence complemented the cool logic of Madison. Even so the vote on June 26 was close: 89 to 79 for ratification and for urging a federal bill of rights.* In New York opposition was even better organized than it had been in Virginia. It was headed by Governor George Clinton, joined by upstate landowners who enjoyed low taxes thanks to the state's income from import duties. Since Anti-Federalists constituted a majority of the ratifying convention, Hamilton's task was to debate and delay. He did both. News of Virginia's decision helped his cause, as did confusion over the precise meaning of the decision finally taken by a 30 to 27 margin; some supported ratification in the belief that another constitutional convention was to take place as a condition of New York's vote. North Carolina and Rhode Island, while far from irrelevant, now seemed less important: North Carolina opposed ratification in August, 1788, but reversed its position in November, 1789; Rhode Island, threatened with commercial isolation, grudgingly ratified by a 34 to 32 vote in May, 1790.

Obviously the new Constitution did not engender immediate reverence throughout the United States. The fight to ratify had been sometimes hard and often bitter. But it had been successful. A second, peaceful, and internal revolution had been completed; like the first revolution, it had been conducted by an articulate minority. And, as with the first revolution, results counted more than means.

Opposition to the Constitution would have been less severe had a bill of rights been incorporated from the outset. Most delegates in Philadelphia had relied on the protection afforded by the states, but they had underestimated popular fears of the new federal power. Without a promise, tacit or explicit, that such a bill of rights would immediately follow establishment of the new government, the Constitution could not have gained approval.

It was left to Cyrus Griffin, president of the expiring Congress, to announce formally the ratification of the new Constitution on July 2, 1788. In August arrangements were completed for the selection of presidential electors, and in September the Congress designated New York the site for the new government. The following month the Congress of the Confederation concluded its business and quietly vacated the New York City Hall to permit renovation for new occupants.

The new nation could now enter into its inheritance.

---

*Virginia acted in the belief that its was the ninth and deciding vote for ratification.

Suggested Reading

John R. Alden's competence as a military historian is well demonstrated in *The American Revolution, 1775–1783** (1954); John Shy examines the British army in *Toward Lexington* (1965), a work that can also serve to introduce Piers Mackesy's *The War for America, 1775–1783* (1964). The internal division within the colonies is best treated by William H. Nelson, *The American Tory** (1961), and Wallace Brown, *The King's Friends* (1965). Social aspects of the Revolution were first reviewed by J. Franklin Jameson in *The American Revolution Considered as a Social Movement** (1926). Jackson Turner Main usefully employs statistical tools in *The Social Structure of Revolutionary America** (1965).

The creation of new state governments is thoughtfully treated by Elisha P. Douglass in *Rebels and Democrats** (1955). J. R. Pole's *Political Representation in England and the Origins of the American Republic* (1966) is a substantial study of the American indebtedness to British ideas about political representation. In *The Creation of the American Republic, 1776–1787* (1969), Gordon S. Wood examines at length the meaning of republicanism for the revolutionaries. John Fiske's *The Critical Period of American History, 1783–1789* (1888)—with which Wood is sympathetic—is still readable. In *The New Nation** (1950) Merrill Jensen is much more favorably impressed with the new republic than are Fiske and Wood, and he relates its establishment in *The Articles of Confederation** (1940). Marion L. Starkey's *A Little Rebellion** (1955) is a lively account of Shays' Rebellion.

Clinton Rossiter has provided a useful treatment of the emergence of the Constitution in *1787: The Grand Convention* (1966), as has Forrest McDonald in *E Pluribus Unum* (1965). Charles A. Beard's much criticized *An Economic Interpretation of the Constitution* (1913) deserves to be read before one turns to Robert E. Brown's devastating *Charles Beard and the Constitution* (1956).

*Available in paperback edition

CHRONOLOGY

1789–1815   Intermittent European war

1789   Federal Judiciary Act
Presidential election: George Washington receives one vote from every elector; John Adams receives a plurality of the remaining ballots and is elected Vice-President

1790–91   Hamilton submits financial program:
1790: Funding Act, including assumption of state debts
1791: Bank of the United States chartered
1791: *Report on Manufactures*

1792   Presidential election: George Washington again receives one vote from every elector

1793   Washington proclaims American neutrality

1794   Whisky Rebellion
Jay Treaty with England

1795   Pinckney Treaty with Spain

1796   Presidential election: John Adams (Federalist) defeats Thomas Jefferson (Democratic-Republican); Jefferson becomes Vice-President
Washington gives Farewell Address

1797   XYZ affair

1798   Alien and Sedition Acts; Kentucky and Virginia Resolutions indicate Jeffersonian protest

1798–1800   Undeclared war with France

1800   Convention of 1800 ends alliance with France
Presidential election: Thomas Jefferson and his running mate Aaron Burr (Democratic-Republican) tie with 73 votes; John Adams (Federalist) receives 65. The House elects Jefferson President.

VI

A NATION EMERGES

Where George Washington led, many of his countrymen obediently followed, for he personified the independent nation that had emerged from two centuries of colonial dependence. Washington's presence at Philadelphia had helped to secure broad acceptance of the new Constitution; his unanimous selection as the republic's first President provided a nonpartisan focus for the loyalty of Americans who were by nature suspicious of central governments and executives.

The unanimity was deceptive. Rivalries of region, race, class, and national origin still divided American society. Nor had political jealousies disappeared, for conflicts flared among and within states over taxes, land grants, currency regulation, and the very purpose of government itself. New Hampshire and New York still disputed title to Vermont. Although returning prosperity eased the currency crisis that had brought on Shays' Rebellion, anxious debtors and impatient entrepreneurs alike eagerly awaited further improvement. And the perpetual argument about the proper function of government went on as it had for generations, between tidewater and back country, between Patriots and Tories, between Federalists and Anti-Federalists; the Constitution had not ended the quest for a perfect balance of liberty and law. As Washington put it, Americans who had

Inauguration of Washington, New York, 1789

matured in rebellion must learn to distinguish between the oppression that justified revolt and a "necessary exercise of lawful authority. . . ." The President's remark foreshadowed much of the subsequent political history of the nation he did so much to establish.

"Nation" was Washington's word for the United States; others used "confederation," or "federal republic," more tactful phrases that deemphasized the central government. During Washington's presidency and that of John Adams which followed, political issues become national—a national debt, a national bank, a national foreign policy to reaffirm national independence, national newspapers supporting national political parties, and finally the beginning of a new national capital. Parochial, colonial ways were changing. The old order resisted, but by 1800 the framework of the Constitution supported a nation that the Federalists had well begun.

Much of the subsequent shape of that nation is the legacy of the brilliant vision of Alexander Hamilton, the rugged independence of John Adams, and the wise and indispensable leadership of George Washington. Even their political opponents acknowledged the preeminence of these Federalists by debating on their terms: by arguing from constitutional provisions, the opposition accepted the Constitution itself; and when Thomas Jefferson, James Madison, and others merged several factions into an opposition party, their unity came from rejection of Federalism, not from agreement on a positive alternative.

THE FIRST ADMINISTRATION

Nation-building is no simple assignment. The Washington administration started with a few clerks, an army of 700 men, and a staggering array of tasks. (Indeed, Washington had more employees to handle the chores at Mt. Vernon than to manage the federal government.) British troops still occupied American soil in the Northwest, and Indians and settlers menaced one another all along the frontier. The national treasury had no resources to placate importunate creditors. Paper currency was so prevalent as to be nearly worthless and specie so scarce as to be overvalued. The United States was a frail new republic with no national courts, no national taxes, and no national mail service to tie Massachusetts with Georgia.

The First Congress straggled into New York in April, 1789, a month after it was supposed to assemble. This tardiness, like Washington's unfeigned reluctance to leave Mt. Vernon, foreshadowed the nation's early difficulty in attracting and retaining the service of able men. Exposed to urban plagues and fevers and deprived of the amenities of home and family, the life of a federal civil servant was hardly gracious. The President's salary provided a degree of comfort, but other honest officials had to scrimp to stay out of debt. No salary compensated for the loss of pride and reputation occasioned by the vehement partisanship of a press unchecked by taste or responsibility. Small wonder that public men preferred to avoid the hazards of travel and the trials of national politics and to serve their states instead. Both Washington and Adams put up with incompetent Cabinet officials rather than face the disheartening task of seeking replacements.

If tardy, the First Congress at least assembled in harmony. Many of the legislators had helped to write the Constitution or had worked to secure its ratification; only a half-dozen had prominently fought the new system. Congress quickly exercised the power to tax with a low tariff and established departments of State, Treasury, and War, to which Washington appointed Thomas Jefferson, Alexander Hamilton, and Henry Knox respectively as chief administrators. To enforce the nation's laws, Congress authorized appointment of an Attorney General and established a federal court system. This statute, the Judiciary Act of 1789, authorized the appeal to the Supreme Court of state-court decisions on constitutional issues, a provision that gave substance to the "supreme law of the land" clause in the Constitution and implied judicial review. Washington appointed Edmund Randolph, a fellow Virginian, Attorney General and John Jay of New York, the first Chief Justice. To fulfill the pledge made to Anti-Federalists during the ratification debate, Congress drafted a dozen amendments of which ten became the Bill of Rights. These amendments protected civil rights that most Americans already assumed to be guaranteed, and thereby skirted the other Anti-Federalist criticism.

Secretary of the Treasury Alexander Hamilton provided direction for the Federalist Congress. His political creativity was at once a great Federalist resource and a major Federalist liability. He meant to nurse the returning prosperity that enhanced public support for the central government; as much as any man. Hamilton strengthened the economic bonds that tied the republic together. But his economic policies also exaggerated political divisions in the country that contributed to eventual Federalist defeat. Hamilton created a national debt and the means for paying it, a national currency and a national bank to issue it. But while his vision was in some respects national, it was in others extraordinarily narrow. His taxes hit most heavily the frontiersman, who had the least cash. He deliberately sought the support of the "rich, the able and the well-born," and in the process alienated much of the rest of the country.

HAMILTON'S POLICIES

Several conditions, Hamilton believed in 1790, menaced healthy economic growth. Insufficient federal revenue and waning confidence in the government's ability to pay its bonded debt impaired the Treasury's capacity to reestablish public credit. The plethora of unreliable currencies complicated efforts of merchants and producers to create a national market. The economy, in Hamilton's view, relied too much on agriculture and slighted industrial development. Hamilton claimed that his master plan would ease economic hardship and cure economic malaise.

Washington with his Cabinet: General Henry Knox, Secretary of War; Alexander Hamilton, Secretary of the Treasury; Thomas Jefferson, Secretary of State; Edmund Randolph, Attorney General

Hamilton proposed to issue new bonds to fund at par the national debt and to meet overdue interest obligations to bondholders at home and abroad. In addition, he suggested that the central government assume state debts since, he argued, they had been contracted in pursuit of the common goal of independence. The new debt would total about $65 million. The government would raise its revenue from an excise tax on whisky, from the sale of public lands, and from a protective tariff that Hamilton asked Congress to enact in order to encourage the growth of manufacturing. He also outlined a twenty-year charter for a national bank to serve as a depository and a source of short-term credit for the government; the notes of this bank would become a national currency. Four-fifths of the capital for the Bank of the United States was to come from private investors, who would elect a proportionate share of the directors. The Treasury provided one-fifth of the initial capital of $10 million and appointed the rest of the board.

Hamilton's program had a political as well as an economic dimension, as he himself was the first to acknowledge. Wealthy citizens had new incentives to support the central government. Funding the federal debt and assuming the state debts created speculative opportunities in a depressed bond market. The new bank and its new currency would open opportunities for investors, merchants, and entrepreneurs. Hamilton's program hurt whisky-producers and those who wanted cheap public land, but these two groups often consisted of the same people—restless individual farmers, remote in the backcountry, who distilled their own grain to carry it more easily to market.

Hamilton's vision of an industrial America was premature, and Congress never passed his protective tariff. Otherwise his program generally succeeded in both its economic and political dimensions. Public confidence in American securities rebounded both at home and abroad. The Bank of the United States served the government, the stockholders, and the national economy well. Wealthy, respected, and educated citizens unflinchingly supported the new Constitution. And when in 1794 frontier farmers in Pennsylvania resisted the tax on spirits, Hamilton advised Washington to crush the Whisky Rebellion and demonstrate the central government's resolution and authority. The rebels dispersed so quickly in the face of overwhelming federal force that the troops had trouble finding the rebellion. The President pardoned the few dissidents arrested in the operation.

Overt rebellion was snuffed out, but opposition remained. "Elective rulers," observed Fisher Ames, a conservative Massachusetts Federalist, "can scarcely ever employ the physical force of a democracy without turning the moral force, or the power of public opinion against the government." Ames himself shared Hamilton's political prejudices and supported his legislation. Not everyone did. When the many vote, a program designed to appeal to a minority must rely on influence instead of numbers. Eventually numbers—farmers, debtors, men on the make envious of men who had arrived—displaced those who had achieved economic and political order. With the foundation for a national economy, the development of the national government, the expansion of the national domain, and the enunciation of a national foreign policy went the formation of national political parties.

Alexander Hamilton, portrait by
John Trumbull

Early opposition to Hamilton's fiscal policies lacked coherence. No one objected seriously to funding the foreign debt, for the republic's international reputation was at stake. Funding the domestic debt, however, roused a good deal of antagonism. Many soldiers and suppliers had been paid with bonds, which had then been sold at substantial discounts to make ends meet during the postwar depression. When the new government seemed likely to make good on the promises of the old, speculators redoubled their efforts to acquire depreciated state and federal securities. Although Hamilton himself did not buy up these certificates, some of his associates and a good many congressmen were less scrupulous.

James Madison denounced Hamilton's proposal to fund the domestic debt at par as unjust and opposed the assumption of state debts as unnecessary. While Hamilton defended the debt as a positive economic and political benefit, Madison thought the financial burden might well be too much for the republic. Further he charged that Hamilton's scheme would benefit profit-seekers at the expense of patriots who had helped the revolutionary cause. Simple justice, he held, demanded compensation at par for the initial holders of the bonds, while speculators should receive only their actual costs. The Treasury's policy, Madison went on, also did the entire southern section of the country an injustice. Southern bondholders owned only one-fifth of the national debt. Several southern states, including Madison's Virginia, had paid off most of their revolutionary bonds. Assumption of state debts would force provident southern taxpayers to meet the bills of improvident ones in the North, where the debts of Massachusetts, for instance, remained largely outstanding. (So did those of South Carolina, a fact that somewhat vitiated Madison's accusation of sectional bias.)

Congress at first returned a split verdict in 1790 by affirming Hamilton's plan to pay bondholders at par but refusing to assume the debts of the states. But congressional maneuvering soon reversed Hamilton's momentary defeat. Southern congressmen voted for assumption in return for support for their effort to move the nation's Capital to the banks of the Potomac. The trade worked. Hamilton had his debt, and planning for the District of Columbia was soon under way.

The South would not barter on the national bank. Jefferson and Madison rallied four-fifths of the southern congressmen, but they did not prevail against the unanimous North. When the President asked his opinion, Jefferson wrote a brief arguing that the "incorporation of a bank, and the powers assumed by the bill" had not been "delegated to the United States by the Constitution." Jefferson interpreted narrowly the elastic clause of the Constitution, which gives Congress the power to make all laws "necessary and proper" to carry out its powers; a bank might be convenient, he declared, but it was not essential. His statement, expanded and embroidered by lesser men in subsequent argument, is the essence of strict construction of the Constitution.

Hamilton responded to Jefferson with the classic statement of broad construction. The Constitution not only delegated some powers expressly, but it also granted others by implication. The elastic clause, Hamilton believed, gave Congress the power to select among various means to legitimate legislative ends. If the end was constitutional, the means were automatically constitutional, unless specifically forbidden. Congress clearly had the right to collect taxes, to disburse federal revenues, to borrow money, to provide for national defense, and to regulate commerce. The Bank of the United States was an entirely appropriate means to any of those ends and should be chartered even if the Constitution did not specifically give Congress the power to establish corporations. Hamilton persuaded Washington, who signed the bill.

Madison and Jefferson did prevent action on Hamilton's *Report on Manufactures,* which requested various bounties for manufacturers including a protective tariff. Hamilton's dream of an industrial nation generated scant political support. Jefferson's belief that "those who labor in the earth are the chosen people of God," that a nation of farmers was a virtuous nation, corresponded to his countrymen's image of themselves. Jefferson's interpretation of human nature and his faith in the endurance of rural virtue were happily combined in his faith in democracy, a faith Hamilton never pretended to share. Jefferson confidently looked for eventual political vindication of his beliefs; Hamilton, who thought it unlikely that any man could be at once right and popular, soon had to rely on manipulation because he did not have the votes.

Jefferson's belief in democracy stopped at the slave quarters. Unlike most of the whites of his day, Jefferson at least worried about slavery. Were black field hands, he wondered, as virtuous as white ones? Did slaves have the inalienable rights Jefferson himself had so eloquently proclaimed as the birthright of humanity? Even though Jefferson sometimes resolved these questions affirmatively, his hesitant response never became either a conviction or the basis for action. Some parts of the country had abolished slavery—much of New England, for instance, and New York—but slavery was abolished only where it was insignificant. Elsewhere, like Jefferson's dilemma, it endured.

SECURING INDEPENDENCE
IN A HOSTILE WORLD

The proud new nation had slim diplomatic and military re-sources with which to preserve independence. No army, no navy, no access to the courts of Europe or to the ports of Europe's colonies—the United States had only the uneasy French alliance and a grudging British accep-tance of independence upon which to found a foreign policy. A rebellious former colony could not expect a sympathetic welcome in a world domi-nated by empires with submissive colonies of their own. The Federalists prudently decided that neutrality would maximize the nation's economic opportunities, reduce its military risks, and thereby best serve the country. The Federalists, as usual, precipitated a political uproar with an entirely sensible policy.

For nearly a quarter-century a European struggle that began with the French Revolution in 1789 upset the Western world. While governments and alliances changed, temporary truces always seemed to give way to renewed war until in 1812 even the United States was finally drawn in. From the initial skirmishes until the settlement in 1815, the bloody encounter de-manded the attention of the American people. For in addition to the danger, the European struggle also created opportunity—the opportunity to restate and perhaps to strengthen the nation's proud independence, the oppor-tunity to discharge the debt for French assistance in the American Revolu-tion, the opportunity to increase the export trade, the opportunity to secure additional territory, the opportunity to capitalize on momentary diplomatic success to secure political advancement of party, program, or person.

Federalists found the French Revolution distasteful. Unlike the Ameri-cans they claimed to be following, French rebels threatened the property rights that Federalists believed good revolutions preserved. War, further-more, was an imponderable that might upset the delicate calculations upon which Hamilton's fiscal policy depended. At the very least, war with Britain would reduce imports and seriously impair the government's revenue. To Federalists, Britain represented stability and order; the British fleet was the first line of American defense. Jefferson, on the other hand, had seen the popular phase of the revolution while in Paris. Subsequently, as Secretary of State, he argued that the Alliance of 1778 bound the nation in honor to assist France; if Washington chose to announce American neutrality and ignore the pledge, he should nevertheless threaten to fulfill the alliance in order to exact concessions from Great Britain. Hamilton countered that our alliance had been with the King, whose death effectively released the United States from its treaty obligations. In 1793 the President officially proclaimed American neutrality.

Neutrality rarely satisfies emotions, and the initial American response to events in France had been emotional indeed. Enthusiastic editorials and toasts welcomed Edmund Genêt, the first diplomatic representative of the revolutionary government, who took advantage of popular good will by commissioning privateers, by authorizing an "allied" army of Americans to invade Florida, Louisiana, and Canada, and by encouraging the formation of "Democratic" societies, some of which became centers of Jeffersonian political intrigue. Washington received Genêt with chilling reserve, and even Jefferson soon decided that the enthusiastic Frenchman had ventured beyond the bounds of acceptable diplomatic behavior. Washington's decision to seek Genêt's recall coincided with a change of government in France. The new government, made up of Genêt's political foes, dismissed the blundering envoy, who then sought and received political asylum in the United States.

Resentment of Genêt's interference in American affairs never became positive support for the British cause. Opportunities for friction with Britain exceeded those for disagreement with France. There seemed an inexorable rhythm to neutrality that brought trouble with one belligerent, which did not completely subside before trouble with the other occurred. Neither Britain nor the United States had faithfully carried out the terms of the Treaty of Paris. Redcoats remained in forts in the Northwest Territory, and planters vainly sought compensation for slaves British troops had carried off after the Revolution. American debtors had not lived up to the spirit of the treaty, nor had Patriots returned confiscated property to the Tories. Frontiersmen thought British garrisons supplied Indian allies and encouraged their interference with American settlement. And the constant encounters of American and British ships created endless friction. The British Cabinet tried to restrict American trade as if the United States were still a colony; an Order in Council in 1793, for instance, authorized seizure of neutral cargoes bound either for France or for French colonies and resulted in the capture of more than three hundred American vessels and a swelling outcry in the United States.

Federalists suffered British interference with neutral trade more willingly than they did French interference. Jeffersonians, soon to be labeled Republicans, conversely excused French actions that would have roused their patriotic wrath if they had been committed under the Union Jack. In 1794 congressional opponents of the Federalists demanded an end to trade with the British Empire. From then on, economic coercion became the standard, and usually ineffective, Republican rejoinder to interference with American shipping. By the margin of the Vice-President's vote, the boycott failed in Congress, and the President decided to use negotiation instead of legislation to keep the peace.

THE JAY TREATY

John Jay resigned as Chief Justice to undertake the thankless mission to England. Jay was to secure compensation for commercial losses and for the slaves British soldiers had taken, evacuation of forts in the Northwest, and expansion of American trading opportunities in the British Empire. But the American envoy had almost nothing to trade for these concessions, especially after Hamilton told the British Minister that the United States would not join a coalition of European neutrals that was organizing to protect the commercial rights of nonbelligerents. James Monroe, the

American Minister in Paris, led British officials to suspect a continued Franco-American alliance, which complicated Jay's task. Jay could only imply that a break in negotiation might lead to war, although he knew his nation was unprepared for the military and economic consequences of hostility with England.

Under the circumstances, Jay did reasonably well. Lacking a compelling threat, he conciliated. Lord Grenville, the British Foreign Secretary, had no wish needlessly to alienate Americans, who might repudiate the large debts owed to British creditors and whose President effectively reduced French influence in the Western Hemisphere. So Grenville agreed to evacuate the posts in the Northwest, where the fur trade was declining in any case. A boundary dispute, claims resulting from commercial interference, and the unpaid debts were all referred to arbitration, with the United States agreeing to pay any award made to British creditors. Britain would permit American ships access to ports in the British Isles and, on humiliating terms, in the West Indies. The West Indian provisions were subsequently eliminated. But the United States did accept Britain's definition of neutral rights, a concession that closed French colonial ports to American vessels and added food and naval stores to the contraband list that Americans could not export to France. The treaty omitted any mention of Britain's impressment of American sailors and of its activity among the American Indians; nor, perhaps because Jay was an abolitionist, was there a reference to confiscated slaves.

His Cabinet colleagues thought Grenville too generous but defended the treaty in Parliament. Generosity was the mildest of the sins Americans attributed to Jay, however, and the Jay Treaty became a rallying point for opponents of Federalism. Frontiersmen and southern planters protested that Jay had ignored their interests in Indians and slaves to secure concessions for eastern Federalist merchants. Referring to the Treaty as "degradation," "submission," and "perfidy," the Republican press alleged that Britain had bought the envoy and the nation's honor, at the very least; the accusation often went on to suggest that the Jay Treaty effectively gave back the national independence won in the Revolution.

Washington hesitated before supporting the Treaty, less because of partisan hyperbole than because of continued incidents on the seas. Finally, convinced that neutrality was essential to national survival and lacking a more agreeable alternative, the President secured the Senate's consent by the closest possible two-thirds vote, twenty to ten. Republicans in the House attempted to block the appropriation that would complete congressional action on the Treaty, but too many representatives from western districts wanted the concessions, however meager, that Jay had obtained. Albert Gallatin of Pennsylvania, who was emerging as a major leader of the Republican forces, and other western representatives muted their criticism and accepted the Treaty to permit continued national expansion.

While Jay was negotiating the evacuation of British troops from the Northwest, federal forces began to drive Indians from the Ohio Valley. In 1794, General Anthony Wayne won an important victory at Fallen Timbers, and in 1795 the defeated tribes formally ceded most of Ohio to the United States in the Treaty of Greenville. In spite of local success against Indians,

American military weakness became embarrassingly evident as the deadline for British evacuation approached. Because of the lack of ready American replacements the United States asked the Redcoats to remain at their posts temporarily to protect frontier settlers. So much for earlier spread-eagle oratory about war with England.

The Jay Treaty brought an unanticipated diplomatic bonus. Suspecting that the Treaty presaged a joint Anglo-American effort to pick up Spanish possessions in the Western Hemisphere, the Spanish government decided to settle several long-standing disputes with the United States. Negotiations with Thomas Pinckney proceeded amicably because Spain soon conceded every American demand. Pinckney pressed for restraints on the Indians in Spanish territory, for uninhibited American use of the Mississippi, for the right to deposit goods duty-free in Spanish New Orleans, and for the thirty-first parallel as the northern border of West Florida. Spain gave in. The delighted Senate gave the Pinckney Treaty a thumping endorsement in 1795.

French reaction to the Jay Treaty was not so friendly. Within a year privateers had captured more than three hundred American vessels. Charles Cotesworth Pinckney, the American Minister, could not even register a formal protest because officials in Paris declined to receive him. Seizures created one tense incident after another while channels for diplomatic discourse were closed. That situation led directly to the nation's first undeclared war, which would take place during the presidency of Washington's successor.

For in 1796 Washington insisted on retiring to Mt. Vernon. He delayed his public announcement long enough to keep Republicans off balance. In the fall, he dusted off a farewell address Madison had drafted four years before. Hamilton and the President polished the piece and released to the public the President's decision not to accept his office again. The Farewell Address became almost an unofficial supplement to the Constitution, although it was preeminently a document of its own time. Washington had, he said, observed geographical and partisan rivalries developing. He warned "in the most solemn manner" against both. He had watched his countrymen become defenders of foreign causes while he himself deplored "permanent . . . antipathies against particular nations and passionate attachments for others. . . ." Even commercial relations abroad should not lead to dependence upon other nations or to a political connection with them. "So far as we have already formed engagements let them be fulfilled with perfect good faith," the President remarked in an obvious reference to the Alliance of 1778. But at that point, "let us stop."

The Farewell Address was a political speech, designed to lay Washington's sanctifying hand on neutrality, commercial expansion, and the rest of the Federalist program. Washington's words provoked Republican editors, who now certified the President's retirement as the only decent action of his second term. John Adams, the heir apparent, also received his share of abuse, which Federalists returned in unrelieved criticism of Jefferson, the candidate of those who opposed Hamilton's fiscal policy, Jay's foreign policy, and Adams' politics.

Hamilton trusted Adams little more than did Republicans. Because the Vice-President was too strong to attack directly, Hamilton schemed to secure additional electoral votes for Thomas Pinckney, popularly supposed to be Adams' running mate, with the hope that Pinckney might finish first in the electoral college. To subvert Hamilton's plan, some of Adams' electors did not vote for Pinckney. When the results were tallied, Adams barely finished ahead of Jefferson, who became Vice-President, the office the Constitution prescribed for the second man in the poll.

THE ADAMS ADMINISTRATION

The Adams family personified the New England stereotype: able, prudent, diligent, educated, honest, faithful to principle, and at the same time, irritable, stuffy, sanctimonious, priggish, and rigid; no one ever accused an Adams of having the common touch. Like the rest of his family, John Adams lacked the political knack that pays off in votes. But he had other qualities of political leadership; he carried out the policies that ensured his nation's survival.

Political partisanship had strained the friendship of Adams and Jefferson, but they approached the new administration in a spirit of conciliation. They agreed that peace was the first priority. Adams suggested that Jefferson might head a delegation to reopen diplomatic contact with France. When Jefferson declined, they settled on Madison. But Washington's Cabinet, all of whom Adams had retained, opposed Madison's nomination and sought advice from Hamilton, whom they regarded as the actual head of the government. In the end, Jefferson reported that Madison would not go to France, and Adams admitted that he could not appoint him. The incident ended the political collaboration of Adams and Jefferson.

The President soon sent John Marshall, a Virginia Federalist, and Elbridge Gerry, an erratic Massachusetts politician inclined to be a Republican in 1797, to join Charles Cotesworth Pinckney, America's unrecognized Minister in France. The mission's instructions ought to have signaled the difficulty of its task. The emissaries were to seek compensation for American vessels already condemned as privateers' prizes and to find an honorable way out of the Alliance of 1778, which obligated the United States to defend the French West Indies. Pinckney, Marshall, and Gerry had little to offer in return for French concessions; they could only agree to commercial arrangements that did not conflict with American obligations under the Jay Treaty.

That Jay Treaty, of course, was central to the problem. Since the United States could only assist France through maritime trade that was forbidden by the Jay Treaty, the French Government really had nothing to say to the American delegation. As long as the three Americans wanted to talk, Talleyrand, the shrewd and none too scrupulous Foreign Minister, decided to seek a loan for his country's beleaguered treasury and a bribe for his own. The proposition itself did not shock the Americans. But the requirement that the funds be delivered before substantive discussion commenced seemed a dubious business arrangement. Talleyrand stalled because his informants assured him Republicans would soon force a conciliatory American policy. In the early months of 1798 Marshall and Pinckney tired of the charade and left France, while Talleyrand flattered Gerry with the idea that he alone could bring peace to the two countries.

Meanwhile friction escalated to undeclared war. While Talleyrand was making vaguely conciliatory promises to the American mission, the rest of the French government had issued a stern new decree that led to further seizures of ships and restrictions on American commerce. The dispatches of Pinckney and Marshall, when released to the American public with "X," "Y," and "Z" substituted for the names of French intermediaries who had demanded payments, whipped up American opinion. Congress talked a good deal about war, but rather less about taxes and appropriations for defense; eventually completion of three frigates was authorized and a loan permitted to equip some militiamen. John Adams began to collect his thoughts for a message requesting a declaration of war. And near the coast French privateers continued to ply their profitable trade, quickly netting a half-million dollars from operations in Delaware Bay alone.

Then, almost as if he were suspicious of his sudden popularity, Adams put his notes away. There would be no war message. And while he was in office, no declared war either, although the war endured through 1798, undignified by a declaration.

When Adams' expected request for a declaration did not arrive, Hamiltonian Federalists, now called High Federalists, discussed congressional initiative. Although they lacked the votes for war, the High Federalists did secure legislation to create and support a national army, to silence the mounting criticism of national policies, and to lengthen the probationary period and limit the activity of aliens who wished to become citizens.

None of this legislation was exactly to the President's taste. The tax on houses and slaves was politically unpopular and led to a small uprising among the conservative Pennsylvania Dutch farmers, who had previously supported the Federalists. Use of the army in 1799 to suppress this Fries Rebellion gave substance to Republican charges that Federalists had created the force to repress dissent. Adams himself thought an army less useful than a navy, but High Federalists believed the British Navy made an American fleet unnecessary. Adams' misgivings increased when Washington, to whom command of the army was offered, insisted that Hamilton be given effective control of the force. Whether the force could ever have been effective is another question. Officers joined readily, but ordinary troops were more reluctant; officers outnumbered enlisted men roughly seven to one, an unwieldy proportion for even the most skilled general.

The Alien and Sedition Acts, Republicans charged, furnished the legal basis for repression. Passed amid feverish preparations for war in the summer of 1798, these acts sought to promote Americanism of the High Federalist brand. Troublesome aliens might be imprisoned or deported on the President's authority; others must demonstrate acceptability over fourteen years instead of the five that had previously been required for citizenship. The Sedition Act outlawed promotion of insurrection, an offense with which both the President and the Vice-President might well have been charged two decades earlier. The statute went on to prohibit writing or speech that tended to "defame" or to "bring . . . into contempt" the President, Congress, laws, and policies of the United States. Although Adams had not asked for this legislation, neither he nor any other prominent Federalist opposed it, except John Marshall, who, once the laws were on the books, wondered whether they were wise.

Republicans thought the Alien and Sedition Acts unconstitutional as well as unwise. The Sedition Act, in particular, seemed designed to stifle political opposition, a criticism that the zeal of Federalist judges who enforced the law did little to abate. In making their case, Republicans relied not only upon the First Amendment's guarantee of free speech and free press; they also advanced the theory that since the states had established the central government, the states themselves, and not the federal judiciary, should decide whether that government had exceeded its legitimate authority. Jefferson secretly prepared for the Kentucky legislature a set of resolutions, based upon this compact theory, that proclaimed the right of each : tate to determine the constitutionality of federal action. The legislature of Virginia agreed in Madison's more moderate words. But other states did not endorse the Kentucky Resolutions, and seven northern states went on record in opposition.

While High Federalists prepared the nation for war, the President decided on another effort for peace. From his son John Quincy Adams, who represented the United States in Berlin, and from Nicholas Vans Murray, the Minister to the Netherlands, the President heard that France seemed more conciliatory. Elbridge Gerry reported that Talleyrand had hinted at more equitable treatment for American commerce. Early in 1799, without the consent of his Cabinet, Adams nominated Murray and two other commissioners to reopen negotiations with France. Convinced that their cresting popularity depended on a probable war with France, High Federalists, including Secretary of State Timothy Pickering, tried to obstruct the President. But Adams had made up his mind. He replaced Pickering with John Marshall, fired the other Hamiltonians in the Cabinet, calmed the country, split his party, and sought peace with France. Negotiations took more than a year, but domestic hysteria dipped while they progressed toward a settlement. In effect, the United States gave up the claims of American shippers in return for an end to the Alliance of 1778. But this Convention of 1800 formally postponed both matters indefinitely and then specified a mutual stand for neutral rights that never seriously bound either signatory thereafter. The unofficial war was officially over.

When it ended, John Adams was on his way out of office. During the campaign of 1800, Hamilton advertised the rift among Federalists with a pamphlet criticizing Adams and advocating the election of Charles Cotesworth Pinckney, whom Federalists in Congress had designated for Vice-President. But Hamilton miscalculated even in his own New York, where Aaron Burr put together a slate of Jeffersonian electors that carried by a few hundred votes. Republicans rewarded Burr by endorsing him as Jefferson's running mate. Republicans evoked memories of British repression with references to the Sedition Act, oppressive taxation, and a threatening and expensive standing army. Federalists answered charges of Adams' tyranny with equally irresponsible allegations that Jefferson's atheism threatened the faith of Christian Americans. Although Adams gloomily and

THE following hand-bill was circulated in the year 1801, by the Federal party. It is now re-published for the *gratification* of those Federal gentlemen who are now supporting "this Cataline." The original may be seen at the office of the Citizen.

Aaron Burr !

At length this Cataline stands CONFESSED in all his VILLAINY—His INVETERATE HATRED of the Constitution of the United States has long been displayed in one steady, undeviating course of HOSTILITY to every measure which the solid interests of the Union demand—His POLITICAL PERFIDIOUSNESS AND INTRIGUES are also now pretty generally known, and even his own party have avowed their jealousy and fear of a character, which, to great talents adds the deepest dissimulation and an entire devotion to self-interest, and self-aggrandizement—But there is a NEW TRAIT in this man's character, to be unfolded to the view of an INDIGNANT PUBLIC!—His ABANDONED PROFLIGACY, and the NUMEROUS UNHAPPY WRETCHES who have fallen VICTIMS to this accomplished and but too successful DEBAUCHEE, have indeed been long known to those whom similar habits of vice, or the amiable offices of humanity have led to the wretched haunts of female prostitution—But it is time to draw aside the curtain in which he has thus far been permitted to conceal himself by the forbearance of his enemies, by the anxious interference of his friends, and much more by his own crafty contrivances and unbounded prodigality.

It is time to tear away the veil that hides this monster, and lay open a scene of misery, at which every heart must shudder. Fellow Citizens, read a tale of truth, which must harrow up your sensibility, and excite your keenest resentment. It is, indeed, a tale of truth! and, but for wounding, too deeply, the already lacerated feelings of a parental heart, it could be authenticated by all the formalities of an oath.

I do not mean to tell you of the late celebrated courtezan N——, nor U——, nor S——, nor of half a dozen more whom first his INTRIGUES have RUINED, and his SATIATED BRUTALITY has afterwards thrown on the town, the prey of disease, of infamy, and wretchedness—It is to a more recent act, that I call your attention, and I hope it will create in every heart, the same abhorrence with which mine is filled.

☞ When Mr. Burr last went to the city of Washington about 2 months ago, to take the oath of office, and his seat in the August senate of the U. States, he SEDUCED the daughter of a respectable tradesman there, & had the cruelty to persuade her to forsake her native town, her friends and family, and to follow him to New-York. She did so—and she is now IN KEEPING in Partition-st. Vice, however, sooner or later, meets its merited punishment. Justice, though sometimes SLOW, is SURE. The villain has not long enjoyed this triumph over female weakness. The father of the girl has at length after a laborious and painful search, found out the author of his child's RUIN, and his family's DISHONOR.—HE IS NOW IN THIS CITY, and VENGEANCE will soon light on the guilty head!—— Fellow-citizens, I leave you to make your own comments on this complicated scene of misery and vice.— I will conclude with a single observation.—Is that party at whose head is this monster, who directs all their motions and originates all their nefarious schemes worthy of your SUPPORT?

Political rhetoric, 1801

Aaron Burr

correctly foresaw his own defeat, his support was more extensive than it had been four years before. No Republican elector omitted Burr from his ballot, so Burr and Jefferson deadlocked in the electoral college.

The house, according to the Constitution, was to break the tie. Through more than thirty inconclusive ballots the rancor of the campaign persisted. Burr made no effort to discourage Federalist schemes to elect him President, although Hamilton, who knew both men well, believed Jefferson the lesser evil. Hamilton's influence among responsible Federalists had dwindled, however, and other men made the arrangement that put Jefferson in the White House and ended the Federalists' reign.

THE FEDERALISTS IN RETROSPECT

In pockets of opposition that fed on their own increasing isolation, the Federalist party lingered. Though it ended in 1800 as an effective national political movement, the theories and policies of Federalism proved more hardy. A strong central government, responding to the direction of the executive branch, backed by the talent and property of influential citizens, and maintaining peace at home and overseas—this was no mean vision, nor was it the exclusive heritage of those crabbed and bitter men who claimed to keep the Federalist faith.

Another legacy of the brief Federalist era was the development of political parties and a responsible opposition. Federalists and Republicans alike accepted constitutional restraints. Both gradually discovered techniques for subordinating internal rivalries to the common pursuit of power, techniques that Republicans applied more successfully than Federalists. Both relied on journals in which partisanship had a priority higher than accuracy. Both developed constitutional interpretations to justify political programs. Both employed political organizers of elastic conscience, whom subsequent generations would call bosses. When Federalists left office, Republicans gracefully adopted portions of the Federalist creed. The tone of Republican government differed, to be sure, but much of the substance of Federalism endured.

Washington, Adams, Hamilton, Jefferson, and Madison served as national rallying points for diverse local factions. But no candidate, no political issue, could for long focus the attention of most Americans upon the central government. The national political climate was less important to a nation of farmers than the weather nearer home, national banks of less concern than local prices of fur, flax, and flour. National parties depended in large measure, then, on the prominence of their local adherents, for hazardous travel and unreliable communication kept national leaders and most voters apart. Local gentry benefited from "deference" voting by citizens who acknowledged their own lack of information by voting for notables who were supposed to be informed. Both parties sought the help of local opinion-makers to secure the broad support they might bring. Neither party sprang up in response to popular demand. Both, rather, were built by their leadership to demand the political program that leaders were ready to supply. The nation was fortunate that by 1800 neither choice was wrong.

Suggested Reading

Marcus Cunliffe, *The Nation Takes Shape** (1959), and John C. Miller, *The Federalist Era** (1960), are reliable, brief surveys of the Federalist period. Miller has also written a judicious biography of Hamilton* (1959) and a study of the Alien and Sedition Acts entitled *Crisis of Freedom** (1951). The latter may be supplemented by James M. Smith, *Freedom's Fetters** (1956). Curtis P. Nettels' *The Emergence of a National Economy** (1962) discusses Federalist fiscal policy and carries the narrative up to 1815.

The development of political parties is examined by Richard Hofstadter in *The Idea of a Party System** (1969), by Joseph Charles in *The Origins of the American Party System** (1956), and by William N. Chambers in *Political Parties in a New Nation** (1963). Noble Cunningham's *The Jeffersonian Republicans** (1957) describes the organization of the Republican opposition.

Stephen G. Kurtz's *The Presidency of John Adams** (1957) is a comprehensive study. Two books by Alexander De Conde focus on the diplomacy of the Federalists: *Entangling Alliance* (1958) and *The Quasi-War** (1966).

Douglas S. Freeman's seven volumes on Washington (1948–57) and the first three volumes of Dumas Malone's work on Jefferson (1948–62) are relevant to this period and are much more than biographies.

*Available in paperback edition

CHRONOLOGY

1803   *Marbury* v. *Madison* establishes judicial review
Louisiana Purchase

1804   Presidential election: Thomas Jefferson (Democratic-Republican) defeats Charles C. Pinckney (Federalist)

1806   Burr conspiracy (trial, 1807)

1807   Embargo Act

1808   Presidential election: James Madison (Democratic-Republican) defeats Charles C. Pinckney (Federalist) and George Clinton (Democratic-Republican)

1810   Congressional election enables "War Hawks" to organize House

1812   Presidential election: James Madison (Democratic-Republican) defeats DeWitt Clinton (Federalist)

1812–15   War against England (Battle of New Orleans, 1815)

1814   Hartford Convention expresses New England's opposition to war

1816   Recharter of Bank of the United States
Presidential election: James Monroe (Democratic-Republican) defeats Rufus King (Federalist)

1819   Adams-Onís (Transcontinental) Treaty negotiated (ratified 1821)
McCulloch v. *Maryland* upholds constitutionality of Bank of the United States

1820   Presidential election: James Monroe (Democratic-Republican) defeats John Quincy Adams (Independent Republican)

1820–21   Missouri Compromise

1823   Monroe Doctrine announced

VII

THE VIRGINIA DYNASTY

Thomas Jefferson's election in 1800 broke the Federalist party's grip on the presidency and initiated a quarter-century of Republican government. Three Virginia patricians—Jefferson, James Madison, and James Monroe—successively occupied the White House during those years and gave the nation dignified and occasionally distinguished direction. By the time these men had finished conducting affairs of state, more Americans were more loyal to the national government than ever before. The Federalists had won the rich, the able, and the well born to the support of the central government; the Republicans won almost everyone else. "We are all Republicans, we are all Federalists," Jefferson remarked in 1801; before the last member of the Virginia Dynasty retired to his plantation, Jefferson's hyperbole had nearly come true.

To be sure, the Republican party changed somewhat over those years. At the outset, in 1801, the Republican creed consisted of the principles Thomas Jefferson had articulated during twenty-five years of public life. Jefferson was preeminently the spokesman for independent farmers, whom he believed to be "the chosen people of God if ever He had a chosen people." As the foremost opponent of Hamiltonian Federalism, Jefferson favored a central government based on the limited powers granted by a strict interpre-

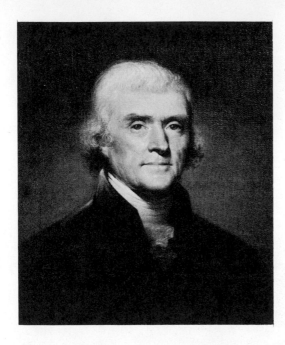

Thomas Jefferson, portrait by
Rembrandt Peale

tation of the Constitution. A corollary of his strict construction was Jefferson's advocacy of rigid governmental economy. In foreign policy, Jefferson leaned toward France and mistrusted England.

Jefferson's critics alleged that his presidency belied every one of his early policies; by 1825 the Republican party certainly had bent some of the old principles and added a few new ones. Although farmers had first claim on federal bounty, Republican policies also fostered the growth of American industry. Once Republicans took over the central government, the Constitution seemed less restrictive than it had when they were out of office, and even governmental economy became less imperative. Before the United States found itself at war with England, Jefferson himself had threatened to ally with England against France. Republican nationalism differed somewhat from the Federalist variety, but it was nationalism nonetheless.

JEFFERSON: POLITICS AND PRINCIPLES

Long after Jefferson had left the White House, he remarked that his election had worked a profound "revolution in the principles of our government." But his inaugural address had given no hint that such a revolution was in the making. The campaign and protracted election of 1800 had been vicious, and Jefferson meant to heal old wounds before new ones opened. He emphasized agreement, not dissension, and he listed the "essential principles of our Government" in a series of carefully qualified statements designed to reassure Federalists as much as to remind Republicans of what they stood for: impartial "friendship with all nations, entangling alliances with none"; "support of the State governments in all their rights," coupled with "preservation of the General Government in its whole constitutional vigor"; "encouragement of agriculture, and of commerce as its handmaid." But Jefferson had begun his list with an affirmation of strict construction; "a wise and frugal government, which shall restrain men from injuring one another [and] . . . leave them otherwise free to regulate their own pursuits."

Although Jefferson courted his opponents in his inaugural address, his hard-headed use of political patronage soon stirred Federalist resentment. By 1803 about half the principal appointive posts in the federal service had gone to Republicans. Federalist legislation, which the President believed the electorate had rejected in 1800, went the way of Federalist officeholders. The Sedition Act expired in 1801 and Jefferson pardoned those who had been jailed under its provisions. Congress reduced from fourteen to five years the time an alien had to wait before becoming naturalized. Many Federalists, appointed to the judiciary in the last moments of the Adams administration, lost their positions when the Judiciary Act of 1801 was repealed. On the advice of Albert Gallatin, a worthy successor to Hamilton as Secretary of the Treasury, Congress removed all internal taxes, including that on whiskey. Convinced that the armed forces could be drastically reduced, the administration budgeted only $1.6 million to support them; in 1799 the military budget had been $6 million.

Jefferson meant to change the style of government as well as its policies. Federalists, he charged, had aped the ways of monarchs; he would bring a seemly simplicity to official Washington. Working dinners for political advisers replaced presidential banquets; the President's informality scandalized foreign representatives accustomed to starchy diplomatic ritual. Jefferson even had a clerk read his annual message to Congress because he thought a personal appearance too reminiscent of the British address from the throne.

But Jefferson spurned only the trappings of leadership. He successfully mustered the support of the congressional Republicans even after Madison and Gallatin, who had provided direction, left Congress for the Cabinet. After their departure John Randolph served for a time as the chief Republican spokesman in the House but in Jefferson's second term Randolph became a waspish obstructionist. Yet his desertion caused hardly a ripple in Republican ranks. Jefferson isolated Randolph and held the party together in support of a program that departed from traditional Republicanism, as Randolph correctly charged.

The Republicans had discovered that they could not undo all the policies of their predecessors. The charter of the Bank of the United States, for instance, had a decade to run when Jefferson took office. Nor could Gallatin and Jefferson repeal the debt Hamilton had contracted. Instead, they undertook to pay it from the revenue derived from Hamilton's tariff. So rigorous was Republican economy that Gallatin spent more than three-fourths of the government's income to service the debt. Before the Napoleonic wars disrupted the world economy, Gallatin even managed to show a small annual surplus.

The Federalists mounted an ineffective partisan opposition to Jefferson's policies. In 1804 a few disgruntled New England Federalists went beyond partisanship and discussed with Aaron Burr a scheme to ally New York and New England in an independent northern confederation. Alexander Hamilton, true to his habitual nationalism, exposed the plot, and Burr, who was still Vice-President, killed Hamilton in a duel not long afterward. Burr then diverted his conspiratorial ambition toward the Southwest.

The Burr conspiracy—or perhaps more accurately Burr's fantasy— has never been completely untangled. Both British and Spanish diplomats in Washington heard that Burr would welcome support for some enterprise he was contemplating in Mexico and the lower Mississippi Valley. Perhaps Mexico was to have served as the center of Burr's empire; perhaps he expected to annex part of the western United States if it seceded or to conquer it if it did not. James Wilkinson, the slippery American commander in Louisiana, whose support the plotters thought they had bought, reported the enterprise to Jefferson. The President ordered the arrest of Burr and his pathetic army of sixty men, who had begun to float down the Ohio toward their rendezvous with dishonor. Jefferson, who in 1798 had so vigorously championed civil liberties, now seem determined to deprive Burr of his. One way or another, he meant to have Burr's conviction for treason, but Chief Justice John Marshall insisted that the letter of the constitutional definition of treason be met. The prosecution failed to produce two witnesses to the same overt act of levying war against the United States, and the jury acquitted Burr.

The Republican party prospered in spite of Burr's disgrace and the defection of other charter leaders, such as Randolph and John Taylor of Caroline, who maintained that Jefferson had forsaken Republican principles. Replacing Burr with George Clinton, another New Yorker, as his vice-presidential running mate, Jefferson crushed the Federalists in the election of 1804. The Republican ticket lost just 14 electoral votes; Republicans took 27 of the 34 seats in the Senate and elected 119 of the 141 members of the House.

Although the election returns seemed proof of political harmony, the ominous division between North and South was visible late in 1806. The House was debating a bill to prohibit further importation of slaves after 1808. Instead of an expected routine discussion, the bill provoked bitter rhetorical exchange. John Randolph saw the issue with characteristic clarity. He derided those who worried about sectional discord between East and West; if disunion came, he predicted, the line would fall between states that permitted slavery and those that did not. Tampering with slavery, Randolph asserted, would "blow up the Constitution in ruins." But banning the slave trade was not the same thing as banning slavery, and eventually Congress made importing slaves illegal.

In his second term Jefferson hesitantly suggested that federal funds might be spent to improve rivers and harbors, to construct roads and canals, and to advance manufacturing and education. Although the President tactfully admitted that such appropriations might require a constitutional amendment, many southern Republicans perceived his proposal as disguised Federalism. Citing the need for governmental economy, Congress refused to appropriate explicitly for such purposes, but the administration diverted some of the income from land sales to improve the roads leading west.

For settlers were pouring across the Appalachians and fanning out in the eastern Mississippi Valley even as explorers pushed on into the trans-Mississippi unknown. At the time the expedition commanded by Meriwether Lewis and William Clark began exploring the Missouri and Columbia valleys, the Ohio Valley had ceased to be frontier. Ohio became a state in 1803 and Louisiana in 1812. Then the pace picked up; Indiana became a state in 1816, Mississippi in 1817, Illinois in 1818, and Alabama in 1819.

To meet the demand for land, Congress passed several laws making purchase easier. The law of 1796 had prescribed a minimum sale of 640 acres at $2.00 an acre and permitted a year's credit on half the purchase price. In 1800 Congress reduced the minimum acreage by half and permitted credit for four years. In 1804 Congress again halved the acreage requirement; now a settler could start farming with a down payment of as little as $80. Although a new law in 1820 stopped installment sale, Congress did permit purchase of units as small as 80 acres at $1.25 per acre. The open space that had inspired Jefferson's vision of "room enough for our descendants to the thousandth and thousandth generation" was fast disappearing.

JEFFERSON'S FOREIGN POLICY

In 1803 the nation's open space nearly doubled with the purchase of the Louisiana territory. To secure Louisiana, Jefferson took full advantage of the struggle for European supremacy that developed from the French Revolution. His failure to influence that struggle decisively was one of Jefferson's great disappointments; but the purchase of Louisiana, in large measure a result of Napoleon's preoccupation with the European war, was one of Jefferson's great triumphs.

Ambitious to erect an empire in the New World to match the one he planned for the old, Napoleon decided to acquire Louisiana to serve as a granary for the French sugar colony on Santo Domingo. In 1800 Spain ceded Louisiana to France in the secret Treaty of San Ildefonso but continued for a time to administer the area. In October, 1802, Spanish authorities notified the United States that the right to deposit goods duty-free in New Orleans had been suspended. Westerners, who were suspicious of all government and the far-off central government most of all, now made reopening the river a test case: success would secure their loyalty to the national government; failure would bring alienation and perhaps separation.

Jefferson knew the stakes. His aversion to Britain, his dedication to governmental economy, his fear of military establishments, and his strict construction of the Constitution, all were subordinated to his need to secure New Orleans. The possessor of New Orleans, he wrote, was "our natural and habitual enemy." Once France had taken possession of the city, he went on, the United States would be driven to "marry . . . the British fleet and nation." Jefferson instructed Robert R. Livingston, the American minister in France, to negotiate for the purchase of West Florida and New

Orleans. When westerners complained that Livingston's mission had had no result, Jefferson sent James Monroe, whom the West respected, to expedite negotiations in Paris. While Monroe was on his way, Napoleon decided to give up his projected New World empire and to renew the war in Europe instead. A slave rebellion in Santo Domingo, brilliantly directed by Toussaint L'Ouverture, combined with the constant loss of French troops to yellow fever, convinced Napoleon that the military cost of a western empire outweighed its potential value. Two days before Monroe arrived, in April, 1803, Napoleon asked if the United States would like to buy all of Louisiana.

Authorized to buy a city for $2 million, Livingston and Monroe bought an empire for $15 million. They promised the French that the United States would protect the religious freedom of the inhabitants of Louisiana and would admit them to citizenship. When asked about boundaries, the French foreign minister observed cryptically that he supposed the United States would "make the most" of its "noble bargain."

Jefferson was both pleased and dismayed. Since the Constitution did not explicitly permit the purchase of territory, Jefferson would have preferred to escape the charge of broad construction with a face-saving amendment. But, fearful that any delay would prompt Napoleon to change his mind, Jefferson sent the treaty to the Senate remarking that "the good sense of our country will correct the evil of [broad] construction when it shall produce ill effects." The Senate sealed the bargain by a vote of twenty-four to seven.

Tripolitan pirates proved almost as annoying as Napoleon. For years before Jefferson took office, the United States had paid various North African chieftains for the privilege of trading in the Mediterranean. In 1801, one of these Barbary potentates chopped down the flagpole in front of the American consulate in Tripoli, and Jefferson decided that a brisk naval war would be cheaper in the long run than perpetual tribute. Without actually declaring war, he sent the Navy to punish the pirates. Several years of intermittent naval skirmishes ended with a treaty in 1805, although the United States paid some tribute until 1816.

More serious than the Tripolitan war was the friction that developed with Britain and France following the renewal of the European war in 1803. Jefferson had sufficient force to do something about Barbary pirates; he could do very little about Britain or France. The American merchant marine occasioned most of the trouble; although Jefferson was never partial to merchants, the prosperity of farmers depended on their ability to market their produce. As the war on the continent intensified, both Britain and France ignored the rights of neutrals. Determined to ruin the British economy, Napoleon closed the entire continent to British shipping. In the Berlin Decree (1806) and the Milan Decree (1807) he announced that France would seize British ships or ships of neutrals that complied with British trade regulations. Britain, in turn, issued a series of Orders in Council that established a blockade of France and all ports under French control. Any neutral ship, therefore, ran the risk of confiscation, for any commerce would breach the regulations of one belligerent or the other. Still, the ship that got through returned immense profits, and many American shippers willingly incurred the risk.

Americans protested against the seizure of goods and ships, but they protested even more hotly against the British practice of impressing sailors. Many British sailors, who found the duty disagreeable, the discipline harsh, the food unpalatable, and the pay servile, jumped ship in American ports and signed on American merchant vessels. British captains, particularly those who found themselves short handed, resorted to impressment to keep their crews at full strength. Great Britain never conceded that British subjects could renounce their citizenship—"once an Englishman," according to British law, "always an Englishman." Since no foolproof test had been devised to distinguish among true Englishmen, Englishmen who had become naturalized Americans, and native-born Americans, mistakes were made—not all of them honest. The most serious incident occurred in 1807, when British naval guns killed three Americans in an attack on the *Chesapeake*, an American frigate. A British patrol then searched the *Chesapeake*, and took off four men. Firing on a naval vessel was an act of war. Had Jefferson wanted a declaration of war, Congress would probably have responded, for public feeling ran high. But Jefferson delayed, Britain eventually apologized, and the crisis evaporated.

Jefferson delayed partly because he hoped Britain might be persuaded to link a general renunciation of impressment with an apology for the *Chesapeake* incident. Since the British cabinet seemed determined to risk war rather than disavow impressment, Jefferson did not insist. Instead, he turned to Congress, which proved much more responsive than British officialdom. In December, 1807, at the President's urging, Congress passed the Embargo, which in effect made all foreign trade illegal. Jefferson believed that the loss of the American market would bring industrial distress to England, that the loss of American goods would create hardship throughout Europe, and that the absence of American shipping would disrupt all international trade and would leave several European colonies stranded. Jefferson confidently expected European distress to force changes in European policy.

Although distress at home initially exceeded distress abroad, the Embargo, in the long run, may have forced a healthy adjustment in the American economy. While some commercial fortunes shrank because goods piled up on the piers and ships rotted at anchor, other merchants invested in manufacturing. The Embargo and the war effectively kept European manufactured goods out of the American market, which domestic industry began to supply. Many seaport artisans remained unemployed, but some found jobs building the magnificent Federal houses that line older streets in even the smaller Atlantic ports. The Embargo unquestionably brought economic hardship, but it did not invariably bring economic ruin.

Farmers also felt the Embargo's economic jolt. As prices dropped with the loss of the export market, the farmers' frustration mounted. Tobacco, cotton, and hemp, the products of the South and the Mississippi

Valley, accumulated in warehouses. Between 1805 and 1809 commodity prices in New Orleans declined about 20 per cent, and then went down still further in 1810 and 1811. Farmers of the South and West reacted with mounting hostility focused on Great Britain, whose Orders in Council they saw as the immediate cause of their economic difficulty. In increasingly strident voices, representatives of cotton and tobacco growers demanded that the United States abandon economic coercion and declare war on Great Britain.

The Embargo had in fact failed to coerce either European belligerent. Jefferson's law played into the hands of the British Cabinet, which had been under pressure from mercantile interests to restrain the American merchant marine. The Embargo deprived Napoleon of his American supplies and at the same time crippled American shipping; the British found both results entirely satisfactory. The American boycott did cause British manufacturers momentary anxiety over the loss of a lucrative market, but the developing market in Latin America more than took up the slack. And Napoleon, for his part, went on confiscating whatever stray American ships reached the continent and brazenly told protesting Americans that he was only enforcing their own laws.

THE MADISON ADMINISTRATION

Domestic unhappiness with Jefferson's policy did not prevent the election of James Madison, Jefferson's chosen heir. In the election of 1808 Federalists gained support in New England and enlarged their congressional minority; but Charles Cotesworth Pinckney, their presidential candidate, ran a poor second, with only 47 electoral votes to Madison's 122. Just before Madison's inauguration, in March, 1809, Jefferson reluctantly agreed to the repeal of the Embargo. But Madison's diplomatic hand was no stronger than Jefferson's had been, and the new President resorted again to economic coercion. The Nonintercourse Act of 1809 prohibited trade with Britain and France until those nations ceased interfering with American rights. But trade with other nations was once more permitted. Negotiations with a British envoy in 1809 seemed to promise repeal of the Orders in Council, so Madison reopened trade with Britain. The British Cabinet, however, repudiated its envoy and his agreement, and Madison had no choice but to reinstitute nonintercourse.

In the face of deteriorating relations with both Britain and France, the Madison administration retreated from nonintercourse to Macon's Bill Number 2. This measure, passed in May, 1810, signaled the abandonment of economic coercion by permitting trade with both Britain and France. But the ghost of trade restriction lingered, for the law required the restoration of nonintercourse with one belligerent in the event the other agreed to respect American neutral rights. Sensing an opportunity, Napoleon promptly revoked his earlier decrees, but he added conditions that practically reimposed them. Madison ignored the qualifications, welcomed Napoleon's deceptive offer, and once more imposed nonintercourse with Brit-

James Madison

ain. Napoleon never stopped confiscating American ships, but nonintercourse did have some economic effect in Britain, which, in 1810, was in the grip of an industrial depression. Pressure in Britain rose until on June 16, 1812, the Cabinet suspended the Orders in Council. Unaware of this gesture, which might not have changed the course of events in any case, the United States declared war on Great Britain on June 18.

The Congress that had been elected in 1810 reflected mounting frustration, especially in the South and West, with the nation's diplomatic dilemma. Young Republicans from southern and western congressional delegations believed that negotiation and economic pressure had failed; only force would convince Europeans of the vitality, honor, and sturdy independence of the American republic. Nourished on stories of their forebears' sacrifice in the Revolution, raised in an environment that respected impetuous courage, trained to value honor above purse, these so-called War Hawks expressed the exhausted patience of their constituents. The War Hawks took control of the House, electing as Speaker Henry Clay, a Kentuckian who had forthrightly advocated war during an earlier term in the Senate. Clay appointed other War Hawks—John C. Calhoun and Langdon Cheves of South Carolina, Felix Grundy of Tennessee, Richard M. Johnson of Kentucky—to key posts in the House. The growing demand for war had found expression.

The President listed the causes of conflict in his war message: impressment, violation of the commercial rights of neutrals, and British encouragement of Indian efforts to forestall American settlement. The ensuing congressional debate revealed other reasons for war. Men fight for intangibles—justice, freedom, honor. But their political leaders insist on tangible memorials—reparations, profit, territory. Inextricably mixed with concern over maritime rights and the need of a new generation to dedicate itself to the cause of American honor and independence was an admitted interest in territorial expansion—at the expense of the Indians in the North-west, the decrepit Spanish regime in Florida, and the British in Canada. All these ambitions antedated 1812; all seemed realizable through war with Great Britain. To be sure, France had also violated American rights, but where could the United States attack France? Canada, as spread-eagle ora-tors had long noted, was a hostage that the United States could seize. Henry Clay thought the conquest of Canada a small matter that might amuse the Kentucky militia for a few weeks.

Removing the British from North America, the War Hawks boasted, would also eliminate the arms that made the Indians dangerous. Settlers pushing into the valleys of the Ohio and the Mississippi were encroaching on Indian territory, and they sought governmental protection when the Indians protested. In 1809 William Henry Harrison, Governor of the Indi-ana Territory, had secured Indian assent to the Treaty of Fort Wayne, which opened most of southern Indiana to settlers. The Indians with whom Harrison dealt probably had no right to make the treaty, and the incident convinced other Indians that only war would preserve tribal territory east of the Mississippi. In 1811 two Shawnees, Tecumseh and his brother the Prophet, put together an Indian confederation pledged to resist the white man's settlement and his corrupting bargains. British officials in Canada, dreading an American invasion, were anxious to enlist Indian support and to persuade their Indian allies to conserve their strength and act in concert with the British when war came. But the Indians could not wait, nor did William Henry Harrison. In 1811 Harrison, fearing a full-scale Indian war, sent a force that destroyed the Prophet's village on Tippecanoe Creek in Indiana.

The Indian menace was not the principal reason Congress voted for a declaration of war, for the western frontier had too few votes to deter-mine a major policy. Nor was the lure of Florida or Canada a primary cause, though annexation of these areas was an important tactical objec-tive. Rather, the basic cause of the War of 1812 lay in the fact that European belligerents, caught up in their own protracted struggle, did not treat the proud, new republic in the manner its pride and recent origin demanded. Great Britain preferred to risk war rather than give up impressment or harassment of American shipping. The United States decided that it could not remain self-respecting and independent if it permitted either impress-ment or harassment to continue. So the war came.

It was a war neither side was ready to fight. Subduing Napoleon was task enough for Great Britain. Madison's administration, never vigorous, was further weakened by immediate resentment of the war, particularly in the Northeast. In the election of 1812, Federalists endorsed DeWitt Clinton, the nominee of anti-war Republicans who opposed James Madison. Madison carried the South and West and won the electoral college by a vote of

128 to 89; if Clinton had been able to add Pennsylvania to his otherwise firm support in the Northeast, he would have been elected. In Congress, the Federalists doubled their strength.

Political opposition and the failure of the Northeast to cooperate made the general lack of governmental competence more critical. The War Department proclaimed a need for 130,000 troops, but it never managed to put more than 30,000 in the field. Congress provided neither conscription nor revenue. The War Hawks voted no taxes to support the fight, for their own South and West resisted internal taxation. In 1814, the Secretary of the Treasury openly admitted that he had no notion where he would find $50,000,000 of his projected annual expenditure of $74,000,000.

Nor was the military effort better managed than the political effort. Americans failed to conquer Canada, partly because they chose to attack near Detroit instead of moving quickly to secure control of the St. Lawrence, upon which the British depended for supplies. American expeditions against Canada often fizzled out when militiamen declined to travel too far from home. The few thrusts that actually crossed the frontier ended in retreat before more determined British forces. The American navy, which faced the world's most powerful fleet, gave a better account of itself. In single-ship engagements early in the war, the *Constitution* and the *United States* defeated British vessels. Americans managed to secure naval supremacy on the Great Lakes after Captain Oliver Hazard Perry's victory at Put-in-Bay. But by 1814 the sheer number of British vessels forced American ships to stay in port. The British blockade along the Atlantic coast grew ever tighter and only the *Constitution* and a few privateers were still operating on the high seas at the end of the war.

Fanciful representation of the burning of Washington, D.C.

The Battle of New Orleans

When defeat loomed for Napoleon in 1814, Britain began to devote more attention to the American war, and the costs of sloppy American leadership rose sharply. British strategists meant to divide the United States with invasions from New Orleans, at Niagara, and along Lake Champlain. These major attacks were coupled with coastal raids, including the spectacular bombardment of Baltimore and the burning of Washington, D.C. A fierce battle at Lundy's Lane, near Niagara Falls, created a stalemate in the Northwest and ended that British thrust. The invasion along Lake Champlain stopped when Captain Thomas Macdonough won naval control of the lake for the United States at the battle of Plattsburgh. And the British attempt to secure the Mississippi failed below New Orleans when southwestern militiamen commanded by Andrew Jackson gave the seasoned British regulars lessons in the uses of fortification, marksmanship, and strategic position. The battle took place on January 8, 1815, about two weeks after a treaty of peace had been signed. British casualties totaled more than two thousand; Jackson lost eight frontiersmen.

New England had never supported the war with the patriotic fervor of the South and West. The region's lack of enthusiasm grew in some quarters into outright hostility as the war dragged on. New England's militia was notoriously unreliable and enlistments in the regular forces lagged. New England's merchants continued their international trade, including a bustling commerce with England and Canada. New England's banks, stronger than those in other regions, declined to provide proportional support for the national treasury. And when the British extended their blockade to New England, the region's dissident leaders redoubled their angry opposition—not toward Great Britain, but toward Washington. Timothy Pickering, the most disaffected of a group of Federalists called the Essex Junto, had advocated secession for some time. In December, 1814, the Essex Junto sought regional support at a secret meeting in Hartford, Connecticut.

But the Hartford Convention stopped well short of secession. The meeting demonstrated that the doctrine of state rights had found a new home in Federalist New England, where once the idea had been anathema. The convention proposed a series of constitutional changes, including the requirement of a two-thirds vote of Congress to declare war, to admit new states, and to enact embargoes. To check the power of the South, the convention demanded the repeal of the three-fifths compromise; to check Republicans, it advocated amendments excluding naturalized citizens from federal office, restricting a President to one term, and prohibiting successive terms for Presidents from the same state. The delegates from Hartford arrived in Washington as the city was celebrating Jackson's stunning victory at New Orleans. Their suggestions disappeared in a flood of postwar nationalism.

Republican view of the Hartford Convention

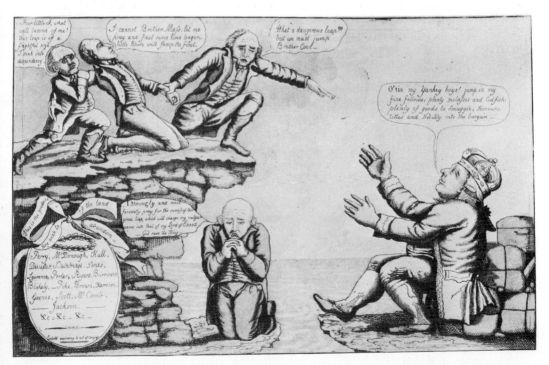

Errors flawed the American war effort, but the peace commissioners at Ghent made few mistakes. Negotiations had begun almost as soon as hostilities, for the British had never really meant to have a war and the Americans soon tired of it. In 1814, a talented American delegation led by Clay, Gallatin, and John Quincy Adams began serious discussions with an inferior set of British representatives. Bargaining positions changed as news arrived from the front; at one time Britain demanded the cession of an Indian buffer state and about one-third of the rest of the United States. In December, 1814, following word of Macdonough's success on Lake Champlain, the negotiators agreed to stop fighting and to restore the status quo ante bellum.

It was a strange peace ending a strange war. None of the great issues that had led to war—impressment, neutral rights, traffic with the Indians, expansion—were seriously discussed, let alone settled. Subsequent treaties in 1815 reopened most of the ports of the British empire to American ship captains. The Rush-Bagot Agreement of 1817 began mutual disarmament on the Great Lakes and initiated steps leading to an unfortified frontier between the United States and Canada. The Convention of 1818 fixed the forty-ninth parallel as the northern boundary of the United States as far west as the Rockies, arranged for Oregon to be left open for ten years to settlement by citizens of either nation, and permitted American fishermen to work the waters off British North America.

The Senate took twenty-four hours in February, 1815, to ratify the treaty and then moved on to more congenial business. The Treaty of Ghent marked the end of an era of international tension that had kept the United States preoccupied with foreign relations; now the nation turned happily to its own affairs. The victory at New Orleans suitably climaxed the "second war for independence." Although the United States had not really won the war, it certainly had not lost it. That was not a bad record for a new nation in conflict with the world's greatest power. Napoleon could not make the same claim.

AMERICAN NATIONALISM

The United States was at peace at home as well as abroad. The war had taught Jeffersonians the wisdom of Federalist ways; at the same time it had so embarrassed Federalists that younger adherents quietly emerged as Republicans. President Madison rediscovered the nationalism he had espoused at the Constitutional Convention and joined Clay, Calhoun, and other young Republicans who made nationalism their political creed. In December, 1815, Madison asked Congress to establish a uniform national currency to be issued by a revived national bank. He also suggested that newly established industries warranted the protection of a tariff. And he called congressional attention "to the great importance of establishing throughout our country the roads and canals which can best be executed under national authority. . . ." One reason the Federalist party soon disappeared was that the Republicans had stolen its program.

As recently as 1811 many Republicans had challenged the utility and opposed the recharter of Hamilton's bank. Difficulty in financing the war persuaded Calhoun, backed in 1816 by Madison, to rally southern and western congressmen to the support of central banking. Although local banking interests dictated opposition from New England and the middle states, the bill passed. By 1817 the Bank of the United States was open for business in Philadelphia, with a twenty-year charter, the right to issue notes and to establish branches anywhere in the United States, and initial capital of $35 million. The government supplied one-fifth of the capital, appointed five of the twenty-five directors, and received a fee—called a bonus—of $1.5 million for the charter and for the Bank's right to serve as the exclusive depository of government funds.

Calhoun had a use for that bonus. He proposed that the bonus itself, and the government's annual dividends from the bank, be spent for roads and canals—"internal improvements," in the phrase of the day—that would enhance the nation's unity, promote its commerce, and add to the comfort of its citizens. "We are great," Calhoun remarked, "and rapidly—I was about to say fearfully—growing." While growth was the glory of nations, it also posed the threat of disunity. "Let us," Calhoun exhorted, "bind the republic together with a perfect system of roads and canals. Let us conquer space." But the nationalism of some Republicans did not extend so far, and the self-interest of others prevented them from following Calhoun's lead. Southern representatives allied with New Englanders, who opposed internal improvements that seemed unlikely to benefit them directly. Westerners divided indecisively. But the middle states, eager to tap the markets of the interior, provided the votes that carried Calhoun's measure to a two-vote majority in the House. As one of his final presidential acts, Madison vetoed this Bonus Bill, perhaps, as he said, because of constitutional scruples and perhaps also because it did not have truly national support.

The tariff, by contrast, did have national support. The American economy needed protection as it adjusted to a world at peace. Nascent industries could not compete with British manufacturers who hoped to bury competition under an avalanche of cheap goods. The tariff was to be moderate and temporary, and it was to protect southern cotton and sugar, Kentucky hemp, Pennsylvania iron, and Ohio wool, as well as New England textiles. Actually, commercial New England, hoping to safeguard its profitable carrying trade, voted against the tariff. Nearly as many Federalists opposed protection as supported it, while Republicans overwhelmingly endorsed it. Madison certified Republican acceptance by signing the tariff of 1816.

For thirty-four years, while Presidents and Congresses came and went, Chief Justice John Marshall's nationalism never wavered. When John Adams appointed Marshall in 1801, the judiciary had neither the prestige nor the power of the other branches of government. But the Court under Marshall resisted Jefferson's attempts to reform or dominate it and continued to defend and enlarge the power of the national government long after Jefferson had gone back to Monticello. The Court was always Marshall's Court, no matter how many Republican justices Republican Presidents sent to join him. Instead of issuing several individual opinions, the Court began to speak with one voice—more often than not that of the Chief Justice. Between 1805 and 1833 the Court decided 919 cases; Marshall wrote the Court's opinion 458 times and dissented on exactly six occasions.

Part of Marshall's genius lay in his persuasive deductions from nationalist premises. Moreover, he had a gift for stating judicial principles so that his decisions were virtually invulnerable, if not above criticism. The earliest, and for Jefferson the most frustrating, demonstration of Marshall's judicial statesmanship occurred in 1803. In *Marbury* v. *Madison* Marshall coupled a gratuitous rebuke to the Republican administration with an assertion of the Court's power of judicial review. For the first time, the Supreme Court claimed the authority to declare federal law unconstitutional, a claim that Republicans disputed. The section of the statute in question had little significance, but Marshall's precedent had great importance, even though the Court chose not to rule against other federal legislation until 1857.

Because Madison won the verdict on a legal technicality, the administration could not directly challenge Marshall's ruling in the *Marbury* case. But Jefferson did intend to limit, or to intimidate, the Court. To ensure the survival of Republican principles, he remarked, the party must secure all three branches of government. Impeachment seemed the only recourse, but that effort bogged down in 1804 when the Senate acquitted Samuel Chase, a Federalist Associate Justice of the Supreme Court.

Over and over again between 1801 and 1835 Marshall recited his constitutional creed: the federal government had sovereignty independent of the states and superior to them in those respects enumerated in the Constitution. "It is true," Marshall answered proponents of state sovereignty in *McCulloch* v. *Maryland* (1819), that the people had "assembled in their several states" to ratify the Constitution. But, asked Marshall innocently, "Where else should they have assembled?" The Chief Justice used the *McCulloch* case to curb the states, which were hampering the Bank of the United States with taxation, and to restate and enlarge the implied powers of Congress. Marshall cribbed his argument from Alexander Hamilton's classic statement to President Washington: "Let the end be legitimate," Marshall wrote, "let it be within the scope of the Constitution, and all means which are appropriate, which are plainly adapted to that end, which are not prohibited . . . are constitutional." In 1821, in *Cohens* v. *Virginia*, Marshall lectured the Virginia judiciary on the supremacy of federal courts. In 1824, in *Gibbons* v. *Ogden*, the Chief Justice defined commerce so broadly that he seemed to claim federal jurisdiction over nearly all economic enterprise.

Marshall protected the rights of private property as zealously as he defended the power of the federal government. In *Fletcher* v. *Peck* (1810) he held that a legislative land grant was a contract worthy of the same protection the Constitution gave other contracts. A notoriously corrupt Georgia legislature had issued a grant that a subsequent legislature had repealed. No matter how dubious the original contract, Marshall declared its repeal an unconstitutional interference with the obligation of contract. In 1819 he ruled that New Hampshire could not convert Dartmouth College into a state university. The corporate charter that had established Dartmouth, Marshall held, was a contract that could not be changed by one party without the consent of the other. This decision, made at a time when businessmen were trying out the corporate form, checked the power of the states to regulate economic activity.

JAMES MONROE
AND THE ERA OF GOOD FEELINGS

Swelling postwar nationalism redounded to the political credit of the Republicans. In 1817 James Monroe inherited the presidency from Madison, seemingly as a matter of right. In the election of 1816 only Massachusetts, Connecticut, and Delaware had cast electoral votes for Rufus King, the able Federalist nominee. Determined to nourish his party's dominance, Monroe undertook a presidential grand tour from Baltimore to Boston and on to Detroit. Splendid patriotic oratory and a gratifying display of political unity marked Monroe's progress. A Boston newspaper provided the new administration with a label by referring to an "Era of Good Feelings." The description was inaccurate in several respects, but it

James Monroe, portrait by Gilbert Stuart

did reflect the temporary suspension of political partisanship and the equally temporary nationalism that marked the period. In the election of 1820 only one stubborn elector failed to vote for James Monroe.

Monroe named John Quincy Adams as Secretary of State, the office that had become the springboard to the White House, and thereby tacitly promised to be the last of the Virginia Dynasty. Adams, like his father, the second President, was a nationalist to the core. Diplomatic nationalism meant enlarging the nation and vigorously reasserting its prestige abroad. Adams and Monroe were equal to both tasks.

More annoying than the failure to conquer Canada in the War of 1812 was the failure to conquer Florida. Although the peninsula was nominally a Spanish possession, Spain no longer made a pretense of ruling it. In 1810, claiming that West Florida was part of the Louisiana Purchase, the United States had annexed the area west of the Perdido River; the seizure of Mobile during the war ended any Spanish challenge. West Florida only whetted the appetite for the rest of the territory, and Spain's failure to control the Seminole Indians and renegade slaves there provided a new excuse to send American forces into the area. In 1818 Andrew Jackson, allegedly acting with indirect authorization from Washington, pushed into Florida with a force of frontier militiamen, burned Spanish forts at Pensacola and St. Marks, and hanged two British subjects, whom he accused of helping the Indians. Jackson's raid set off a tense debate in Monroe's cabinet; most of the members, including Calhoun, who as Secretary of War was Jackson's immediate superior, wanted to disavow the impetuous general.

But John Quincy Adams, at first alone and then with Monroe's backing, defended Jackson. Already negotiating with the Spanish minister Don Luis de Onís to establish boundaries for Louisiana, Adams now added a demand that Spain reimburse the United States for the expenses of Jackson's expedition. He hinted that if Spain could not keep order in Florida the United States would be forced to annex it to protect the residents of Georgia and Alabama against raiding Indians. Jackson's exploit had demonstrated that Spain could not hold Florida, so Onís set out to salvage what he could. In 1819 Adams and Onís agreed to a "transcontinental treaty" that ceded Florida to the United States in return for the Treasury's assumption of $5 million in American claims against Spain. The United States renounced a shadowy claim to Texas by fixing the boundary of Louisiana at the Sabine River. Spain in turn renounced its claim to any territory north of the forty-second parallel, the northern boundary of California. Adams and Onís drew a line along the Arkansas and Red rivers and north to the forty-second parallel, thereby finally defining Jefferson's bargain of 1803. The Senate promptly approved the treaty, but Spain, less pleased with the outcome, delayed until 1821, when ratification became final.

Having eliminated Spain's claims to the northern Pacific coast, Adams did not propose to allow Russia to add the territory to Alaska. When the Czar closed the waters off Alaska and pushed its southern limit to the fifty-first parallel, Adams protested sharply. "The American continents," Adams

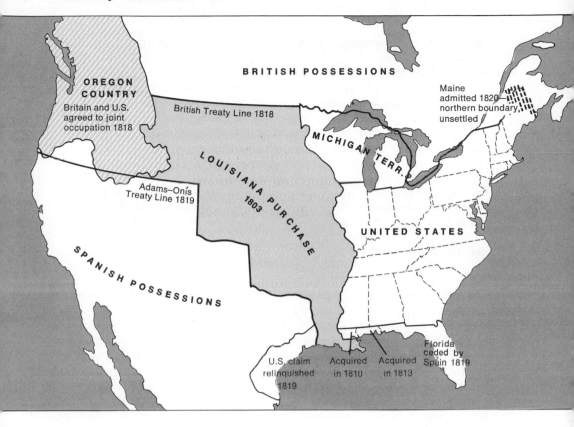

told the Czar's minister, "are no longer subjects for any new European colonial establishments." The Czar did not think the area vital to his empire, and in 1824 he revoked the maritime restriction and set Alaska's southern boundary at 54°40′.

The principle of noncolonization that Adams tried out on the Czar was destined for a wider audience. Since the beginning of Monroe's presidency, the administration had been puzzling out a policy toward the Latin American republics that were gradually winning their independence from Spain. Although France and Russia were vaguely interested in assisting Spanish efforts to regain the empire, no European nation could intervene in the western hemisphere without the cooperation of the British fleet, which commanded the Atlantic. Since British merchants welcomed the Latin American independence that ended Spain's mercantilistic restrictions on trade, the British Cabinet did not encourage European efforts to subdue the former Spanish colonies.

Secretary Adams too was anxious to keep European powers out of the western hemisphere. During 1818 and 1819 Adams had suggested that both Britain and the United States recognize the new Latin American republics. Britain was not then ready to appear to condone revolution. But in

1823 George Canning, Britain's Foreign Minister, proposed a joint statement opposing intervention in Latin America. Although he lacked precise instructions, Richard Rush, the American minister in London, replied that Britain ought first to extend diplomatic recognition to the new republics as the United States had done the year before. Rush then forwarded Canning's suggestion to Washington, where Monroe, who liked the idea, sought and received the blessing of both Madison and Jefferson. But Secretary Adams opposed a joint declaration lest it make the United States seem the pawn of British policy—"a cockboat in the wake of the British man of war." Adams also opposed any step that might be interpreted as barring intervention by the United States in Latin America or the acquisition of territory there. Adams persuaded the President to spell out this policy, and Monroe devoted part of his 1823 State of the Union message to enunciating it.

The Monroe Doctrine—as it came to be called in the 1840s—began with the standard assumption that America was part of a new and better world, while Europe was different and decadent. According to Monroe, Americans were "interested spectators" of European events and cherished "sentiments the most friendly" toward their trans-Atlantic forebears. But in matters strictly European, he continued, "we have never taken any part, nor does it comport with our policy, so to do." So much, Monroe implied, for those who suggested that the United States should aid the Greek revolt that was raging in the 1820s. On the other hand, the United States was, in the President's opinion, directly concerned about the Western Hemisphere, and any effort by European powers "to extend their system to any portions of this Hemisphere" would be construed as "dangerous to our peace and safety." The United States, Monroe reassured his European audience, would not interfere with existing colonies. But henceforth "the American continents" were "not to be considered as subject for future colonization by any European powers."

Even before Monroe decided to shun Canning's offer, Canning had withdrawn it. And before Monroe read his speech, the French government had assured Canning that France had no intention of repressing Latin American insurrections. Without France and Britain, Spain could not regain its colonies and Monroe's statement of policy was superfluous. Congress listened to his message politely, took no action on it, and appropriated no money for ships to enforce it. European capitals dismissed the Monroe Doctrine as Yankee bombast. But nationalistic Americans, whose only memory of the War of 1812 was the victory at New Orleans, thought the United States a good match for all continental Europe.

THE END OF GOOD FEELINGS

The nation stood behind the President's foreign policy, but on domestic matters, unity—and good feelings—disappeared well before 1823. Prosperity was essential to harmony, and the financial panic that began in 1819 exposed rifts between sections and classes that nationalism had earlier obscured. In 1818 the price of cotton had reached 32.5 cents a pound; in

1819 the average was slightly over 14 cents. Before 1819 plantation land in Mississippi had sold at spirited auctions for as much as $100 per acre; in 1819 the market was placid and the price depressed. Jefferson reported that land in Virginia could not be sold for a year's rent; rents in Baltimore dropped by half. Unemployment mounted in Philadelphia. In Pittsburgh the unemployed simply deserted the city, and the population suddenly decreased by nearly one-third.

Like all panics, that of 1819 had no single cause. In part the panic grew out of worldwide economic dislocation that accompanied the wars at the beginning of the century. Irresponsible American banking, from the Bank of the United States to the wildest "wildcat" bank in the West, further weakened the economy. And in part the panic resulted from the expansive postwar mood of Americans, whose optimism blinded them to economic reality. When optimism vanished in the panic, the American public tended to blame the Bank of the United States, the keystone of postwar nationalism. This popular explanation was too simple, but extensive criticism of the Bank aroused once more those who had always feared the power of the national government.

These fears of state-rights advocates multiplied during two years of intermittent wrangling over slavery. In 1819 Missouri applied for admission to the Union with a constitution that routinely guaranteed slavery, since 10,000 of Missouri's inhabitants were slaves. Missouri's application for statehood became anything but routine, however, when James Tallmadge, Jr., a congressman from New York, moved to prevent new slaves from entering Missouri and to emancipate gradually those already there. The Tallmadge amendment threatened not only slavery in Missouri but slavery everywhere, which southerners believed must either spread or die. If slavery could be ended in Missouri, where it was already established, it could be kept out of other territories and perhaps even abolished in existing states. The amendment also threatened the equality in the Senate of free and slave states, a condition that had become a tacit sectional agreement. And finally Tallmadge's motion threatened the unity of the Republican party. Jefferson warned that Rufus King and other opportunistic Federalists thought opposition to slavery might unite Northwest and Northeast against southern Republicans.

Anxious to preserve Republican unity, Henry Clay put together the legislative package called the Missouri Compromise. Clay linked Maine's application for statehood in 1820 with that of Missouri, thereby preserving the sectional balance. He then incorporated the proposal of Illinois Senator Jesse Thomas that no other part of the Louisiana Purchase north of 36°30′ (the southern boundary of Missouri) should be open to slavery. Southern representatives supported Clay's compromise with more enthusiasm than did representatives from the free states. But unless new southern territory was added, or unless the 36°30′ line was revoked, two or three more of a dozen potential northern states would end southern equality in the Senate. For the Compromise left only Arkansas and the Indian Territory as future slave states.

The revised constitution Missouri submitted to Congress late in 1820

The Missouri Compromise, 1820

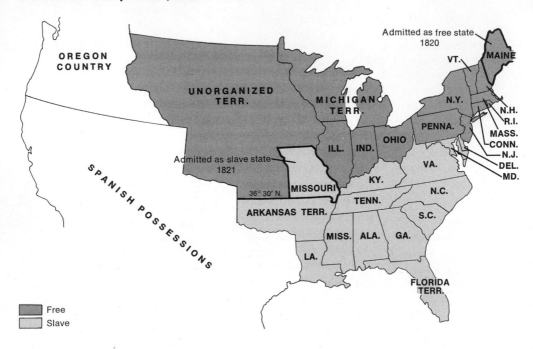

OREGON COUNTRY

UNORGANIZED TERR.

MICHIGAN TERR.

SPANISH POSSESSIONS

Admitted as slave state 1821

36° 30' N.

MISSOURI

ARKANSAS TERR.

ILL. IND. OHIO

KY.

TENN.

MISS. ALA. GA.

LA.

Admitted as free state 1820

VT. MAINE

N.Y.

PENNA.

VA.

N.H.
R.I.
MASS.
CONN.
N.J.
DEL.
MD.

N.C.

S.C.

FLORIDA TERR.

Free
Slave

threatened to undo the Compromise before it could take effect. The constitution made slavery as permanent as law could make it by requiring the consent of each slaveowner to leglislative emancipation. In another section the document forbade free blacks to enter the state "under any pretext whatever." Since blacks were citizens of some northern states, this second provision violated the privileges and immunities clause of the Constitution of the United States. Those who had supported Tallmadge's amendment once more opposed statehood for Missouri. But Henry Clay borrowed from a Tennessee senator a pacifying resolution that required Missouri's promise not to construe her constitution so as to violate the privileges or immunities of citizens of other states. The promise and Clay's formula were equally worthless after Missouri was admitted in 1821, but for the moment most politicians were relieved to have the issue buried.

The Virginia Dynasty occupied the political middle ground between the uncompromising nationalism of John Marshall and the state-rights Republicanism of John Randolph. Sensing that the nation was changing and courageous enough to discard outworn political principles, the three Virginians at first used the powers of government on behalf of sections and classes that Federalists had overlooked. Popular confidence in the central government mounted. For a few years Republicans acted as if they were genuinely convinced that the good of the whole nation transcended personal preferment, sectional prejudices, and parochial interests. But an energetic and restless people, itching to exploit the resources of a broad continent, soon rediscovered old rivalries and then developed some new ones.

Suggested Reading

Henry Adams wrote nine volumes of *History of the United States During the Administrations of Jefferson and Madison* (1889–91); his study begins with an account of American society that has been published separately as *The United States in 1800** (1955). Adams' brief account of American society may be compared with Thomas Jefferson's *Notes on the State of Virginia,** written in the 1780s. Marshall Smelser has provided the most recent and certainly the best-written study of the Jefferson and Madison administrations, *The Democratic Republic, 1801–1815** (1968).

Irving Brant completed a multivolume biography of James Madison in 1961 and Dumas Malone is studying Jefferson on a comparable scale; four volumes carry the Virginian through his first term as President. The letters and papers of both Republican Presidents are being collected and published, as are the papers of the Adams family. Samuel F. Bemis' *John Quincy Adams and the Foundation of American Foreign Policy* (1950) is excellent.

Several studies have focused on the War on 1812, including two detailed works of Bradford Perkins, *The First Rapprochement* (1967) and *Prologue to War** (1961), which together trace Anglo-American relations from 1795 to 1812. Julius Pratt's *Expansionists of 1812* (1925) is a persuasive statement of the case for land hunger as the cause of the war; Roger H. Brown, *The Republic in Peril: 1812* (1964), argues that national pride was more fundamental.

Two accounts by George Dangerfield, *The Awakening of American Nationalism** (1965) and *The Era of Good Feeling** (1952), survey the period from 1815 to 1828. David H. Fischer, *The Revolution of American Conservatism** (1965), examines the Federalist party, while Noble Cunningham, *The Jeffersonian Republicans in Power** (1967), deals with the Federalists' successful opponents. James S. Young, *The Washington Community, 1800–1828* (1966), discusses the ways politicians functioned in the nation's unfinished capital city.

*Available in paperback edition

CHRONOLOGY

1824   Presidential election: The House of Representatives selects John Quincy Adams. In the election, none of the four candidates—Adams, Andrew Jackson, William H. Crawford, and Henry Clay—received an electoral-vote majority; all are nominally Democratic-Republicans.

1828   "Tariff of abominations"
Presidential election: Andrew Jackson (Democrat) defeats John Quincy Adams (National Republican)

1830   Senators Webster and Hayne debate principles of state sovereignty and nationalism
Indian Removal Act

1831, 1832   *Cherokee Nation* v. *Georgia* and *Worcester* v. *Georgia* decisions hold Indians are entitled to federal protection

1832   Tariff of 1832 precipitates nullification crisis
Jackson vetoes renewal of charter for Bank of the United States
Presidential election: Andrew Jackson (Democrat) defeats Henry Clay (National Republican), William Wirt (Anti-Masonic Party), and John Floyd (dissident National Republican)

1833   Compromise tariff of 1833 passed

1836   Specie Circular requires government land be bought with hard money
Presidential election: Martin Van Buren (Democrat) defeats William Henry Harrison, Hugh L. White, Daniel Webster, and W. P. Mangum (sectional Whig candidates)

1837   Financial panic
Charles River Bridge case attacks "privileged corporations"

1840   Independent Treasury Act passed (repealed in 1841)
Presidential election: William Henry Harrison (Whig) defeats Martin Van Buren (Democrat)

1841   John Tyler succeeds Harrison

VIII

THE POLITICS

OF THE COMMON MAN

In 1829, for the first time, many ordinary citizens celebrated the solemn inauguration of the President of the United States. Dignity did not long endure; alcohol and popular enthusiasm for Andrew Jackson turned the ensuing reception into an uninhibited romp. As if to reassert their title, the guests milled around *their* White House, stood on *their* furniture, smashed *their* china, drank *their* punch, and exhausted *their* President with cheers and good will. The crowds, wrote a puzzled Daniel Webster, really seemed "to think that the country ha[d] been rescued from some dreadful danger."

Webster's incredulity disclosed not only his failure to sense the popular mood but also his estimate that the administration of John Quincy Adams had not endangered the republic. When Adams began his career in the eighteenth century, and even as late as 1812, when Webster first won office, governing was almost exclusively a gentleman's profession. Yet, in the 1820s and 1830s education, experience, and gentility began to count less with the expanded electorate than heroism and identification with ordinary folk. In a sense, the presidency of John Quincy Adams marked the end of a political generation; that of Andrew Jackson opened a new and more democratic era, when to be popularly called "Old Hickory" signified popular affection and no lack of respect.

Carved figurehead for the ship
Andrew Jackson

When the Constitution was adopted, many of the original states had religious qualifications for suffrage, and all either limited the vote to taxpayers or retained a property qualification. The fourteenth state, Vermont, admitted in 1791, permitted universal manhood suffrage. Upon admission to the Union, Indiana, Illinois, Alabama, Missouri, and Maine adopted white manhood suffrage. In the dozen years after 1815 state after state modified its constitution to enlarge the number of eligible voters, to establish legislative representation on the basis of population instead of tax receipts, and to increase the number of elective offices.

A nudge toppled the old order. Those who had hoped to keep political office a preserve of the rich, able, and well-born argued at length but in vain. At bottom, the dispute stemmed from differing views of the nature of man: advocates of limited suffrage worried about man's follies, vices, and sins; optimistic democrats believed man perfectible, trustworthy, decent. To Americans, who thought they had just trounced the greatest power in Europe and who were exploiting the apparently limitless resources of an apparently limitless continent, a gloomy view of human nature and of man's future seemed entirely inappropriate.

And so James Kent, the learned Chancellor of New York, who eloquently defended the rights of property in the state constitutional convention of 1821, lost his case. He believed that tax-paying property owners were more entitled to representation than "men of no property" or the "crowds of dependents connected with great manufacturing establishments" or the "motley and undefinable population of crowded ports." He scoffed at the "notion that every man who works a day on the roads or serves an idle hour in the militia" was the equal of more substantial members of society.

Like many conservatives, he feared that liberty would degenerate into "wild and savage licentiousness"; like most conservatives he preferred a familiar order to the uncertainty of change. But the future lay with men of more faith, more imagination, and less property. In 1821 New York adopted a more democratic constitution.

THE ELECTION OF JOHN QUINCY ADAMS
◆

Not everyone who had the right to vote did so in the presidential election of 1824. About 350,000 men, perhaps one of every four eligible, bothered to cast ballots. Lack of interest did not result from lack of candidates, for four distinguished Americans sought the office, and a fifth, John C. Calhoun, had carefully considered the race before deciding to settle for the vice-presidency, which he won easily. Henry Clay, John Quincy Adams, William Crawford, and Andrew Jackson were all nominally Jeffersonian Republicans. As long as one dignified Virginian had followed another in agreed succession, the party had remained united. Republican members of Congress had assembled in a caucus that apparently selected the party's presidential nominee but actually only ratified the obvious choice. Faced with a contest for the first time in 1824, the caucus failed, and Jefferson's coalition broke apart.

A rump session of the caucus nominated William Crawford, the Georgian who had served Monroe as Secretary of the Treasury. Crawford's stict construction, his southern residence, and the source of his nomination made him appear the Jeffersonian heir. But the quasi-official status of Crawford's candidacy became a liability. For the caucus seemed an undemocratic survival from the days when gentlemen decided political matters, and its nominee, while capable, seemed uninteresting.

Nobody, on the other hand, had ever thought Andrew Jackson dull. Jackson personified the economic and social success of which all Americans dreamed; he was the poor orphan who grew up to own a prosperous plantation, to serve in both houses of Congress, and to sit as a judge. His duels, his Indian wars, and his victory at New Orleans made Jackson the symbol of the popular preference for deeds over words. His life displayed the rugged independence, the healthy acquisitiveness, and the unpretentious good fellowship his countrymen admired.

Henry Clay also liked good fellowship, and perhaps no legislator before the Civil War had more close congressional friends than the magnetic Kentuckian. He had been elected Speaker of the House at his very first appearance in that body and, except for one year, was reelected as long as he served in the House. More clearly than any other candidate, Clay advanced a specific program, which he called "the American system." He argued that the central government should finance internal improvements with income from the sale of land at a reasonable price. And he advocated both a protective tariff and a stable national currency regulated by a national bank. Taken together, Clay held, his policies would produce a prosperous, unified nation. His genius was in transforming vaguely felt needs and aspirations into concrete legislative measures. The components of his American system were the major issues of American political discussion until slavery made any political discussion impossible.

John Quincy Adams, the fourth candidate in 1824, was immune to Clay's charm but agreed with his program. The son of the second President inherited both the stubborn integrity and the political ineptitude of his father. John Quincy Adams had been brought up to govern; no man who ever competed for the presidency was apparently better prepared. His brief appearance in the Senate and his distinguished diplomatic service revealed that Adams was intelligent, frank, and conscientious to a fault. Above all, he was an uncompromising nationalist.

For all his nationalism, however, Adams had the support only of the Northeast and ran second in both popular and electoral vote to Jackson, whose appeal was more nearly national than that of any other candidate. Old Hickory won many of the southern and western states that Clay had believed were safely his. In spite of a paralytic stroke late in 1823 that left him virtually helpless, Crawford ran slightly ahead of Clay in the electoral college, although Clay had a few hundred more popular votes than did the Georgian.

Yet popular votes did not a President make. The Twelfth Amendment held that when no candidate had a majority, the House of Representatives had to choose among the three candidates with the largest electoral total. Henry Clay could use his immense prestige in the House only to make another man President. And Clay really had no choice. Crawford's illness

John Quincy Adams: He lacked the common touch.

The Election of 1824

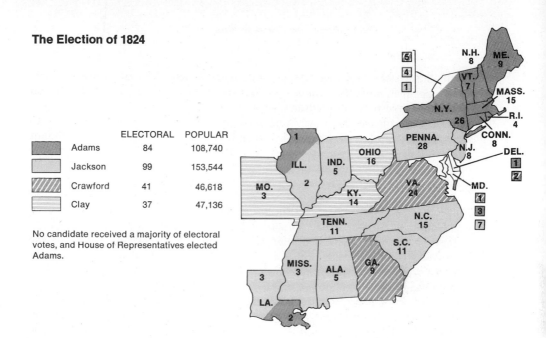

	ELECTORAL	POPULAR
Adams	84	108,740
Jackson	99	153,544
Crawford	41	46,618
Clay	37	47,136

No candidate received a majority of electoral votes, and House of Representatives elected Adams.

eliminated him. Although Jackson's political principles were unclear, his rivalry with Clay for political support in the West and South were evident indeed. Adams, on the other hand, shared Clay's economic nationalism and seemed to the Kentuckian a lesser political obstacle than the General. Both sides pressured and flattered Clay, but his decision could never really have been in doubt. He chose Adams, who won on the first ballot in the House.

If the cooperation of Adams and Clay had stopped with the election, the Adams administration might have been less acrimonious and Clay's political future more bright. But Clay joined Adams' Cabinet as Secretary of State, a position that seemed to confer the right of succession to the White House. Jacksonians promptly charged that a "corrupt bargain" had mocked the people's will, and the presidential campaign of 1828 began in 1825 with Clay's appointment.

John Quincy Adams' presidency was, as one of his grandsons later wrote, a "lurid administration," illuminated by crackling political lightning. The President's proposals were plentiful and imaginative, but Congress refused to enact them. Internal improvements, in Adams' vocabulary, meant more than roads and canals; in 1825 he deluged Congress with suggestions for varied national projects. Government ought to encourage exploration and scientific research and to charter a national university. Statesmen must not only develop programs to stimulate the nation's economic growth, but must also respond to "the spirit of improvement" that was "abroad upon the earth."

Congress found politics in the here and now more to its taste. Anything might serve as an occasion for partisanship. Adams' nomination of two delegates to discuss hemispheric cooperation at a Congress in Panama provoked a filibuster that lasted most of the winter of 1825–26. The endless talk itself was unimportant, but it furnished an opportunity to broadcast the charge that Clay and Adams had corruptly secured their offices. Debate also permitted private discussions that knit several state organizations into a formidable political coalition. Martin Van Buren, an astute senator from New York, pledged his own "Albany Regency" to Jackson and undertook to secure the support of others, like Isaac Hill of New Hampshire and Thomas Ritchie of Virginia, who had been Van Buren's allies in the Crawford campaign of 1824. Calhoun also talked with Van Buren and enrolled in Jackson's camp. Thomas Hart Benton in Missouri, Major William Lewis and John Eaton in Tennessee, Amos Kendall and Francis Preston Blair in Kentucky, James Buchanan in Pennsylvania—all Jacksonians with budding political machines—redoubled their effort to discredit the President and his Secretary of State. It did not matter that eventually Adams' nominees to the Panama Congress were approved; one of the envoys died, and the other arrived too late to accomplish anything. The political cost of the President's seeming victory was immense. The coalition of Jacksonians, soon proudly to call itself the Democratic party, was able to limit Adams to one troubled term in the White House and to prevent Henry Clay from ever taking up residence there.

The fight over the tariff was also politically expensive. In 1827 the House heeded pleas of Massachusetts and Rhode Island woolen-manufacturers for protection. When the vote in the Senate was tied, Vice-President Calhoun killed the bill. A second bill in 1828 became the center of a thick political intrigue and eventually emerged as the "tariff of abominations." To provisions that were slightly less generous to the woolen interests than those of 1827 were added duties on iron, lead, flax, hemp, and raw wool. Jacksonians hoped to woo the middle states, whose products the tariff of 1828 protected, and simultaneously to blame Adams for the law in the South, where any tariff was an abomination. A Democratic coalition prevented any amendment, perhaps in the expectation that disgusted northern representatives would find the bill unsatisfactory and join southerners, who voted overwhelmingly against it. Although Daniel Webster and sixteen New England congressmen grudgingly supported the measure, twenty-three New Englanders opposed it. But overwhelming support from the middle states and the Northwest was enough to put the new tariff on the President's desk. Political criticism would greet whatever action Adams took, and fully aware of the hazard, he signed the bill. The intricate Jacksonian strategy was probably unnecessary, for tariff or no tariff, John Quincy Adams was a sure loser in 1828.

The campaign of 1828 had begun in 1825 with doubtful accusations, boisterously stated, and then proceeded to degenerate. By election day voters had heard that the profligate Adams had used public funds to install sinful games in the White House. While Ambassador to Russia, the Jacksonians said, Adams had supplied a virtuous American girl for the pleasure of the debauched Russian Czar. The President's campaigners were hardly less imaginative. They exaggerated Jackson's exploits as a frontier brawler and distributed a broadside edged in coffins, representing the men Jackson was alleged to have murdered during the War of 1812. Jackson's opponents seized upon the fact that his wife had married him under the mistaken impression that her previous husband had secured a divorce. The charges against Old Hickory boomeranged. His duels and his military reputation were the stuff of legends and evidence of courage, decisiveness, and patriotism. His wife, the retiring Rachel, personified defenseless womanhood, and her death before inauguration enhanced her symbolic tragedy.

It was the most exciting campaign in a generation, perhaps since the birth of the republic. Not issues, but furor and a developing party organization lured people to the polls. Each candidate received more votes than the total cast four years earlier; perhaps 55 percent of those eligible voted. More than 55 percent of those ballots were for Andrew Jackson, who won 178 electoral votes, while Adams won only 83. Calhoun remained as Vice-President. The electoral college, once intended to check such popular enthusiasms as that for Jackson and to keep the choice of chief magistrate from the people, had become responsive to the popular will. By 1832 only in South Carolina did the legislature choose presidential electors; elsewhere the voter had a direct choice.

ANDREW JACKSON'S FIRST ADMINISTRATION

Andrew Jackson's inaugural address was equivocal and dull; his administration began slowly. The Cabinet contained more friends of Calhoun than some politicians thought seemly, but Martin Van Buren, Calhoun's rival as the General's heir, was Secretary of State. An informal group of advisers, called the "Kitchen Cabinet" by the envious, included Isaac Hill, Amos Kendall, and Francis P. Blair, all experienced editors whose newspapers sparked local Democratic organizations and spread the Jacksonian word.

Democrats claimed the spoils of victory by displacing officeholders at all levels of the federal bureaucracy. The administration actually removed only about one out of nine federal appointees. But as other jobs fell vacant, Jacksonians filled them. The President regarded this turnover as a reform, for there had been no wholesale change since 1801, and some appointees, grown musty in office, regarded their positions more as a right than a trust. In a democracy, Jackson held, office ought to be open to all citizens, and his idea that positions should be rotated among the party faithful was the counterpart of extended suffrage.

Like Madison and Monroe before him, Jackson questioned the federal government's right to appropriate funds for the internal improvements his western supporters demanded. In 1830 Jackson restated his constitutional qualms by vetoing a bill to subsidize a road in Kentucky called the Maysville Road. But he shrewdly conciliated the West by approving expenditures to improve rivers and harbors; indeed during Jackson's presidency appropriations for internal improvements were considerably larger than those of the Adams administration. Only four days after vetoing the Maysville Bill, Jackson signed a measure to finance part of the National Road, which, Jackson carefully noted, was an interstate project. Perhaps only the President thought these two actions consistent. But he retained both his constitutional scruples and the loyalty of the West at the minimal cost of part of a road in Henry Clay's state.

If Jackson's policy on internal improvements seemed devious, his Indian policy was uncompromising and direct. He asked Congress in 1829 to establish a western Indian territory, and the Indian Removal Act of 1830 provided for forced migration, which continued through the decade. Earlier, when Georgia began to crowd the Creeks from tribal lands, John Quincy Adams had unsuccessfully attempted to ease the process for the Indians; when, a few years later, Georgia wanted to push the Cherokees out too, Andrew Jackson had no objection. In two cases, *Cherokee Nation v. Georgia* (1831) and *Worcester* v. *Georgia* (1832), Chief Justice Marshall held, in substance, that the Indians were entitled to federal protection. The President is supposed to have remarked that Marshall would have to enforce his own decision. Cherokees got scant protection from the old Indian-fighter in the White House, and Georgia forced their migration along the "trail of tears" to Oklahoma.

The South applauded both Jackson's Indian policy and his constitutional reservations about internal improvements. But before the end of his first term the South discovered that Old Hickory differed from many southerners in his interpretation of the rights of states, for Jackson seemed to think the Union vastly greater than the sum of its sectional parts.

The first open indication of trouble came early in 1830, during a Senate debate on a resolution introduced by Senator Samuel Foot of Connecticut that suggested the sale of public lands be temporarily restricted. Missouri's Senator Benton assailed the resolution. Southern Senators, including Robert Y. Hayne of South Carolina, who may have been coached by Calhoun, supported Benton in an apparent attempt to create a political alliance between West and South. Hayne's attack on the Northeast went beyond land policy to add a denunciation of the section's broad view of federal power. In introducing constitutional interpretation, Hayne had shifted the topic of debate, and Daniel Webster seized the opportunity.

Webster knew the peril of discussing economic and land policy, about which sections differed. Rather he attacked southern doctrines of state sovereignty and strict construction. He appealed to the mystic bonds that knit many interests and many regions into one great nation, and he concluded that liberty and union were perpetual and inseparable. Some months later, in a dramatic confrontation with Calhoun, Jackson affirmed a similar nationalism in a toast to the preservation of the Union.

The rift between President and Vice-President had personal as well as political causes. Jackson discovered that in 1818 Calhoun, then Monroe's Secretary of War, had supported an attempt of the Cabinet to discipline Jackson for his conduct in Florida. Jackson demanded that the Carolinian explain his action and found Calhoun's reply unsatisfactory. Jackson was also outraged because Calhoun's wife seemed to have stirred a tempest that swept through Washington society. John Eaton, Jackson's friend and Secretary of War, married saucy, attractive Peggy O'Neale, whose reputation was none too good and whom the scandalized wives of the rest of the administration shunned. Perhaps because his own wife had been slandered, Jackson defended Mrs. Eaton, as did Martin Van Buren, who used the apparently trivial controversy in his effort to supplant Calhoun as heir apparent. By the spring of 1831 Calhoun's friends were forced from the Cabinet; before the end of 1832 Calhoun resigned as Vice-President and returned to Washington as Senator from South Carolina.

THE TARIFF AND NULLIFICATION

Even if Jackson and Calhoun could have patched up their personal disagreements, the tariff would have divided them irreparably. Jackson's position on the issue before 1830 had been ambiguous, although he conceded that protective duties were constitutional. In 1831 he recommended that the "tariff of abominations" be reduced, and in 1832 Congress passed a new measure that lowered some duties while remaining basically protective.

Calhoun's native South Carolina had made the tariff a scapegoat for chronic agricultural depression. Actually, crop after crop of cotton had taken from the soil fertility that only money, fertilizer, and time could replace. But Carolinians argued that the tariff depressed the price of cotton by reducing their market abroad, and that the duty simultaneously raised the price of goods they had to buy. Unhappy about the act of 1828, South Carolinians had expected Jackson to scrap the tariff; the act of 1832 suggested that ordinary political action would not provide redress.

The attack on the tariff concealed a defense of slavery. The tariff, Calhoun wrote in 1830, was only the "occasion, rather than the real cause of the present unhappy state of things." Calhoun saw protection as part of a national assault on "the peculiar domestick [sic] institutions of the Southern States," which he proposed to protect by shoring up "the reserved rights of the states." If the federal government grew too powerful —and a protective tariff indicated to Calhoun the existence of that condition—then southern states "must in the end be forced to rebel, or submit to have . . . themselves and their children reduced to wretchedness."

When politics failed to shield the South, Calhoun was ready with an ingenious substitute. In 1828 he had secretly written the *South Carolina Exposition and Protest*, which asserted state sovereignty and from that premise deduced the power of any state to nullify federal law. In 1831 Calhoun openly restated these views in the *Fort Hill Address*. Only the states, Calhoun wrote, could determine the limits of legitimate federal authority. If, after solemn consideration, a state found federal legislation oppressive and unconstitutional, the state might formally nullify the law, which would then be unenforced. The state would not abide by such a federal law until three-quarters of the states had specifically delegated to the central government the power in question. If the state still found the statute unacceptable, secession was the final recourse. The protective tariff provided an immediate test.

Calhoun's theories were a major issue in South Carolina's legislative election held in 1832. Although unionists made up a substantial minority, most legislators favored nullification. In accordance with Calhoun's formula, the legislature called a convention that officially nullified the tariffs of 1828 and 1832, forbade collection of duties, and prohibited appeal of the issue to the federal courts. The legislature appropriated money to equip a force to resist federal coercion. South Carolina then waited for Andrew Jackson.

The President thought himself a protector of the rights of states. Like Calhoun, Jackson believed his interpretation of the Constitution was based on the Jeffersonian principles of the Kentucky and Virginia Resolutions. No one, Jackson wrote Hayne in 1831, had a "higher regard and respect than myself" for the rights of the states. Jackson acknowledged that the central government might occasionally exceed its constitutional powers but suggested that political action was the remedy for such usurpation, which, in any case, could not "be of long duration in our enlightened country where the people rule." Once the people had spoken, he warned, opposition became revolution, and all the evils of revolution "must be looked for and expected. . . ."

So Robert Hayne, Governor of South Carolina in 1832, could hardly have been surprised by the vehemence of Jackson's response to nullification. The title itself—*A Proclamation to the People of South Carolina*—brushed off state sovereignty, Calhoun's basic precept. Phrase after phrase showed the President's impatience with South Carolina's constitutional pretense: nullification carried "with it internal evidence of its impractical absurdity"; South Carolina's constitutional argument was dismissed as a "strange position," or worse, as a "metaphysical subtlety." The President thought "every man of plain unsophisticated understanding" agreed that no state could disobey legitimate federal law. Plain, unsophisticated Andrew Jackson used italics to make the point: "I consider, then, the power to annul a law of the United States, assumed by one state, *incompatible with the existence of the Union, contradicted expressly by the letter of the Constitution, unauthorized by its spirit, inconsistent with every principle on which it was founded, and destructive of the great object for which it was formed.*" The Union could, Jackson asserted, coerce a disobedient state. While he hinted at the horror of disunion, he emphasized the advantages of Union in the grand manner of Daniel Webster. The central government linked the states "in one bond of common interest," defended them, encouraged their flourishing literature, arts, and commerce, and conferred on their people that proud title, *"American citizen."*

Martin Van Buren, anxious to preserve a united party, worried that Old Hickory had said too much. The President's belligerent nationalism might, Van Buren feared, alienate those Democrats whose devotion to state rights exceeded their devotion to Jackson. Van Buren wrote, and the New York legislature adopted, wordy resolutions that applauded Jackson's presidency but stopped short of endorsing his uncompromising affirmation of central power. Apparently Van Buren hoped to indicate agreement with Jackson's action and at the same time to reassure those, especially in the South, who were alarmed at the sweeping assertion of national authority.

Van Buren's subtlety was probably unnecessary. Northern legislatures endorsed the President's course, usually without quibble, and southern legislatures also disavowed nullification. Some self-styled defenders of the Republican tradition deserted Jackson; John Tyler, for instance, became a state-rights Whig, but neither state-righters nor Whigs were very comfortable in the alliance, as Tyler's unhappy, accidental presidency subsequently made clear. In confronting South Carolina, Jackson sought and secured national support.

Nationalism was equally visible in Congress, where legislators tried to preserve the Union. A force bill, which authorized the President to use national troops to uphold national legislation, demonstrated that the legislature's determination complemented Jackson's. Compromisers meanwhile sought a face-saving formula to make force unnecessary. Early in 1833 Henry Clay, after consulting Calhoun, proposed that the tariff be annually reduced until, in 1842, the rates reached the level of 1816. South Carolina then withdrew its nullification of the tariff, but nullified the superfluous Force Act. Both state and nation had decided, for the moment, that political action remedied hardship more safely than a stand on constitutional principle.

The controversy over nullification disclosed the President's political philosophy. Strict construction of the federal Constitution lay at the center of Jackson's creed and at the core of the Jacksonian party. Old Hickory had intuitively combined the Federalist-Whig vision of a strong, unified nation with Jefferson's concern that liberty might disappear if the country were too much governed. Jackson's strict construction assumed organic union of states and sections under a federal Constitution; but he believed that Constitution restricted the government and liberated the individual.

THE BANK WAR

Although Jackson appeared to South Carolinians as a nationalist, those who simultaneously sought recharter for the Bank of the United States thought his construction of the Constitution uncommonly strict. The Constitution, as Jackson read it, required the central government to coerce a disobedient state but did not authorize the establishment of a national bank. The BUS, Jackson believed, limited the opportunity for enterprising Americans to get ahead. "The monster," as Jacksonians called the Bank, had too much power and was not sufficiently subject to public control.

Two incompatible groups opposed the Bank on economic grounds: one faction argued that the BUS did not permit sufficient note issue by local banks, and the other opposed issuing any bank notes at all. Through its monopoly on government deposits, the BUS accumulated the notes of state banks, which it returned for regular redemption. This cycle curtailed note issue, provided a more stable currency than would have resulted without central restraint, and in a crude way controlled the availability of credit. But in the rapidly expanding Jacksonian economy borrowers demanded more credit to finance more expansion, so the Bank's caution made enemies.

On the other hand, those who disliked any paper currency preferred specie, or hard money, and instinctively disliked all banks, no matter how prudently managed.

The BUS had not been prudently managed from 1816 to 1819, but had permitted a dangerous expansion of credit. Langdon Cheves, who guided the Bank between 1819 and 1823, adopted the economically necessary, but politically unpopular, policy of reducing loans to produce gradual deflation. The Panic of 1819, although short, was sharp and brought economic hardship, particularly in the West and South, where land prices had soared well above land values. Criticism of the Bank, never entirely stilled, grew sharper, and neither anger nor criticism subsided when John Marshall announced in *McCulloch* v. *Maryland* (1819) that the Bank was not only constitutional but practically immune to state regulation.

When Nicholas Biddle succeeded Cheves in 1823, the Bank was economically secure and had survived the assaults of panics and politicians. An arrogant Philadelphia aristocrat, Biddle enlarged the institution's resources and power. Bank notes circulated at a minimal discount; government deposits were secure; federal funds were efficiently transferred; and short-term loans to the Treasury were readily available. Biddle, in short, proved to be a competent banker.

But he blundered politically. In 1832, perhaps advised by Clay, who was running against Jackson, Biddle unwisely pressed for renewal of the Bank's charter. Four years remained on the first charter, but Biddle apparently concluded that the President would not risk interference with the Bank in an election year, particularly when a crisis approached over nullification. Jackson's attitude toward the BUS had seemed ambiguous; in his first annual message, he had wondered whether the BUS was either legitimate or appropriate. Yet, Jackson had written Biddle to thank him for meeting so efficiently the fiscal needs of the government, and the secretaries of state and of the treasury whom Jackson had appointed were known to favor recharter. Congress investigated Biddle's management of the BUS and then voted a new charter by relatively small margins in both houses.

Jackson interpreted Biddle's request as a personal and political challenge, and Old Hickory seldom backed away from a fight. He returned the new charter to Congress with a prompt, unwavering, and superbly political veto. He appealed to a young nation's pride by imagining the harm that foreign stockholders might do to national security through their influence on the Bank. Unmoved by Marshall's decision in the *McCulloch* case, Jackson indicted the Bank as unconstitutional; it was, he held, neither necessary to the financial tasks of government, nor proper as an exercise of legislative power. Strict construction demanded that the central government refrain from "invasions of the rights and powers of the several states"—strange language, South Carolinians must have thought a few months later, when the thundering presidential proclamation denouncing nullification arrived. But Jackson's strict construction tried less to secure the power of states than to secure the liberty of individuals. And the President thought the Bank undemocratic and potentially dangerous to individual liberty because

Cartoonists fight the Bank War.

its economic influence was virtually beyond public control. No matter how well-managed and economically beneficial the Bank was, free people could not place so much power in private hands.

The veto held. Enough senators resisted the persuasive arguments of Webster and the financial pressure of Biddle to sustain Jackson and send the issue into the campaign of 1832. Biddle printed and distributed 30,000 copies of Jackson's veto message. But this tactic probably backfired, for the Bank had numerous enemies: those who wanted larger quantities of paper money and the inflation that would result, those who wanted no paper money at all, those who sincerely believed the establishment of such an institution invaded the rights of states, and those who owned state banks and longed both to eliminate officious regulation by the Bank, and to secure a share of federal deposits.

Jackson determined to distribute those deposits among deserving state bankers and deny the BUS the use of federal funds even before the charter officially expired in 1836. Following his triumphant reelection in 1832, when Jackson's electoral vote was more than three times that of Henry Clay, the President ordered Secretary of the Treasury Louis McLane to remove the government's funds from Biddle's bank. When McLane demurred, Jackson elevated him to the State Department and appointed Joseph Duane to the Treasury. When Duane also refused, Jackson fired him without ceremony and moved Attorney General Roger B. Taney to the Treasury. In spite of a resolution that Congress considered federal funds secure, Taney reduced the government's balance; new deposits were made in state banks, called "pet banks" because political favoritism usually dictated their selection.

Before state banks could use their new resources to expand business, Biddle called in loans and raised the interest rate. Such steps ultimately would have been necessary, but Biddle reacted more promptly and more drastically than the situation required, perhaps because he wanted to demonstrate the Bank's utility, perhaps because he wanted the complaining business community to pressure the President. Jackson, however, turned complaints about the recession of 1833–34 to his own purpose. The economic distress, he argued, precisely illustrated his contention that private individuals and private corporations could never safely be entrusted with unchecked economic power.

Many state banks had fewer economic inhibitions than the BUS. Federal deposits often encouraged uncontrolled expansion of credit. Foreign investment, particularly in roads and canals, also contributed to an inflationary spiral that showed, for instance, in soaring land sales, prices, and speculation. Sales of government land in the 1820s had dispersed about 1 million acres annually; between 1835 and 1837, 40 million acres were sold, and the resulting revenue far exceeded that from any tax, including the tariff.

But the revenue was in the form of state-bank notes of uncertain value. As paper currency proliferated, its reliability and stability declined. To protect the Treasury, in 1836 Jackson issued the Specie Circular, which required that government land be purchased with hard money. The policy was intentionally deflationary, for the resulting demand for specie forced banks to curtail credit. By late spring of 1837 many banks could no longer exchange notes for hard money; before the end of the year more than 600 banks had failed. But Old Hickory had retired with the affectionate gratitude of his countrymen before the consequences of his destruction of the Bank of the United States became apparent. Along with the party and the presidency, Martin Van Buren inherited a financial panic that soon matured into a dismal depression.

THE VAN BUREN ADMINISTRATION

The nation's economic paralysis was no less acute than the political paralysis of Van Buren's administration. Martin Van Buren won an impressive victory in 1836, but he could not translate it into an impressive legislative record. Congress refused to permit a periodic gradual reduction in the price of less desirable federal land that remained unsold years after an area had been surveyed. Nor could Van Buren persuade Congress to establish permanently the system of preemption, a policy first temporarily adopted in 1830, which allowed squatters to purchase land they had improved before the area was legally opened for settlement and sale.

Like Jackson, Van Buren was an advocate of laissez faire. He believed that government must keep its fiscal affairs in order and rely on private initiative to restore public prosperity when depression struck. Van Buren's response to the financial crisis, then, was essentially negative. He would not revoke the Specie Circular, in spite of the fact that even Democrats argued that repeal would restore public confidence and raise land values. Critical of state banks, he would not permit the Treasury's surplus to be distributed to the states, as had been done late in the Jackson administration. Instead, he asked Congress to establish an Independent Treasury system that would divorce the government from banking by establishing subtreasuries in major cities to hold federal funds. Since these subtreasuries were not to lend money, deposits would be secure at a time when bank failures were legion. But with security went deflation, for the failure to make economic use of government reserves deprived the economy of a major source of credit.

On July 4, 1840, when the Independent Treasury was enacted, Jacksonians hailed it as a declaration of economic independence comparable in importance to the great Declaration written sixty-four years before. The "Locofoco" wing of the party, with which Van Buren was identified, believed that the national government should keep taxes, appropriations, and economic activity to an absolute minimum. The Locofocos, who were so named because locofoco matches had once saved the faction from confusion after more conservative Democrats had extinguished the lamps at a convention, included reformers and workingmen. The coalition opposed monopoly, privilege, all banks, and paper money and held that each individual must have an equal opportunity to push aside all rivals in the race for riches.

The government's responsibility was to see that the race was fair, not to enable everyone to reach the goal more quickly, as advocates of federal activity would have it, nor to encourage a favored few with such privileges as corporate charters.

Even the Supreme Court of the United States, that last bastion of Federalism, succumbed to Jacksonian economic ideas. Roger B. Taney, who succeeded Marshall as Chief Justice in 1835, had helped write Jackson's message vetoing recharter of the BUS and then had removed the government's deposits; in 1837 he stiffened Van Buren's resolve to retain the Specie Circular. It was also in 1837 that Chief Justice Taney turned some Jacksonian economic principles into legal precedents in the *Charles River Bridge* case.

Chartered by Massachusetts in the eighteenth century, the Charles River Bridge Company collected substantial profit from the tolls on the only bridge between Boston and Charlestown. In 1828 the legislature granted another company the right to construct a second bridge not far from the first. After construction costs of the new bridge were paid, moreover, tolls would be abolished. The Charles River Bridge Company, maintaining that its franchise was exclusive, sued to prevent Massachusetts from breaking the contract implied in its corporate charter.

Taney could find nothing in the charter making the original grant a monopoly. The company had "no exclusive privilege . . . over the waters of the Charles River," and "no right to prevent other persons" from erecting a competitive bridge from which the community would benefit. To be sure, Taney admitted, "the rights of private property are sacredly guarded," but, he added, "the community also have rights and the happiness . . . of every citizen depends on their faithful preservation." Governments did not by implication surrender these rights to "privileged corporations."

Both the attack on privilege and the finding that a popular majority could curb a corporation were sound Jacksonian doctrines. Although conservatives complained that private property was no longer safe, in fact Taney's decision unquestionably encouraged economic growth. For had the Court protected monopoly, technical innovation and economic enterprise would have been stifled.

THE WHIGS ORGANIZE

Opponents of the Jacksonians gradually gathered in a coherent party called Whig. In 1836 Whigs had so little resembled a national organization that different candidates, each calculated to appeal to his own section, had carried the party's hopes. Daniel Webster failed to carry the Northeast, but William Henry Harrison showed surprising strength in the Northwest, and Hugh White carried Tennessee and Georgia. Whig strategists had hoped for a scattered vote that would require the House to elect the President. But Van Buren secured a majority of both the popular vote and the electoral college.

Failure to agree on a single candidate in their first campaign was symptomatic of deep divisions among Whigs. Insofar as it had a program, the party preferred Clay's American system, but Whigs organized initially more to oppose Jacksonians than to advance a program. Adherents ranged from southern advocates of state sovereignty, who found Jackson's stand on nullification intolerable, to northern advocates of strong central authority. Whigs drew support from plantation-owners like John Tyler, representatives of northern manufacturing and commercial interests like Daniel Webster, and ambitious frontiersmen like Abraham Lincoln. Composed of diverse interests, classes, and varying political philosophies, the Whigs soon discovered that unity and victory could be achieved only by imitating the formula the Jacksonians had evolved in 1828: they emphasized what they opposed and nominated a candidate whose heroic reputation concealed uncertain political views.

The election of 1840 revealed how well Whigs had learned the techniques of mass politics. William Henry Harrison led the national ticket, which was judiciously balanced with John Tyler, a Virginian who championed state rights. The party maintained popular ignorance of Harrison's political convictions by adopting no platform at all. In lieu of issues, they provided songs, slogans, symbols, fireworks, food, drink, parades, and the reiterated accusation that Van Buren had inappropriate, aristocratic taste in wine, china, and furnishings, which he indulged at public expense. Harrison, by contrast, was depicted as a simple son of the frontier, born in a log cabin, weaned on hard cider. Excitement, plus local effort by both parties, brought more people to the polls than had participated in any previous national election; nearly 80 percent of the eligible voters cast ballots. The interest of the ordinary voter turned the campaign into a contest to determine which candidate was more common. By a slim popular majority, but a wide margin in the electoral college, Harrison won.

Whigs campaigned better than they governed. Harrison named Web-

Harrison's partisans, 1840

ster Secretary of State and appointed several of Clay's followers to key posts, apparently to administer the American system that was to be enacted. But a month after his inauguration Harrison died, and the new President, John Tyler, was hostile to concentrated federal power and the American system. Clay rallied the party's legislative forces and introduced a tariff, a bill to revive the Bank, and a measure to finance internal improvements from land sales. In a complex political maneuver in 1842, Clay abandoned his scheme to finance internal improvements, and Tyler accepted a tariff that restored the protective duties of 1832. Although the Independent Treasury was repealed in 1841, Tyler twice vetoed bills to charter a third national bank.

But if Tyler's presidency was legislatively almost barren, it was nevertheless politically important. Following the second failure to secure Tyler's approval of a bank bill, his Cabinet resigned, with the exception of Webster, who was concluding a treaty with England. The Whigs then read Tyler out of the party, whose program he had never found congenial. At the end of his term, Tyler invited Calhoun, another man without a party, to join the administration as Secretary of State. Together, the two southerners secured the annexation of Texas, an action that the voters had apparently endorsed a few months earlier by electing James K. Polk, an expansionist Democrat, to succeed Tyler. Calhoun and Tyler, both of whom had left the Democratic party because of Jackson's nationalism, rejoined the Democrats after 1845. Their presence among Democrats tipped that party yet further toward the South, while the Whigs became perceptibly less Southern. And the preservation of the Union depended upon a precarious sectional equilibrium in the nation's two political parties.

Suggested Reading

A good recent survey of Jacksonian Democracy is Edward Pessen's *Jacksonian America** (1969), which includes an excellent bibliography. Douglas T. Miller, *The Birth of Modern America, 1820–1860* (1970), focuses on socioeconomic developments. Glyndon G. Van Deusen's *The Jacksonian Era** (1959) is a balanced narrative. Influential interpretations include Arthur M. Schlesinger, Jr., *The Age of Jackson** (1945), which stresses the political rivalry between classes, and Lee Benson, *The Concept of Jacksonian Democracy** (1961), which stresses the similarities between Whigs and Democrats. The perceptive account of Alexis de Tocqueville, *Democracy in America** (1855), is in a class by itself.

Jackson's election is treated in Robert V. Remini, *The Election of Andrew Jackson** (1963), and in John W. Ward, *Andrew Jackson: Symbol for an Age** (1955). Marvin Meyers deals with the rhetoric of Jacksonian politics in *The Jacksonian Persuasion** (1957). The crises of Jackson's first administration are analyzed in William W. Freehling, *Prelude to Civil War** (1966), which suggests that slavery as well as the tariff precipitated nullification, and in Bray Hammond, *Banks and Politics in America from the Revolution to the Civil War** (1955).

Francis P. Prucha's *American Indian Policy in the Formative Years** (1962) discusses legislation and administration.

Jacksonian politics is the focus of Robert V. Remini's *Martin Van Buren and the Making of the Democratic Party** (1959) and of Richard P. McCormick's *The Second American Party System** (1966). Among the several state studies of Jacksonian politics is Donald B. Cole's *Jacksonian Democracy in New Hampshire* (1970).

*Available in paperback edition

CHRONOLOGY

1817–25 Construction of Erie Canal

1819 *Savannah* becomes first steamer to complete trans-Atlantic run

1822 Textile factories open in Lowell, Massachusetts

1828 Construction of Baltimore and Ohio Railroad begins

1831 First issue of *The Liberator,* Garrison's abolitionist magazine

1838 The National Road reaches Vandalia, Illinois

1842 Massachusetts Supreme Court permits labor organization in *Commonwealth* v. *Hunt*

1844 Samuel F. B. Morse sends first telegraph message

1846 Elias Howe invents sewing machine

1847 Mormon migration to Utah begins

1851 Herman Melville's *Moby Dick* published
Clipper ship *Flying Cloud* sails from New York to San Francisco in 89 days

A PEOPLE IN MOTION

In the years between the Battle of New Orleans and the shelling of Fort Sumter, a swiftly increasing population rushed to settle a swiftly expanding American nation. New Americans from Ireland, Scandanavia, and Germany poured down gangplanks and either went west to small, trim farms, or stayed in bustling cities, where they joined established Americans who had found their depleted farms no longer profitable. And all Americans grew more crops, wove more cloth, distilled more whisky, and traded with more frenzy in their headlong dash for prosperity.

Many succeeded. Optimistic Americans needed only to look about them to vindicate their faith in the perfectibility of man. While population jumped fourfold, productive capacity more than kept pace. While territory increased, canals, railroads, and telegraphs simultaneously made distances shrink. The rapid expansion of political democracy also testified to the nation's faith in the dignity of the individual. Progress seemed the inevitable result of human activity and almost an additional right of American citizenship.

Yet some, who wanted to create a new heaven in the New World, were not satisfied. Visions of utopia varied. As each peddler had his own brand

Immigrants landing: steerage and stereotypes

of snake oil, each reformer had his own panacea. New millennial sects promised salvation following an imminent day of judgment. Secular prophets preached vegetarianism and phrenology and decried the evils of yeast with a fervor worthy of better causes. And better causes—free, universal public education, equality for women, abolition of debtors' prisons, compassionate treatment of the insane—did attract energetic reformers. A few daring souls even suggested that the black population might share the nation's progress and bounty, but the public was not yet ready to listen sympathetically to those who advocated the abolition of slavery or racial equality.

THE REVOLUTION IN TRANSPORTATION

In 1816 an American importer paid about nine dollars and waited about fifty days for a ton of merchandise to cross the Atlantic; for another nine dollars, he could ship the same goods thirty miles over miserable roads into the interior, a trip that might take several days. Such expense discouraged internal trade, and each settlement consequently sought to supply most of what it consumed. Farmers produced for their table, not for market. Farmers' wives preserved food, made cloth, and bargained with itinerant venders for pots, pans, and clocks. What manufacturing there was usually took place in the home, for factories were rare and machinery not widely available.

In 1860 an American importer paid less than five dollars to bring a ton of goods across the Atlantic in less than two weeks. He could ship these goods the 450 miles from New York to Buffalo in about the same time and at about the same expense that thirty miles had required in 1816, so internal trade flourished. American farmers grew most of the world's cotton and had begun to export grain on a large scale. Farmers' wives bought cloth from dry-goods counters; the peddler was almost a memory. Flour mills, textile mills, iron foundries, and distilleries processed the products of mine and soil. Sewing machines, reapers, and steam engines multiplied the nation's output. Some Americans, particularly on the frontier or on rural ridges in both North and South, clung to self-sufficiency; for the rest of the country, the still incomplete market economy revealed the shape of the future.

Since transportation seemed to mean prosperity, political controversy surrounded construction of roads, canals, and railroads. Internal improvements, the politician's phrase for building such facilities, had an important claim on state treasuries in the years before the Civil War. Occasionally the central government paid construction costs with revenue from the sale of public lands; in 1803 the enabling act that admitted Ohio to the Union appropriated 5 percent of the receipts from public land for roads. Eventually railroads were given federal land as a direct subsidy. Sometimes private capital built roads or, more rarely, canals; mixed corporations, established by public and private capital, carried on a few construction projects.

Although federal aid for construction continued to be a live political issue, action was inconsistent. States pushed ahead with their own projects, of which the most important was New York's Erie Canal connecting the Great Lakes with the Atlantic through the Hudson. The results of that venture were staggering: the population of New York City increased more than 250 percent in the twenty years after 1820; freight costs between New York and Buffalo dropped 95 percent between 1817 and 1857. The canal permitted settlement of part of the Northwest that lacked access to the Mississippi, for the large, accessible, eastern market made a settler's products more valuable, while decreasing freight charges made his supplies less expensive.

The Erie's success set off an epidemic of canal-construction. Philadelphia, Boston, and Baltimore tried to surpass New York and secure a sector in the interior. Canal-building did not seem formidable; amateur engineers had supervised construction of the Erie, which initially was just an overgrown ditch with only four feet of water. But the way west from Philadelphia, Boston, and Baltimore proved more intractable; it required more locks and such improvisations as hoists to haul canal boats over hills. Ohio, Illinois, and other western states also dug canals, which could not compete with the railroads completed only a few years later. With the immensely important exception of the Erie and a very few other projects, canals disappointed investors. In the depression of the late 1830s, some states discovered they could not afford their canals and repudiated bonds that had financed construction, an action that outraged investors on both sides of the Atlantic.

River traffic required no bond issue and comparatively little investment. Yet the river steamer transformed American life no less than did the canal. Between 1815 and 1860 steamboats cut by about four-fifths both time and cost of shipment on the Mississippi River system. Between 1820 and 1850 the value of goods arriving in New Orleans from the interior increased more than thirteen times and amounted to more than $185 million. New Orleans in these years grew more rapidly than New York, and Cincinnati, St. Louis, and other river towns handled more commerce than many ocean ports. The volume of traffic on the rivers partly caused and clearly demonstrated the economic vitality of the hinterland.

In 1860 all water routes faced stiff competition from 30,000 miles of railroad track. That year rails carried as much bulk freight as did waterways, and the value of commodities carried by rail was substantially larger. Yet so healthy was the economy that efficient carriers had cargo to spare; although rivers and canals carried a declining percentage of the nation's goods, tonnage continued to grow. The advance of the rail net was even more striking than the canal boom. In 1830 about 1,200 miles of canals, mainly in New York, Pennsylvania, and Ohio, had no competition from 73 miles of track; by 1840 canal and railroad mileage was nearly equal at 3,300 miles. While canal-construction virtually ceased, railroad mileage nearly tripled before 1850 and more than tripled again before 1860. Once across the Appalachians, railroads rapidly spread through the Midwest; in 1860 Illinois contained more track than New York or Pennsylvania, and Indiana had almost twice as much as Massachusetts.

The Erie Canal

Routes to the West, about 1840

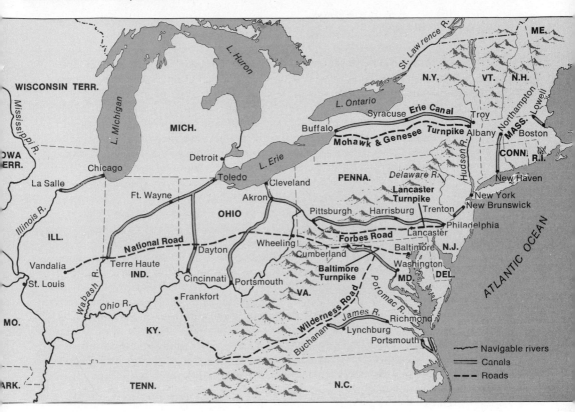

Trains cut distances and costs even more than did earlier innovations in transportation. Passengers traveled more comfortably, more cheaply, and at least twice as fast as in the best stagecoach; steamers and canalboats could compete with railroads in cost and comfort, but they were usually much slower. Between 1816 and 1860, passenger fares dropped about 60 percent and freight rates fell even faster. Reduced freight charges enabled midwestern farmers to supply eastern markets more cheaply than less efficient local farmers. Some of the less prosperous eastern farmers joined the urban population; a few rode the railroads to new lands in the West.

Perhaps more than any other economic change the growth of the rail network pushed the United States into the future. Railroads emancipated the nation from parochialism by fostering the growth of cities and by breaking down the isolation of outlying settlements. Rivalry among cities, states, and sections for the control and location of railroads baffled political leaders who tried in the 1850s to balance competing interests. The economic effect, even beyond the impact on freight rates, was immense. Railroads were themselves an insatiable market for iron, coal, and immigrant labor. Together with improved river transportation and canals, they permitted the development of a national market, without which manufacturing, which requires masses of buyers, might have been indefinitely delayed.

Once the nation's surplus produce arrived by river or rail at New

York or New Orleans, the thriving American merchant marine hauled it to markets abroad. Although the glamorous American clippers were the fastest vessels afloat, most freight was carried in slower ships of greater capacity. Clippers reduced sailing time from New York to San Francisco by nearly half; on all the world's oceans American ships and shippers set records and made money. But perhaps dazzled by the clippers' success, Americans were slow to invest in iron vessels and steam power, and when the age of wood and sail ended, so too, for some time, did the prestige and prosperity of the American merchant marine.

FARM AND PLANTATION

The nation's richest resource was its soil. Even in New England, the most urban part of the United States, only one-third of the population lived in towns in 1860; in the South and Midwest, more than 85 percent of the population was rural. Many of these farmers remained nearly self-sufficient, and most of the economy passed them by. But for the ambitious, progressive farmer in 1860, agriculture was a business; he grew a crop that he could convert to cash in the market. Cash-crop farming required a heavy investment, whether in a reaper to harvest wheat or in slaves to pick cotton. But the return was better than that of the small farmer with a patch of beans and a few hogs.

Those who remained self-sufficient did so partly because independent farming was more than a way of making ends meet; it was a way of life. These sturdy yeoman—tough, thrifty, hard-working, self-reliant—raised few surplus crops. Such pioneers cut the trees of Wisconsin, broke the sod of Illinois, and planted a little cotton in the virgin soil of Alabama. Abraham Lincoln's family illustrates the pattern. Lincoln's father, a rootless farmer, migrated from Virginia to Kentucky, where Abraham was born. Before young Lincoln was twenty-one, the family had moved twice more, first to Indiana and then to southern Illinois. The hardship of Lincoln's early years is proverbial, but life for the Lincolns was no more severe than it was for thousands of other farm families. Combat with the wilderness, ague, Indians, climate, and creditors was constant; each day contained as many working hours as daylight and strength permitted. And the long working day was as common on self-sufficient farms in the hills of New Hampshire or Virginia as it was on the frontier. All these farmers, vaguely suspicious of the comfort for which they apparently toiled, itched to move on when neighbors moved too close.

Since land speculation was the national pastime, moving on was easy. The pioneer sold his land and buildings, usually at a profit, to a speculator or perhaps to a nearby farmer who enlarged his operation to produce for market. Sale of federal land kept the government solvent between 1815 and 1860, but revenue varied enormously from year to year. In the years immediately following the War of 1812, and again just before the Panic of 1837, settlers surged into new cotton lands in Alabama, Mississippi, Louisiana, Florida, and Arkansas. The same waves of migration settled grain lands in the old Northwest, Missouri, and Iowa.

The first crop in the upper Mississippi Valley was corn, which went to market in the form of hogs. Hogs could harvest the crop themselves, thus freeing labor for improving the property; if necessary, the hogs could walk some distance to market. But the world preferred wheat to corn or hogs, and in the 1840s, attracted by better prices and greater profits, farmers shifted to wheat where soil permitted. In the 1850s, wheat-production climbed about 75 percent; widespread use of the mechanical reaper, which Cyrus McCormick began to market extensively in the 1850s, seemed to promise that farmers could produce still greater yields.

McCormick's reaper was only one of several technological changes that permitted the rapid expansion of northern agriculture. In 1837 John Deere perfected a steel plow, which others improved in the 1850s. Deere's implement, unlike earlier ones, cut prairie sod cleanly. The revolving disc harrow, invented in 1847, and a device to knot twine, which improved harvesting machinery, further reduced time and labor required on northern fields.

But machinery and good land cost money, particularly as thicker settlement drove all land prices up. And so, even before the Civil War, the Jeffersonian dream no longer corresponded to the reality of commercial farming. For the commercial farmer was as much a businessman as the owner of any store or small manufacturing establishment. He produced crops for sale, not for personal consumption—and money, not independence, was the object of his game.

Planters, as the South called its commercial farmers, invested their capital in land and slave labor. The world price of sugar, cotton, and tobacco was as crucial to the plantation-owner as the price of wheat was to the northern grain-producer. In a sense, the price of cotton affected the whole nation, although southern spokesmen claimed too much on the eve of the Civil War when they boasted that national prosperity depended upon their crop. Yet even in the 1850s, when production leveled off following a three-fold increase in the preceding twenty years, cotton still made up about one-half of all American exports. The South's crop earned much of the nation's foreign exchange, provided the raw material for many of the North's mills, and gave both North and West an important economic boost, for the plantation did not supply its own needs. Grain and pork to feed slaves came from the Northwest; cheap cloth to clothe them came from New England. Northern merchants collected shipping and insurance charges, commissions on sales of cotton, and profits on consumer goods. When the planter spent his receipts, the cash barely paused on its way North, where it circulated throughout the more diversified economy, stimulating more investment and creating more capital.

Rich soil, the high price of cotton, and while it lasted, prosperity made the South indifferent to other forms of economic activity, except for an occasional angry outburst against Yankee profiteers. When cotton prices fell, seaboard planters fared less well than those with newer, more fertile plantations in the Gulf States. South Carolina, economically pinched in the early 1830s, was quick to blame the tariff for its trouble; although other southern states were less vehemently opposed, the entire region eventually came to regard protective tariffs as a device to enrich northern manufacturers at the expense of Southern planters.

Northern and European economists suggested that planting would be more profitable if the labor force were hired instead of owned. The slaveholder, the argument went, incurred unnecessary costs because he supported unproductive children and aged slaves. Slaves required capital that could have been used to improve agricultural methods. In addition, the investment was risky, for slaves occasionally ran away or died in epidemics that swept the quarters.

Whatever the risks, whatever the costs, southerners believed slavery profitable, permanent, and even humane. Southern defenders pointed with pride to the extra expense of supporting the sick and disabled. Critics of slavery had once included such distinguished Virginians as Washington, Jefferson, and Madison; by the 1830s southern critics were rare, and by the 1840s they were silent. The price of a prime field hand climbed from between $400 and $500 in 1800 to between $1,200 and $1,800 on the eve of the Civil War. But plantation records indicate that some masters clothed, housed, and bought medical care for slaves with an average annual cash expenditure of less than $40. At that rate, it was a poor slave who did not earn his master a tidy profit.

Profit alone did not explain the persistence of the South's "peculiar institution." Only about one-fourth of the heads of southern households owned any blacks at all; of those who did, the vast majority owned fewer than ten slaves, beside whom the master worked in his fields. Slavery was more than a system of agricultural labor; it was also a system of racial control. Had slaves been white, slavery might well have disappeared with indentured servitude. But white southerners believed that blacks were shiftless, deceitful, and innately inferior; only a thin veneer of white man's Christianity hid the blacks' native barbarism, which might, if vigilance were relaxed, engulf the South.

Vigilance rarely relaxed. Active insurrections, such as that led by Denmark Vesey in South Carolina in 1822 or by Nat Turner in Virginia in 1831, were rare. Blacks generally found more subtle ways to resist. Petty theft, malingering, and low productivity, for instance, which whites took to be inherent characteristics of blacks, were ways of protesting the slave system. Neither rebellion nor resistance, however, broke white control over the entire black population, and this control became tighter throughout the South until 1860, when some southern states compelled free blacks to emigrate or return to bondage.

Every aspect of life in the South showed the presence of slavery, although the system was not everywhere the same. Individual peculiarities of masters and slaves and differing customs in different areas meant that treatment varied from plantation to plantation. Some masters provided comfortable housing and hearty food, and required only a reasonable day's work. Slaves, after all, cost money, and those who were undernourished, ill, or abused were less valuable in the market and less useful in the field. But the value of the investment did not keep every planter from inhumanity: branding, whipping, and chains were not, as self-righteous defenders of slavery sometimes claimed, mere figments of the active imagination of abolitionists. And bondage itself, even if decently practiced, was an offense to human dignity. The slave trade inevitably broke up families; the slave could not defend his back from the lash or his spirit from reminders of his servility; he could make no contract, incur no debt, swear no oath, own no property, nor legally read and write. Having defined blacks as legally irresponsible and having prescribed social subservience for them, whites persuaded one another that blacks were frivolous and obsequious by nature and that only slavery made them tolerable in white society.

MILLS AND WORKERS

Defensive southerners sometimes charged that northern manufacturers practiced wage slavery, that industrial workers in those new northern mills were more abused than slaves. These charges ignored the racial basis of slavery, but they contained an element of truth because northern mill workers did in fact work as long hours as some plantation hands. Machinery, moreover, made those hours more productive than manual labor on plantations, and the economic growth of factory towns like Lowell, Massachusetts, soon outstripped that of the planting regions. In 1815 Lowell was a sheep pasture; in the 1830s Lowell boasted nine churches, a school budget of $7,000 for about 3,000 children, a canal, the beginning of a railroad to Boston, and perhaps 15,000 inhabitants. Lowell boomed because the textile industry boomed, as revealed by the mounting number of spindles used. In 1820, the American cotton industry used 22,000 spindles.

Cotton mills in Lowell, Massachusetts

In five years, the number had nearly quadrupled, and by 1840 it had more than tripled again. In the forty years before 1860 the activity of American cotton mills increased twenty-five times, to 5,235,000 spindles. And in 1860, when 3 percent of Americans were employed in industry, 36 percent of Lowell's citizens were at work in the mills. Lowell was the prototype for other industrial cities, where mass production developed to meet the growing demand of a national market.

The Napoleonic wars interrupted commerce and stimulated domestic production of some formerly imported goods. Such manufacturing often took place in farmhouses, where families performed part of a manufacturing operation to supplement their income and occupy their time during the winter. A middleman left raw material and collected finished produce, which perhaps was left at a nearby farmhouse, where another stage in the process took place. In factories, such as those established at Lowell, all these operations were performed more efficiently under one roof.

Factories required capital, which paid a return that varied from 5 to perhaps 20 percent; the syndicate that established Lowell put $600,000 into its initial venture. Before 1860 investment in Lowell's mills alone exceeded the cost of constructing the Erie Canal. Businessmen in search of funds to build factories and buy machinery increasingly employed the corporate form. Early in the nineteenth century state legislatures chartered corporations with special laws that sometimes implied monopoly and often aroused popular hostility against what seemed to be privilege. The charter typically permitted a corporation to accumulate capital through public sale of shares, to engage in a specified business, and to establish rules for management of the company. Stockholders could invest without direct responsibility for day-to-day operation of the firm. And unlike other forms of business organization, in the event of failure owners were liable only to the extent of their investment; other personal property could not be seized to satisfy the corporation's debts. So fast was the nation's economy expanding, and so handy was the corporate form, that many states by the 1840s had enacted standard laws of incorporation. Since legislatures no longer had to pass individual charters, popular prejudice against corporations as privileged enterprises gradually subsided.

Labor for these new businesses came from the farms. But to work in mills, workers had to move to cities, where the mills were. The proprietors of the Lowell mills built dormitories and actively recruited young ladies from the farms of northern New England; the girls were properly chaperoned, and various after-hours cultural activities were offered for their self-improvement. The modesty, appearance, conduct, and attitude of Lowell's "mile of gals," as Davy Crockett called them, charmed the visitors that endlessly flowed through the mills. During the 1840s and 1850s Irish immigrants shattered the homogeneity of Lowell's mill population with the result that culture, chaperones, and decorum vanished in the race for wages.

The labor of women and children was especially prevalent in the textile industry, although the proportion of children declined after 1820. Probably about forty of every hundred textile workers were women in the 1830s, and entire families occasionally worked in the mills. Wage statistics are unreliable, and a cost-of-living index is unavailable. If estimates are accurate, however, an urban family of five needed at least ten dollars per week for immediate expenses; frequently a man could not earn that much in a factory. Women and children worked, then, because their wages were essential. The conventional working day, like that on the farm, ran from sunrise into the evening, between eleven and fourteen hours.

In the usual American pattern, urban workers asked for legislation to improve their condition. They wanted education and land, two conventional nineteenth-century panaceas, and sought laws to guarantee universal, free public education as well as a Homestead Act to provide free federal land to settlers. In the 1830s a Workingman's Party championed both of these demands in New York. Workers also asked for immediate relief through legislation limiting the working day to ten hours. In 1840 President Martin Van Buren responded to this demand with an executive order that limited to ten hours the workday on federal projects. State legislatures in New Hampshire, Maine, Pennsylvania, Ohio, New Jersey, and Rhode Island passed ten-hour laws by 1857. But the acts were widely violated and badly enforced.

And the workers could not yet organize to protect themselves. Artisans and skilled craftsmen, like those in the construction and shoe trades, occasionally formed local unions. But the general public was almost always hostile to a strike, and the rare strikes were almost always futile. Industrial workers had less bargaining power than craftsmen, and unions failed in most mass-production industries until the twentieth century. The state, furthermore, was apt to regard any labor organization as a conspiracy in restraint of trade and a violation of the common law. In 1842, in *Commonwealth* v. *Hunt*, the Supreme Court of Massachusetts ruled that trade unions were within the law and that they could legitimately use strikes to back their demand for exclusive employment. In spite of the precedent, unions continued to meet legal obstacles for decades afterward.

Discontented or not, the labor force pushed goods out of the factories at an astounding rate. The value of manufactures in 1860 was twelve times the figure for 1815, whereas population increased only four times in that period. In 1850 American industrial production topped a billion dollars and for the first time surpassed the annual total of all American agriculture, including cotton. Although by 1860 agriculture regained the lead with nearly two billion dollars in crops, industrial production climbed nearly as rapidly. The census of 1860 held bad news for those who thought cotton still king; the combined production of the iron, leather, and boot and shoe industries surpassed in value all the South's cotton.

Yet cotton was still the raw material for one of the most important industries. Manufacturers of cotton goods employed almost 115,000 workers, a number surpassed only by the total in the boot and shoe industry. Cotton manufacturing was second to no other enterprise in value added by manufacture, that is, in the difference between cost of raw material and value of finished product. Lumber, once the chief American finished product, was second in 1860, followed by boots and shoes, flour, men's clothing, iron, machinery, and woolens.

Unlike agriculture, manufacturing was not a national enterprise. More than half the mills were in New England or the middle states, where nearly three-quarters of the capital was invested and two-thirds of the total value of all manufactured goods produced. Industry was also firmly established in the Midwest. But only about one-tenth of the nation's industry was located in the slave states.

Americans invented some of the machinery essential to industrialization, and they applied the ideas of others as well. American inventions included the telegraph, which Samuel F. B. Morse first demonstrated in 1844, the rotary press, perfected by Richard Hoe in 1846, the sewing machine, invented by Elias Howe in 1846, and various adaptations of Howe's machine for use in manufacturing shoes. Equally significant were American modifications of methods and inventions borrowed from other countries. The unification of manufacturing under one roof and the use of steam power to run boats, trains, and belts and pulleys in factories were not initially American ideas. Nor was mass production, which depends upon interchangeable parts, although Eli Whitney and other arms manufacturers were among the first to try it.

Buoyed by a swelling economy, then, the American industrial revolu-

Cincinnati, 1838: Manufacturing was not a monopoly of New England.

tion had started before the Civil War began. Entrepreneurs were already combining technology, transportation, labor, capital, market, and raw material to produce more goods for more Americans. Government, geography, and fate also cooperated. Both land sales and the inclination of politicians kept taxes and appropriations to a minimum. Two oceans and two weak neighbors made unnecessary the expensive military establishments that might have precluded more productive uses of capital. This generation of Americans became involved in two wars, to be sure, but the Mexican War more than paid for itself in territory, and the Civil War, while tragically expensive, interrupted industrial growth only temporarily.

PROGRESS AND REFORM

Not many Americans before 1860 expected the Civil War to come; such a gloomy outlook would have belied the spirit of the age. Most Americans believed their national experience proved that reasonable men could choose wisely between justice and injustice and could rationally solve problems. It was an optimistic time, when progress seemed the nation's birthright, as prosperity seemed its economic destiny, when America really was the land of opportunity where each individual was entitled to the fortune, status, and respect he earned, unless, of course, he was black.

It was also an age of dozens of causes and countless prophets. Neal Dow, Lyman Beecher, and a flock of college presidents organized temperance or prohibition societies that persuaded individuals to take the "cold-water pledge" and legislatures to regulate or forbid the sale of spirits. Lucretia Mott, Elizabeth Cady Stanton, Margaret Fuller and a few other women, regarded as brazen by most of their contemporaries, argued for educational opportunities, legal rights, and equality for women. Dorothea Dix finally persuaded some authorities that the insane were ill, not criminal. And Horace Mann persisted in what was for too long a lonely crusade for universal, free public education.

Unable to sway society and unwilling to wait for results, some reformers sought isolation for their utopias. John Humphrey Noyes and his followers settled in Oneida, New York, where their unconventional habits in religion, economics, dress, and sex excited the hostility of their neighbors until the utopian community's prosperity converted enmity to envy. A group of intellectuals established a community near Concord, Massachusetts, at Brook Farm, where many New England writers visited, and Nathaniel Hawthorne briefly lived. But the hope that common living, working, and conversing would improve the living standard and the minds of the participants was disappointed.

Socialism was a by-product of settlements at Oneida and Brook Farm, but it was the principal goal of the British industrialist Robert Owen, who established a model community at New Harmony, Indiana. Étienne Cabet, a French theorist, led a small band of socialists from Texas to Illinois and then to Missouri. The ideas of Charles Fourier, another French socialist, inspired some Americans to found a phalanx (as Fourierist experiments were called) at Red Bank, New Jersey. After failing as a haven for intellectuals Brook Farm also failed as a phalanx. These communities differed in detail, but all sought to make the quality of life better by sharing income, expenses, and essential tasks.

All the causes of the era required an act of faith, and some were explicitly religious. Evangelists, of whom Charles Grandison Finney was perhaps the most impassioned, saved souls and stirred the spiritual aspiration of frontiersmen; Finney himself forthrightly opposed slavery as a moral outrage, but not all revivalists read the Bible that way. The Oneida community was one outpost of those who believed man could make himself perfect on earth. William Miller, a displaced Vermonter who preached in upstate New York, led an excited flock that believed the day of eternal judgment would arrive in 1843; faith survived one postponement, but the next year, after some followers had for the second time dressed in white robes and perched in trees to secure an unobstructed view of Christ's coming, the Millerites disbanded.

Yet another Vermonter who migrated into upstate New York founded the Church of the Latter Day Saints in 1830. Joseph Smith, Mormons believe, with the aid of an angel, discovered and translated the Book of Mormon in the 1820s. Smith and his followers formally founded a church and moved first to Ohio and then to Missouri before settling in Nauvoo, Illinois, in 1839. Earlier features had been costly, but hard work and faith in Smith's driving leadership brought prosperity. Smith developed considerable influence in Illinois politics, which he abruptly lost in 1843 by inept bargaining with both political parties. That same year Smith told his flock about his recent divine revelation permitting polygamy. The prophet himself soon had more than twenty wives, and word of the practice roused the righteous citizens of Illinois to demonstrate against the Mormons. In 1844 a mob snatched Smith from the jail where he was awaiting trial on other charges, informally sentenced him to death, and carried out its own verdict. Brigham Young, one of Smith's lieutenants, led the remaining Mormons out of Illinois and temporarily out of the United States to the Great Salt Lake, where the penniless faithful made the desert bloom.

Joseph Smith, Horace Mann, Dorothea Dix, and Nathaniel Hawthorne were very different people. But they and other reformers of the period were linked by more than chronology. They shared with other Americans an optimistic faith in the future; they believed that every individual, regardless of social station, could contribute to the quality of life in the whole society; they wanted desperately to improve that quality and were impatient with those of less conviction. Individualism and equality were the essence of their creed; these same ideals also motivated the simultaneous effort to secure political democracy and economic opportunity. The age was all of a piece.

With the usual exception of slavery. While other reformers met scoffing and skepticism, abolitionists encountered undisguised hostility in the 1830s. A Boston mob put a noose around the neck of William Lloyd

Garrison, the strident abolitionist editor, and led him through the streets; other mobs in Connecticut and New Hampshire destroyed schools to which idealistic teachers had admitted blacks. In 1838 Elijah Lovejoy, an abolitionist printer in Illinois, replaced several presses his neighbors destroyed but died trying to stave off a final assault. Most Americans with a reform impulse found less dangerous outlets for their zeal.

But opponents of slavery kept trying. Factions in the antislavery movement became sects, each with its own leader, body of literature, and variation of the program. The most aggressive abolitionists, whose voice was Garrison's *Liberator*, demanded the immediate end of slavery without compensation to the slaveowners and insisted on full equality for the black. Garrison, who was contemptuous of politics, urged the North to secede from the wicked Union that permitted slavery and denounced the Constitution as "a covenant with death and an agreement with hell." Theodore Dwight Weld, an eloquent preacher whose parish was the nation, and James G. Birney, an Alabama planter who freed his own slaves, were only slightly less militant. They admitted that complete abolition might be delayed, and Birney in particular thought political action potentially useful. Twice Birney was the Liberty party's nominee for President, but the results were disheartening: about 7,000 votes in 1840 and 63,000—less than 3 percent of the total vote—four years later.

Two other groups opposed not only slavery, but the black as well. One rather wistful proposal was to end slavery, either by purchase or by the generosity of masters, and simultaneously to end the racial dilemma by sending freed slaves back to Africa. The American Colonization Society, organized in 1817 with such prominent supporters as Henry Clay, actually sent a few blacks to Liberia. But most free blacks preferred to remain in America, and the Society never raised enough money to purchase and deport many slaves.

The Free-Soil movement, which sprang up in the late 1840s, was only incidentally concerned with slaves in the South. Free-Soilers proposed to keep slavery out of the territory Americans had secured from Britain in the Northwest and taken from Mexico in the Southwest. They opposed the expansion of slavery partly because they did not like it, but mostly because they wanted to keep the black population penned up in the South. Oregon, for instance, simply prohibited blacks from settling in the state.

LETTERS, POEMS, AND TRANSCENDENTAL THOUGHT

Although most Americans in the second quarter of the nineteenth century preferred doing to writing, printed words tumbled from American presses. As if to answer the smug inquiry of a British critic who asked, "Who reads an American book?" volumes of respectable literary quality began to appear. Some, like Washington Irving's *Legend of Sleepy Hollow*, derived from the American folk idiom. James Fenimore Cooper set his *Leatherstocking Tales* on the American frontier and seemed uncertain that civilization had improved the wilderness. Edgar Allen Poe, impoverished, pathetic, and dissipated, wrote stories and poems of macabre genius that influenced stylists on both sides of the Atlantic. William Cullen Bryant produced poetry, Jacksonian journalism, and then literature on behalf of the antislavery cause. During the early 1840s, Herman Melville went to sea, and for the next half-century he used ships, sailors, and salt water as the setting for his reflections on sin and salvation, man and God. IIis *Moby Dick*, perhaps America's greatest novel, was published in 1851.

A host of articulate intellectuals collected around Boston. Poets of some talent and more reputation, like Oliver Wendell Holmes, Henry Wadsworth Longfellow, James Russell Lowell, and the abolitionist John Greenleaf Whittier; essayists and slightly eccentric reformers, like Margaret Fuller and Henry David Thoreau; religious thinkers and metaphysicians like William E. Channing, whose sermons decisively influenced Unitarianism, and Theodore Parker; historians like George Bancroft, who told the nation's story as the triumph of good over evil and served the Democratic party to make sure virtue continued victorious; novelists like Nathaniel Hawthorne, the descendant of Puritan divines, who brooded over the tension among the materialism of his contemporaries, the abundance of his country, and the Calvinist ethic—all these and many more lived in or around Boston and sharpened their ideas in conversation with one another.

In many ways the most representative intellectual of them all was Ralph Waldo Emerson, who symbolized the vigor of American talent as Andrew Jackson stood for the simultaneous vigor of American democracy and economic enterprise. Emerson's family was better educated and both socially and economically a cut above Andrew Jackson's. Emerson's father, a Unitarian clergyman, died when his son was small; Jackson's father did not live to see his child. Both boys knew money was short as they grew up. Jackson matured quickly as British prisoner during the Revolution; he knew very little about books and a great deal about making his way in the world when he arrived in frontier Tennessee. He practiced law there, speculated in land, established a handsome plantation, and became a frontier aristocrat. Emerson, on the other hand, grew up at home in Boston, studied hard, and worked his way through Harvard. He conducted a successful finishing school for polite young ladies of Boston and used the profits to return to divinity school at Harvard. Neither divinity school nor subsequent pastorates really satisfied Emerson, and he eventually settled down in Concord where he made thinking and writing his profession, supporting himself, eventually quite well, with lectures and essays.

Emerson wrapped optimism, nationalism, and individual independence in striking prose, and his countrymen avidly absorbed it. Their response was predictable, since Emerson was merely stating well the same ideals that made Andrew Jackson the political hero of the time. In 1837, Emerson asked American scholars to dare to think their own thoughts and have done with European conventions. His country, Emerson optimistically believed, would create "a new race, a new religion, a new state, a new literature. . . ." Confident individuals would bring these wonders to reality by their own efforts. In one of his most famous essays, Emerson exhorted his readers to self-reliance. "Insist on yourself," he wrote, "never imitate." Man only had strength when he stood alone, and was "weaker by every recruit to his banner." Emerson was ashamed of humanity's capacity to submerge individuality in "badges and names, . . . large societies and dead institutions." Happiness did not come to groups, but to the individual who had "put his heart into his work and done his best. . . ."

Emerson did more than make striking phrases to express his countrymen's clichés. In his religious quest and in his unorthodox answer, called transcendentalism, he reflected the interests of his time, although he differed sharply from the evangelical preachers of the day. Emerson wrote of a mystical union between man and nature, of an impersonal, universal spirit that he called the Over-Soul. His mysticism had no place for church or clergy; the individual must discover his own unity with the infinite, must merge his own transient self with the eternal Over-Soul. In this exalted state, Emerson declared, "this world is so beautiful that I can hardly believe it exists."

And Americans, including many of Emerson's friends, tried to make that beautiful world yet better, an effort he regarded with detached good humor. "What a fertility of projects for the salvation of the world!" Emerson wrote with amusement as he catalogued the contradictory crusades for and against yeast, manure, insects, marriage, and Christianity. Yet in the 1850s Emerson also became committed to a cause: the crusade against slavery. The gallows, he remarked after John Brown's execution, had become "glorious like the cross." With that remark, Emerson ceased to be a mirror for his generation and became a somewhat tardy seer.

Suggested Reading

George R. Taylor's *The Transportation Revolution* (1951) is an indispensable beginning for the study of pre–Civil War economic history. W. W. Rostow, *The Stages of Economic Growth** (1960), argues that industrial growth became self-sustaining in the 1840s. Robert W. Fogel argues in *Railroads and American Economic Growth** (1964) that the role of railroads in that growth has been exaggerated. In *The Economic Growth of the United States** (1960) Douglass C. North interprets a great deal of economic data.

Stanley Elkins' *Slavery** (1959) is a psychological interpretation and has provoked much scholarly controversy. Ulrich B. Phillips, *American Negro Slavery** (1919), and Kenneth M. Stampp, *The Peculiar Institution** (1956), differ in interpretation from one another and from Elkins. Eugene D. Genovese's *The Political Economy of Slavery** (1965) is the view of a Marxist; see also his *The World the Slaveowners Made* (1969). David B. Davis, *The Problem of Slavery in Western Culture** (1966), puts the subject in a broader perspective. Frank L. Owsley, *Plain Folk* *of the Old South** (1949), shows slavery's impact on whites who were not slave-owners.

Alice F. Tyler's *Freedom's Ferment** (1944) remains the most satisfactory survey of the reform movements of the 1840s. Louis Filler's *The Crusade Against Slavery** (1960) is a sound account of the abolitionist movement. Van Wyck Brooks, *The Flowering of New England** (1938), shows the literary vitality of New England, and Frederick J. Turner, *The Frontier in American History** (1920), stresses the pervasive influence of the West on American society.

*Available in paperback edition

CHRONOLOGY

THE GAINS AND LOSSES

OF GROWTH

In February, 1817, John C. Calhoun warned his fellow congressmen that the breadth of the country endangered its unity. The House, Calhoun cautioned, must "counteract every tendency to disunion," and members must not yield to "a low, sordid, selfish, and sectional spirit" that would bring separation and "misery and despotism." During the next three decades Calhoun changed his warning to a threat; prophesies of disunion became part of every itinerant sectional politician's stock in trade. But in the 1830s and 1840s, most unreflective Americans shrugged off sectional differences as a geographic fact, not a portent of disaster.

The sections, after all, had common interests and complemented one another in their diversity. The New England textile mill needed both southern cotton and customers in the West. The frontiersman needed credit from the East and markets in both the South and East for his surplus. The southern plantation-owner was only too aware that he needed Yankee ship captains and Yankee merchants as well as Yankee mills; sometimes he also needed corn and hogs from northwestern farmers.

Since no section was economically homogeneous, political questions cut across regional lines. Subsistence farmers everywhere thought taxes too high; frontiersmen from Texas to Minnesota thought government land too expensive. The merchant in New York and the cotton-planter in South Carolina both opposed protective tariffs, while the manufacturer in Massachusetts, the ironmaster in Pennsylvania, and the sugar-planter in Louisiana were all protectionists. And interests everywhere changed. Daniel Webster began by opposing a protective tariff and ended as protection's most distinguished advocate. Henry Clay opposed rechartering the Bank of the United States in 1811 but in 1832 ran for President as the candidate of recharter. And John C. Calhoun, once a war hawk and in 1817 a fervent nationalist, later forecast secession at the first sign of nationalistic legislation.

With so many imponderables, many politicians decided to transcend sectionalism, ignore economic differences, and focus on noncontroversial issues. Thus, William Henry Harrison's log-cabin simplicity in 1840. Thus, James K. Polk's expansionism in 1844. Thus, the well-advertised heroism of generals Zachary Taylor and Winfield Scott in 1848 and 1852. Thus, mention of the menace of immigrants and Catholics in the American, or Know-Nothing, movement of 1856. Thus, finally, Abraham Lincoln's split rails to disguise the exclusively northern basis of his party in 1860. But economic and sectional issues refused to go away; after 1850 they were not even well hidden. In front of Harrison's log cabin ran Henry Clay's federally financed roads, and behind it lurked the rest of the American system. Before Polk's expansion was well begun, an upstart member of his own party set off a fifteen-year wrangle with the apparently innocent query "Expansion—for whom?" That simple question dominated General Taylor's brief presidency and so weakened General Scott's party that it did not survive his campaign. By the time Know-Nothings tried to distract public attention to papal plots, voters thought domestic subversion more dangerous—whether by the "slavocracy" or the abolitionists depended upon one's sectional point of view. And no number of split rails won Abe Lincoln any votes in the South.

Expansion was the most promising of these camouflaging expedients, for land speculation was the national game. But each section played by its own ground rules, so expansion only created a bigger pay-off and made the competition more fierce.

JACKSONIAN FOREIGN POLICY

Foreign policy was not the first concern of either Andrew Jackson or Martin Van Buren. Jackson's activity before his presidency indicated more faith in force than in diplomatic discussion. Martin Van Buren, whom Jackson made Secretary of State and Minister to London, treated foreign affairs as a lesser branch of domestic politics. Yet, in 1830 Jackson was surprisingly tactful in negotiating a new commercial treaty with Great Britain that enabled American merchants for the first time to trade directly and legally with the British West Indies. Old Hickory was less tactful with France as he tried to collect twenty-year-old claims for French interference with American shipping during the Napoleonic wars. In 1831 France agreed to begin payment and promptly defaulted. When Jackson threatened to seize French property, he set off a wave of jingoism that eventually brought a suspension of diplomatic relations. Without seeming to do so, Jackson then backed off from his outbursts, and without calling attention to the fact, France paid the American claims.

Martin Van Buren's diplomatic difficulty grew out of chronic trouble along the Canadian border. Always anxious to export American democracy and perhaps to add a little territory in the process, Americans thought every sign of Canadian-British friction heralded an eventual revolution. Canadian rebels counted upon American sympathy, occasional informal aid, and refuge and hospitality if a coup failed. In December, 1837, the *Caroline*, a small American steamer, made three trips across the Niagara River with supplies for dissident Canadians. A detachment of Canadian militiamen crossed the river at night, killed an American while overpowering the *Caroline's* crew, set fire to the vessel, and cut her adrift. As tension along the border mounted, Van Buren urged Americans not to provoke British retaliation. Throughout 1838 and into 1839, Americans enlisted in secret lodges whose object was Canadian liberation, but enthusiasm evaporated in the face of evident Canadian apathy.

Meanwhile, frontier argument moved eastward. The dispute over the boundary between Maine and New Brunswick, which had been going on since 1783, flared into the Aroostook War of 1838–39. In 1838 an "invasion" by Canadian lumberjacks provoked the Governor of Maine to mobilize the militia. Congress appropriated $10 million and authorized a force of 30,000 men, but General Winfield Scott, Van Buren's trouble-shooter, arranged a truce in 1839 before any blood was shed. The argument was taken out of the Maine woods and referred to a diplomatic commission.

Daniel Webster headed the State Department when discussion of the northern boundary began again in 1842. Webster and Lord Ashburton, Britain's congenial and conciliatory special envoy, met for productive negotiations in the heat of a Washington summer so oppressive that Ashburton swore he would "positively not outlive this affair." The negotiators scrapped the confusing provisions of the treaty of 1783 and drew the present northern boundary of Maine, which left 7,000 of the disputed 12,000 square miles to the United States. Britain also agreed to one minor adjustment in the frontier at the northern end of Lake Champlain and another in Minnesota that awarded the Mesabi iron deposits to the United States.

The Webster-Ashburton Treaty also resolved a potentially explosive impasse over slavery and maritime rights. In the 1830s Britain had abolished slavery throughout the empire and in the 1840s tried to stamp out the remnants of the African slave trade. Although the United States had outlawed importation of slaves in 1808, some American vessels were still engaged in the traffic and other vessels used the Stars and Stripes as a ruse. The United States refused to permit the British Navy to stop and search American ships and Webster eventually promised that the United States would maintain its own African squadron and enforce American law on American vessels. The promise was indifferently kept.

MANIFEST DESTINY

John L. O'Sullivan was impatient. For months the politicians had talked about treaties and titles, but what O'Sullivan wanted was land. The Oregon Territory was a long way from New York, where O'Sullivan wrote editorials, but in 1845 he wrote one that caught the spirit of many of his countrymen. "Away, away," he wrote, "with all those cobweb tissues of rights of discovery, exploration, settlement, contiguity, etc." America's claim to additional territory was "the right of our manifest destiny to overspread and possess the whole of the continent which Providence has given us for the development of liberty and federative self-government." Britain would not settle Oregon, but in American hands "it must fast fill in with a population destined to establish . . . a noble young empire of the Pacific."

Whether applied to Oregon, Texas, New Mexico, California, Cuba, or Central America, O'Sullivan's editorial contained all the elements of the creed called manifest destiny that swept the United States in the 1840s with all the fervor of a religious revival. The West, so the faith went, was God's gift to Americans, whose responsibility was to settle it, to cultivate it, and to produce not only crops and cash but virtue as well. The western dream combined the early Spanish explorers' visions of gold with Jefferson's picture of fertile prairies and sturdy yeomen, added the greed of the common land-speculator, and cloaked the result in the Puritan's vocabulary of divine mission. Manifest destiny had other roots deep in the American tradition: the assumption that Americans were a divinely chosen people, fit to furnish a shining example to the world; the fervent faith in self-government; the compulsion to people empty space. It was a strange creed, full of contradictory elements—nationalism, sectionalism, and narrow state rights; historical inevitability and an eagerness to shove fate; Christianity and arrogant acquisitiveness.

Title mattered less than possession when in the 1820s Americans began moving into the Mexican province of Texas. The Mexican government, glad to have the thinly settled area grow, granted land to Americans and winked at their use of slaves to till it, for slavery was illegal in Mexico. But in 1830, when Americans in Texas had become annoyingly self-assertive, Mexico prohibited further American settlement and refused subsequent demands for Texan autonomy. In 1836 the Texans declared independence and secured it when an army under Sam Houston defeated Mexican forces at San Jacinto. Before the end of the year, the Republic of Texas had a constitution and had begun to negotiate for annexation to the United States.

Neither Jackson nor Van Buren was ready to add territory that might bring war with Mexico and that surely would create political trouble within the United States. Texans then opened discussions with Britain, which was interested in a barrier to American continental growth, a source of cotton,

Trails to the Far West

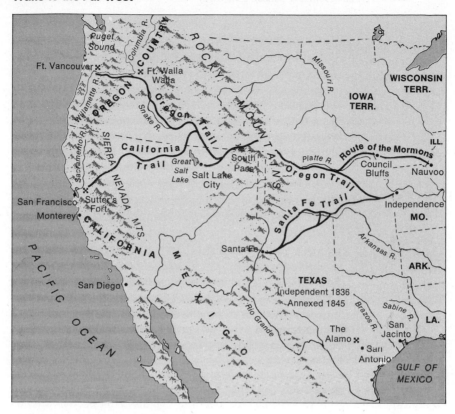

and an unprotected market for British goods. These negotiations probably would have had no result, for Texas' ties to the United States were too close and Britain's opposition to slavery too strong. But the possibility of British influence in an area many Americans already thought of as their Southwest raised enthusiasm for annexation.

Britain was more directly concerned about American settlement in the Oregon territory. Joint occupation, established in 1818, had been renewed indefinitely in 1828. Then in the 1840s, merchants and missionaries combined to extol the virtues of Oregon to other Americans. Even seventy-eight-year-old John Quincy Adams, about to end his magnificent career as an antislavery spokesman in the House, waxed ecstatic about Oregon. We claim the whole territory, Adams declared, to "make the wilderness blossom as the rose, to establish laws, to increase, multiply, and subdue the earth, which we are commanded to do by the first behest of God Almighty." By 1845 more than 5,000 Americans had followed the Oregon Trail from Missouri to the Willamette Valley, and they wanted to end anomalous joint occupation and substitute exclusive American rule all the way to 54°40′, the southern boundary of Alaska.

A few hundred venturesome Americans settled in California, where the land was as fertile and vacant as Oregon and where the climate and the harbors were better. John Sutter, a German-American who had acquired Mexican citizenship and an immense tract of land in the Sacramento Valley, expedited the American migration. The bustling American colony expected control from Washington soon to replace the loose rein from Mexico City, but the seizure of Monterey in 1842 by a misinformed American naval officer was a few years premature and had to be disavowed.

Some experienced statesmen, in their concern for banks and tariffs, mistook manifest destiny for a fad. In 1844 Henry Clay, the probable Whig nominee for President, met with Martin Van Buren, who seemed likely to be Clay's Democratic opponent. A debate over expansion, they agreed, risked reopening sectional squabbling; they decided to keep the issue out of the campaign by separately opposing immediate annexation of Texas or any other territory.

The agreement cost Van Buren the nomination. Word came from the Hermitage that Andrew Jackson favored annexing Texas and thought Van Buren had made a mistake. The Democratic convention deadlocked when Van Buren received slightly more than a majority but less than the required two-thirds of the votes. Unable to decide among more prominent aspirants, the delegates settled on James K. Polk, an intense, humorless Tennesseean with a puritanical sense of purpose. The Whigs, who nominated Clay as expected, joked about his dark-horse opponent. "Who," they asked from the campaign stump, "is James K. Polk?" They need not have inquired. Polk had spent fourteen years in the House, the last four as Speaker; he had twice been Governor of Tennessee; he was Andrew Jackson's candidate after Van Buren fumbled the expansion issue; he was, as one of the delegates put it, "a pure, wholehogged democrat" from the Jacksonian mold. He was called "Young Hickory" and foreshadowed the arrival of a new political generation and a brief, blustering political movement called "Young America"; when he was inaugurated at fifty, he was the youngest President the United States had ever had.

The Democratic platform stood forthrightly for expansion, pledging "the reannexation of Texas" and "the reoccupation of Oregon," which campaigners transformed into "Fifty-four Forty or Fight!" However dangerous Henry Clay thought the issue, large parts of the electorate—in eastern cities, on northwestern farms, and on southwestern plantations—obviously supported expansion. But Clay hedged his opposition to more territory just enough to drive some voters to the abolitionist Liberty party, which polled 16,000 of its total 62,000 votes in New York. If Clay had carried New York, which the Democrats won by 5,000 votes, the presidency would have been his.

THE MEXICAN WAR

John Tyler sensed the popular temper well before the election and ordered Secretary of State Calhoun to prepare a treaty annexing Texas. Calhoun's treaty went to the Senate simultaneously with a vigorous note to Great Britain defending slavery. Linking the two documents, abolitionists charged that annexation was a slave-owners' plot to extend the boundaries of bondage; Calhoun's treaty died in the Senate with only sixteen proponents and thirty-five opposed. Undismayed, Tyler read the election results as a mandate for immediate annexation. Lacking the two-thirds majority for a treaty, he suggested that a joint resolution would serve as well. The Senate finally accepted the resolution by two votes three days before Tyler left the White House. Before the end of 1845 Texas was a state.

But the boundaries of the new state were disputed. Texas claimed the area south to the Rio Grande, but Mexico, which hotly resented American annexation of territory it still believed to be Mexican, argued that Texas had never extended south of the Nueces River. In 1845 President Polk ordered General Zachary Taylor into the disputed region; in the spring of 1846 Taylor moved to the north bank of the Rio Grande near a concentration of Mexican forces at Matamoros.

While Taylor's troops were moving south, John Slidell, a special American envoy to Mexico, tried to accomplish American aims without war. Slidell was authorized to offer Mexico as much as $30 million for the disputed part of Texas, all of California, and the intervening territory called New Mexico. While Slidell waited, one Mexican government fell and another no less stubborn replaced it. No one would officially receive the American diplomat, and no Mexican government could offend its proud citizenry by releasing so much territory. Slidell wrote Polk that only a beating would induce Mexico to discuss American propositions seriously. Foreseeing no chance of success, Slidell started home.

In May of 1846 Polk asked his Cabinet whether the insulting treatment of Slidell, together with other Mexican-American friction, justified

As a general, Zachary Taylor helped secure the Mexican cession, but as President he could not find an acceptable formula for governing the territory.

war. Most of the Cabinet agreed with the President's decision to ask for a declaration; later news that Taylor's troops had clashed with Mexican forces at Matamoros converted the others. The foe, Polk told Congress, had "invaded our territory and shed American blood on American soil." Congress was aware that Polk bore some responsibility for provoking hostilities but passed the declaration by large majorities in both houses; measures to raise troops and supply followed.

Polk reinforced Taylor's force and ordered him to move his troops into northern Mexico. Taylor, popularly known as Old Rough and Ready, met and defeated a Mexican army at Monterrey in September. Taylor won a national reputation, but he lost Polk's confidence by allowing the defeated Mexicans to retire after an armistice. Polk diverted part of the Army to a planned assault on Vera Cruz and ordered Taylor to mark time at Monterrey. Convinced that a Democratic President was restraining him because of his Whig politics, Taylor took the offensive again in 1847 and blundered into a far larger Mexican force at Buena Vista. The American army won a

The Mexican War, 1846–1848

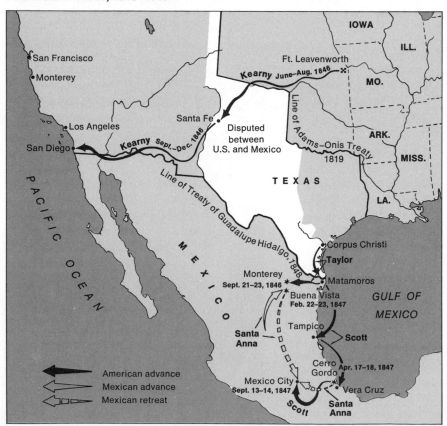

decisive victory—in spite of its disobedient commander, the President noted acidly—and Taylor's reputation at home climbed.

American settlers in California declared their independence and mounted their own "Bear Flag Revolt" against Mexico. An American "surveying" expedition commanded by John C. Frémont joined the rebels, and an American naval squadron soon arrived at Monterey. By the time overland forces had arrived from Kansas by way of Santa Fe, where they had secured American control of New Mexico without a shot, Mexican rule in California was largely finished.

But Mexico seemed not to understand the war was lost. To make the point, Polk sent an expeditionary force under General Winfield Scott to Vera Cruz in March, 1847. Scott secured the port and retraced the route of the Spanish conquistadors to the capital. Mexican armies contested Scott's slow advance, but following a decisive victory at Cerro Gordo in April, Scott moved triumphantly into Mexico City in September.

Nicholas P. Trist, the Chief Clerk of the American Department of State, accompanied Scott's troops and carried Polk's conditions for peace. Trist's instructions offered Mexico virtually the same terms Slidell had presented before the war. But the Mexican government would no more deal with Trist than it had with Slidell. The disgusted President ordered Trist home just as the envoy began conversations that seemed promising. He sent Polk a patronizing note, continued the negotiations, and completed the Treaty of Guadalupe-Hidalgo in February, 1848. The Treaty disguised conquest as purchase, for Mexico received $15 million and the United States agreed in addition to pay claims by its citizens against Mexico. In return, Mexico ceded California, New Mexico, and the disputed portion of Texas. Although Polk was irritated with Trist, the Treaty corresponded to his instructions. The President submitted the Treaty to the Senate, which promptly ratified it. And the area of the United States jumped by one-fifth.

CONTINUING SECTIONAL CONFLICT

Victory brought no new laurels to the Polk administration. Early congressional support for the war soon disappeared in sectional and partisan sniping. Whigs criticized the President for causing the war. Abraham Lincoln spent much of his term in Congress introducing resolutions demanding to know the precise spot where the first clash occurred. Alexander Stephens, a Georgia Whig, called it "not only dishonorable, but disgraceful and infamous" to wage war against a friendly neighbor. Thomas Corwin rhetorically transformed himself from an Ohio congressman into an outraged Mexican: "Have you not room in your own country to bury your dead men?" Corwin shouted. "If you come into mine, we will greet you with bloody hands and welcome you to hospitable graves."

Some northern criticism grew out of Polk's settlement of the Oregon dispute. In 1845 Polk had publicly claimed the entire territory to the southern boundary of Alaska at 54°40'. But he had also offered to settle for extending the 49° boundary to the Pacific, an offer that Great Britain asked to have repeated in 1846. Under political pressure from northwestern Democrats, who really meant to fight for 54°40′, Polk momentarily refused. But both sides moved toward agreement. By 1846 the rush of American settlers had reduced the number of furs the Hudson Bay Company was taking out of Oregon, and British interest in the area dropped proportionately. Anxious not to have to fight Mexico and Britain simultaneously, Polk asked the Senate's advice when Britain formally revived the compromise of the forty-ninth parallel. Over the protest of northwestern expansionists, the Senate advised acceptance and then formally ratified the treaty.

More divisive than the Oregon Treaty was the argument about slavery that the Mexican War precipitated. The Massachusetts legislature believed that the object of the war was new territory for slave-owners and new states to increase the "slave power" in national politics. Massachusetts legislators formally resolved that the war was "wanton, unjust, and unconstitutional in its origin and character," and that "the highest honor of the country" and "Christian duty" as well "should arouse all good citizens to join in efforts to arrest this gigantic crime."

The administration's request for $2 million to pay for negotiations with Mexico seemed a routine bill in August, 1846. But when David Wilmot, a good Jacksonian Democrat from Pennsylvania, finished presenting his amendment, the bill was anything but routine. For the Wilmot Proviso made prohibition of slavery in any territory acquired from Mexico "an express and fundamental condition" of expansion. Concern for free, white labor, not disgust with slavery, probably determined Wilmot's stand. He meant to preserve, he remarked subsequently, "a fair country . . . where the sons of toil, of my own race and color, can live without the disgrace which association with negro slavery brings upon free labor." Whatever his motive, the Wilmot Proviso provided a rallying point for all who opposed the war, for all who opposed slavery or its spread, and for those northerners who had supported the war in an initial burst of expansionist enthusiasm but regretted the consequences of manifest destiny. Polk thought the Proviso the device of "demagogues & ambitious politicians" who hoped "to promote their own prospects."

Polk correctly estimated the Proviso's appeal to the North. Legislatures in every free state but one endorsed Wilmot's rider, and northern congressmen voted for it time after time. Although the House passed the Proviso several times, the Senate always struck it out. And each debate stirred further the sectional quarrel that expansion was supposed to calm. It was not clear at the time, but the Wilmot Proviso made slavery an open political issue, one that would be at the very core of political rivalry for the next fifteen years. Other issues began to disappear from political discourse: ". . . day after day," one weary congressman grumped, "nothing can get a hearing that will not afford an opportunity to lug in something about negro slavery."

Calhoun countered the Wilmot Proviso with four congressional resolutions asserting that Congress could not constitutionally restrict slavery at all. Congress did not vote on Calhoun's resolutions, but there was no lack of heated talk about them and about the state-rights view of union upon which they were based. The Alabama legislature wrote its own resolutions. Alabamans declared the Missouri Compromise unconstitutional, pronounced slavery guaranteed in every federal territory, and threatened to secede if the Wilmot Proviso ever passed. Other southern legislatures toned down the language of the Alabama Resolves while repeating their substance.

As the hardening of sectional lines after 1846 demonstrates, expansionism was a peculiar form of nationalism that only temporarily concealed sectional ambitions. John L. O'Sullivan, who coined the phrase "manifest destiny" and in 1846 called for "more, more, more! . . . till our national destiny is fulfilled," was a proponent of state rights and eventually an apologist for the Confederacy. Southern zeal for expansion did not extend to annexing Oregon nor to taking all of Mexico; Calhoun, the most farsighted of southern spokesmen, did not vote for the declaration of war against Mexico and never developed any enthusiasm for Polk's expansionist schemes. Parts of the Northwest lost interest in manifest destiny when its northern limit became 49°, and new land had not been a primary concern of northeastern residents for generations. Polk himself was a Jacksonian nationalist of the strict-construction school, but some other expansionists used nationalistic rhetoric to serve sectional ends.

The domestic record of Polk's administration also demonstrates how sharply Democratic nationalism differed from the Hamilton-Marshall-Clay variety. Polk vetoed bills for internal improvements. He meticulously set four goals for his presidency: he wanted to acquire California, resolve the dispute over Oregon, lower the tariff, and reenact Van Buren's Independent Treasury. Like Jackson, but without Old Hickory's zest, Polk loved the Union and believed it should be bigger; like Jackson also, Polk took a narrow view of the federal government's economic responsibility.

Congress renewed the Independent Treasury in 1846 with an act almost identical to that of 1840. The tariff caused more controversy. Arguing that protection cut consumers off from foreign suppliers and doubled the profits of domestic manufacturers, Secretary of the Treasury Robert Walker suggested moderate reductions from the levels of 1842. His bill included a duty of 30 percent on iron and 25 percent on cotton cloth, neither of which seemed adequate to the industries involved. Polk cracked the whip of patronage in the House, and except for Democrats from the middle states, his party responded; Whigs voted seventy-six to one against the bill. Polk appealed to party regularity in the more evenly divided Senate, where the Walker Tariff passed in 1846 by one vote.

Before his inauguration, Polk announced that he would serve but one term. He established his goals, fulfilled them, left the White House, and died within a year. But he left his party in disarray. Van Buren Democrats resented the convention of 1844, and Polk's patronage policy had done nothing to ease the sting. Far from burying sectional controversy, the new territory Polk had acquired brought slavery back into the political arena; only with emancipation was the subject banished again. The Wilmot Proviso, popular in their constituencies, put political pressure on northern Democrats. One or another of Polk's policies annoyed Democrats in the northwest, who wanted all of Oregon and internal improvements, and those in the middle states, who wanted tariff protection. Whigs had won the congressional election of 1846, and 1848 looked like another Whig year.

Most of the Democratic presidential hopefuls had only local backing. Lewis Cass, an able, honest Senator from Michigan, had fewer enemies than his rivals and received the nomination. The platform was perfunctory, but Cass was known to believe that settlers themselves should choose whether to permit or prohibit slavery in their territory. Its supporters, chiefly northwestern Democrats, called this plan popular sovereignty; opponents—northerners who wanted absolute prohibition of slavery in the territories and southerners who demanded an absolute guarantee—called Cass's plan squatter sovereignty.

Shut out at the Democratic convention, Van Buren's New York followers held their own and joined Liberty party members, anti-slavery Whigs, and other dissidents and reformers in establishing the Free-Soil party. With the exception of a few abolitionists, Free-Soilers opposed only the expansion of slavery; they agreed on the Wilmot Proviso because it reserved the territories for white settlers and kept blacks out. The party nominated Van Buren for President and campaigned for "Free Soil, Free Speech, Free Labor, and Free Men." The former President had no following in the South, but in the North, and especially in New York where he ran ahead of Cass, Van Buren hurt the Democratic ticket.

Young, ambitious Whigs moved to snatch the opportunity. Those like Webster and Clay who had represented Whiggery for a generation were elbowed aside. Even before the convention met, Thurlow Weed, a New York editor whose first love was politics, William H. Seward, a former governor of New York who in 1848 went to the Senate, Alexander Stephens, a staunch unionist from Georgia, Abraham Lincoln, whose single term in Congress was nearly over, and a host of Whigs from the border states, had settled on Zachary Taylor. If Taylor had any political convictions, they were unknown, and his backers proposed to keep them that way. Taylor owned a plantation and slaves in Louisiana, yet his military service demonstrated a firm commitment to the nation. And although Old Rough and Ready had occasionally proved inept on the battlefield, he was a winner. That was not a bad qualification for a presidential nominee.

THE COMPROMISE OF 1850

Whatever Taylor's program, the election gave him no mandate. Cass carried as many states, but Taylor won, partly because Van Buren split the Democratic vote. Democrats organized the Senate, but neither party controlled the House, where Free-Soilers held the balance of power, and three weeks were consumed in just electing a speaker. A divided Congress, an inexperienced, untutored President, two split parties, and several self-righteous factions were slim resources for meeting the political problems

that piled up for attention. And every issue furnished an opportunity for someone to talk about slavery, which made every rift wider and every error more serious. Southerners, angry at the lack of northern cooperation in returning runaway slaves, pressed for a stiff new fugitive-slave law. Northern politicians, for their part, objected to the highly visible slave trade in Washington, which Congress had the unquestioned constitutional authority to abolish.

Even more vexing was the need of the new territories for government. Flooded by gold-seekers in 1849, California was ready for statehood. There was more to California than the picturesque gold rush, with its delightful place names, its vigilantes, its vice, its tall tales, and its claim jumpers. Ordinary Californians wanted law, order, and a fixed legal code to confirm land titles. President Taylor suggested that California skip territorial status, draw up a constitution, and apply for immediate statehood; he hoped thereby to sidestep southern demands for protection of slavery in federal territories. But California would upset the sectional balance, carefully maintained in the Senate since 1820, and there was no evasion of southern demands for the territories of Utah and New Mexico, neither of which was ready for statehood. The claim of Texas to much of eastern New Mexico and the related claim of Texas bondholders to federal redemption of their securities complicated any final arrangement in the Southwest.

The Wilmot Proviso and Calhoun's rejoinder that slavery must everywhere be protected were the extremes of the debate over territorial slavery. Polk, Buchanan, and many other moderate Democrats favored extending the Missouri Compromise line to the sea. Stephen A. Douglas, the shrewd Senator from Illinois who was emerging as the chief Democrat in the Northwest, had, like Lewis Cass, endorsed popular sovereignty. President Taylor and many northern Whigs wanted to handle each region separately. California, they held, had drafted a constitution that happened to prohibit slavery; California met the ordinary requirements for statehood and ought to be admitted. Other cases could be considered when they arose.

But unless statesmen could forge a legislative majority from these

The Compromise of 1850

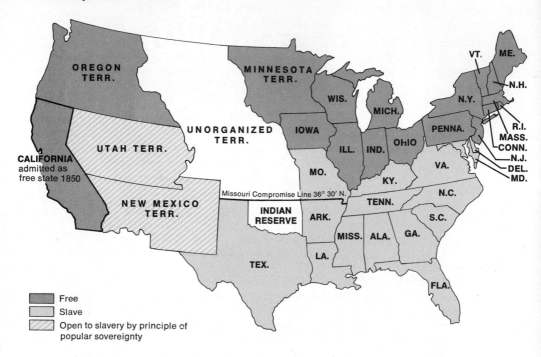

Free
Slave
Open to slavery by principle of popular sovereignty

disparate views, nothing would be done about anything. By common consent, Henry Clay undertook the task with a series of resolutions he introduced in the Senate early in 1850. The resolutions provided for admission of California as a free state; organization of the rest of the Mexican cession, without restriction on slavery; Texas' surrender of the disputed territory to New Mexico and federal assumption of the Texas debt; enactment of a stringent fugitive slave law; and elimination of the most offensive slave depots in Washington, coupled with a congressional promise not to abolish slavery there without the consent of the people of the District and of Maryland as well. Eventually Clay rolled all the resolutions into one "omnibus bill," and the prolonged debate over the Compromise of 1850 began in earnest.

It was not, on the whole, an edifying debate. Senator Calhoun, so ill that he would die before the bill came to a vote, had to have his speech read for him. Calhoun scorned compromise, ignored the specific issues under discussion, pointed out that social bonds between sections were already snapping, and demanded that Congress protect the right of southerners to take their slave property wherever they pleased. Jefferson Davis, a fiery Mississippian, spoke in a similar vein. Senator Seward answered for many northern Whigs, who, with President Taylor, opposed compromise. Seward's speech had a tone of moral self-righteousness that outraged southerners, for he rested his case against slavery, and against compromise, on "a higher law than the Constitution"; his was a new variant of manifest destiny that reserved the territories for free men.

While oratory continued on the floor, Clay encouraged the public to articulate its demand for peace through compromise. Businessmen, who blanched at the economic consequences of war, circulated petitions. Resolutions from mass open meetings poured into Congress. Representatives of influential Texas bondholders lobbied for compromise. Stephen A. Douglas and other Democrats worked to hold their party in line. And Daniel Webster gave a courageous address that cost him the support of the growing number of Massachusetts abolitionists but inspired unionists throughout the land. Webster asserted that slavery could not survive in New Mexico's deserts, a point that Clay and other compromisers reiterated. Why, they asked, insist on the Wilmot Proviso merely to taunt the South? Webster condemned his own section for not returning runaways as the Constitution required. And he condemned even more sternly the ease with which partisans of both sides contemplated disunion. For Webster knew that talk of peaceful separation was drivel. The old nationalist wanted no part of war, but he wanted disunion less.

Nothing moved Old Rough and Ready. But the President's intransigence was almost providentially removed when Zachary Taylor stayed too long in the July sun, cooled off with too much ice water and cold milk, ate too many cherries, and died of an acute digestive disorder. Millard Fillmore, who succeeded, was Seward's rival in New York's complicated cut-throat politics. When he was Vice-President, Fillmore's disagreement with Seward and Taylor had been widely assumed; President Fillmore promptly applied the power of the executive branch to achieve a compromise. But quite suddenly and unexpectedly the Senate stripped the omnibus bill of all its controversial provisions and passed only a fragment organizing the Utah Territory. Weary and discouraged, Henry Clay left to repair his health and spirit at the shore. Stephen A. Douglas salvaged the Compromise of 1850.

Called the Little Giant because of his small stature and outsize energy, ambition, and competence, Douglas was the busiest prominent politician in the nation during the 1850s. A convinced democrat and a nationalist to the core, Douglas made too many enemies to reach the White House. But the fear of making enemies never paralyzed him, and whatever the issue, Douglas labored to find a unifying answer. He was not always right; but he was always active. In 1850 he broke Clay's omnibus bill into its components, mustered bipartisan support for each measure, and before the end of September he delivered the whole package to Fillmore's desk for signature. So varied was the support for each bill that only twenty-eight congressmen voted for every provision of the Compromise; twenty-five of those congressmen were Democrats; twenty-six were from the North.

The laws, then, were never based on the spirit of compromise and never had either broad national or official bipartisan support. Several of the measures disappointed the fondest hopes of their supporters and the bleakest fears of their opponents. The New Mexico and Utah territories were organized and permitted to make their own arrangement about slavery. Texas accepted its present frontiers and a grant of $10 million to redeem the debt. California became a free state, broke the balance in the

Senate, but before the Civil War regularly voted with the South in Congress. The slave trade in the District of Columbia continued apace, even though the law closed down the most notorious slave pen. Most notably, the Fugitive Slave Law neither deterred slaves from flight nor secured northern cooperation in their recapture. Relieved Americans greeted the Compromise with cheers and fireworks. The cheers and relief were premature; the fireworks were only beginning.

But the compromisers had their moment. Rabid southerners hoped a convention in Nashville would endorse the Calhoun-Davis stand; instead, Nashville delegates suggested mildly that the Missouri line be drawn westward to the Pacific. Jefferson Davis himself lost a gubernatorial race in Mississippi. Moderate Georgians endorsed the compromise, although they underlined the importance of whole-hearted northern enforcement of the Fugitive Slave Law. Most presidential candidates for the election of 1852 supported sectional accommodation. Douglas, Cass, and Buchanan, the front-running Democrats, and Webster, Fillmore, and Winfield Scott, rivals for the Whig nomination, all professed their faith in compromise. When Democrats eventually settled on a dark horse, Franklin Pierce, he unequivocally added his endorsement. Faithful to their formula of nominating generals, Whigs picked Winfield Scott, who was less forthright than Pierce and who southerners feared shared Seward's outlook. Only Free-Soilers outspokenly denounced the legislation of 1850, and they were seriously weakened when Van Buren's Democrats loyally supported Pierce.

THE COMPROMISE BREAKS DOWN

Pierce's smashing victory (Scott carried only four states) seemed ultimate proof of the popularity and universal acceptance of compromise. But the election in fact signaled no surge of sentiment for union; rather, it marked the demise of the Whig party and a consequent growth of sectionalism. For twenty years men of all regions had come together in the Whig party. Inspired by Webster's oratorical nationalism, Whigs had consistently tried to enact Clay's nationalistic legislation. To be sure, they had only successfully suppressed internal divisions by nominating politically unknown generals. But in 1852 not even a politically unknown general could hold the party together. After 1852 only Democrats claimed a national constituency, and their precarious unity depended upon keeping slavery out of politics.

The Fugitive Slave Law, however, almost guaranteed that bickering would continue. For the act failed by a large margin to meet the test of northern opinion. Ralph Waldo Emerson referred to the law as a "filthy enactment" and vowed not to obey it. A Maryland planter was shot while chasing his runaways in Pennsylvania. Authorities in Detroit had to call out troops to calm a mob enraged by the recapture of a fugitive on his way to Canada. State legislatures had earlier passed "personal liberty" laws, which had effectively prevented slave-owners from reclaiming their runaways and which had been a major reason for the southern demand for federal legislation in 1850. After the Compromise, northern legislatures pounced on a southern device: in 1859 the Wisconsin legislature solemnly denounced federal enforcement of the Fugitive Slave Law as an invasion of Wisconsin's reserved rights as a state.

The provisions of the act provoked part of the furor. Appointed commissioners, sitting without juries, were not bound by the ordinary rules of judicial procedure in hearing cases. Accused blacks could not testify. The commissioner pocketed a ten-dollar fee if he found for the owner; five dollars sufficed if the black were released.

For years, Harriet Beecher Stowe wrote, she had "avoided all reading upon or allusion to the subject of slavery." She broke her resolution with a vengeance. No Christian or humane people, she thought, had any moral duty to obey the Fugitive Slave Law. Her *Uncle Tom's Cabin*, which first appeared in installments in 1851 and 1852, glorified slaves who escaped and whites who helped them. The book was not a one-dimensional abolitionist tract: Simon Legree, the villain of the piece, was a transplanted Connecticut Yankee; feckless white southerners had more compassion for

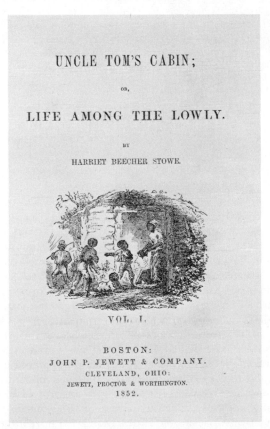

UNCLE TOM'S CABIN;

OR,

LIFE AMONG THE LOWLY.

BY

HARRIET BEECHER STOWE.

VOL. I.

BOSTON:
JOHN P. JEWETT & COMPANY.
CLEVELAND, OHIO:
JEWETT, PROCTOR & WORTHINGTON.
1852.

Harriet Tubman: an escaped slave who returned to the South to lead others out of bondage

blacks than did patronizing, pretentious northerners. But unsophisticated northern audiences who watched countless road companies perform dramatizations of the book, and unsophisticated northern readers who made it the first of the best-sellers, condemned the slave-owner and the Fugitive Slave Law, and poured out their tears for Uncle Tom, Topsy, and Eliza.

Outside of fiction, fugitives were few. If official statistics are accurate, only 16 of 400,000 slaves in South Carolina escaped in 1850. Although losses in the border states were higher, perhaps 1 slave for every 5,000 who remained in bondage succeeded in escaping every year. Yet southerners, especially those in the deep South, conjured up a gigantic northern conspiracy called the underground railroad that spirited countless blacks to freedom. There *was* an underground railroad, and a few blacks did travel it, at great risk to themselves and to their courageous hosts. But it was either less successful or less ubiquitous than worried southerners fancied.

ECHOES OF MANIFEST DESTINY

So the Compromise of 1850 settled few of the old arguments and created a few new ones. And Franklin Pierce, a man of little imagination, had no fresh ideas as mounting sectional gales buffeted his floundering administration. For lack of creative statesmanship, some Democrats experimented again with an active expansionist foreign policy as a cure-all for acute domestic disharmony. President Pierce supported the mission Fillmore had authorized to open Japan to American commerce. Commodore Matthew Perry, who commanded the expedition, signed a treaty in 1854 allowing American traders to use two ports. Pierce sent Townsend Harris to exploit this initial concession; in 1858 Harris persuaded the Japanese to open other ports and to establish an embassy in Washington.

Prodded by Secretary of War Jefferson Davis, Pierce also secured about 45,000 square miles of southern New Mexico and Arizona in the Gadsden Purchase from Mexico. The most convenient route for a southern transcontinental railroad ran through the area, and Davis argued that such a prize was worth $10 million.

Cuba, sought by American expansionists from Jefferson on, was worth up to $130 million, or so William L. Marcy, Pierce's Secretary of State,

Perry's troops drill in Japan, 1854.

informed Pierre Soulé, the United States Minister to Spain. In 1854 Soulé consulted at Ostend, Belgium, with John Y. Mason, the American Minister to France, and James Buchanan, the Minister to England. The three Americans tried to devise a strategy for prying Cuba loose from Spain without arousing the hostility of France or England. Their dispatch to Marcy, initially confidential but soon published and called the Ostend Manifesto, gratuitously advised Spain to get rid of its troublesome colony. Although Cuba was a burden to Spain, they argued, paradoxically the island would be a great boon to the United States. Should Spain refuse to sell Cuba, the three ministers discovered laws both "human and divine" that authorized the United States to seize it. The Ostend Manifesto was too much for northern Democrats, who feared another debate over the expansion of slavery, and too much for the cautious Marcy, who rebuked Soulé, the Manifesto's principal author.

If not in Cuba, perhaps slavery might expand in Central America. American and British interests had clashed in Nicaragua during the Polk administration. As part of the Clayton-Bulwer Treaty of 1850, Great Britain and the United States had promised not to colonize Central America nor to claim exclusive rights to any future canal, which was the major reason for interest in the area. But William Walker, an American who made manifest destiny a profession, saw a different future for Nicaragua. At the head of a band of filibusters, Walker took over the country in 1856. He won the support of southern expansionists by opening the republic to slavery, but his tenuous hold on Nicaragua was soon broken and with it the slim chance for new southern territory.

American expansion in the 1850s was only a faint echo of the boisterous manifest destiny of the 1840s. Trade treaties with Japan, a slice of Mexican desert, a bombastic, disavowed demand for Cuba, and some free-enterprise filibustering in Central America aroused no enthusiasm comparable to that Americans felt for possession of Texas, Oregon, and California. Nor could talk of renewed expansion distract Americans from the sectional rancor their earlier growth had already aggravated.

Suggested Reading

Four quite different older works are still useful. Francis Parkman's *The Oregon Trail** (1849) is the narrative of a nineteenth-century historian. Henry Nash Smith, *Virgin Land** (1950), deals with the West as a compelling symbol for Americans. Albert K. Weinberg's *Manifest Destiny** (1935) is a standard account of expansion in the 1840s. No one should study the 1850s without rereading Harriet Beecher Stowe, *Uncle Tom's Cabin* (1852).

Allan Nevins has edited *Polk: The Diary of a President* (1952) and written a distinguished study of the period. *The Ordeal of the Union* (1947). The best recent biography of Polk is the two-volume work by Charles Sellers completed in 1966. A lively account of part of the Polk administration is Bernard DeVoto's *The Year of Decision: 1846** (1943).

Holman Hamilton's *Prologue to Conflict** (1964) is a careful study of the Compromise of 1850. Otis A. Singletary, *The Mexican War** (1960), covers that conflict. Frederick Merk's scholarship distinguishes his *Manifest Destiny and Mission in American History** (1963). In *The Far Western Frontier, 1830–1860** (1956), Ray A. Billington provides a useful survey. William C. Binkley's *The Texas Revolution* (1952) is a basic book on the subject.

*Available in paperback edition

CHRONOLOGY

1854   Kansas-Nebraska Act

1856   Presidential election: James Buchanan (Democrat) defeats John C. Frémont (Republican) and Millard Fillmore (American)

1857   *Dred Scott* decision
       Lecompton Constitution
       Financial panic

1858   Lincoln-Douglas debates

1859   John Brown raids Harper's Ferry

1860   Presidential election: Abraham Lincoln (Republican) defeats John C. Breckinridge (Southern Democrat), John Bell (Constitutional Union) and Stephen A. Douglas (Democrat)
       South Carolina secedes

1861–65   The Civil War:
           1861: Fort Sumter bombarded
           1862: Preliminary Emancipation Proclamation, to take effect in 1863
           1863: Battle of Gettysburg; Battle of Vicksburg
           1864–65: Battle of Virginia

1862   Pacific Railway Act
       Homestead Act
       Morrill Land Grant Act

1863   National Banking Act

1864   Presidential election: Abraham Lincoln (Republican) defeats George B. McClellan (Democrat)

XI

THE UNION DIVIDES

North and South lost touch during the 1850s. Social contact diminished as churches and political parties divided on the Mason-Dixon line and as more and more southern boys stayed in the South for college. The compromise that opened the decade was supposed to begin an era of sectional peace; slightly more than ten years later, the first shell went screaming toward Fort Sumter, and the war was on.

The 1850s had been full of misconceptions. A growing northern audience accepted the abolitionist caricature of the South, with its spacious plantations where masters flogged discontented slaves part of the day and spent the rest plotting ways to snatch the public domain from white yeomen. The abolitionist idealized the slave as his master's equal, capable of immediate integration into the white man's society; yet most northerners did not see the few blacks in their own midst that way.

Southerners too had their share of misconceptions, even about the South. Southern whites assumed that their slaves were indolent, dishonest, and happy in their bondage. Trouble, the masters believed, came from elsewhere—from anywhere but the plantation itself. Social discontent would end when the abolitionists were still; cotton prices would go up when the tariff was repealed; political problems came from Washington, and reasoned solutions only from nearby state capitals. Abolitionists, "Black

Republicans," and eventually all Yankees were scheming, grasping, self-righteous hustlers who cloaked their greed in high-sounding phrases. Somewhere under the angry words was a trace of reality; the anger too was real.

The central reality, and the cause of the anger, was the presence of black bondsmen in the South. Slavery governed the behavior and social relations of both races in the South and, southern whites believed, preserved the section from barbarism. Increasing numbers of northerners, on the other hand, perceived bondage as a moral outrage. Since Americans have always sought political resolutions for their disagreements, slavery and the attendant questions of race relations constantly appeared on the nation's political agenda. Ultimately the issues defied political accommodation and nearly ruptured the nation.

The nation required political leadership, but the parties responded with timid time-servers or political unknowns, because strong men with strong convictions endangered party unity. Whigs sought the illusion of strength by nominating generals whose obstinance masqueraded as conviction. The Democrats' expedient was the "doughface," a northern man with southern principles. When evasion failed, the Whigs disappeared and the Democrats divided. Northern Democrats deserted their party because it refused to prohibit slavery in the territories where it did not exist; southerners pulled out because the party would not guarantee slavery in those same territories, where most Americans agreed that it could not profitably survive.

In spite of all the resources of the central government to help reclaim runaways, southerners still believed illogical secessionists who claimed that independence would make recapture less difficult. Slavery drove logic and reason and compromise out of political discourse and replaced them with moral absolutes—right and wrong.

The defense of the South's "peculiar institution," like the abolitionist attack, had been outlined in the 1830s, and partisans reiterated these arguments through the next two decades. In 1836 James H. Hammond proclaimed slavery "the greatest of all blessings which a kind Providence bestowed upon our glorious region." Slavery, indeed, made "our southern country proverbial for its wealth, its genius, and its manners." As a senator from South Carolina in 1858, Hammond had not changed his mind. Because of slavery, the South enjoyed a perfect society with "an extent of political freedom . . . such as no other people ever enjoyed upon the face of the earth."

So the South no longer hesitated to defend slavery; it was, as Calhoun said in 1837, "a positive good." The institution gave the uncivilized black man Christianity, subsistence, and the white man's culture; all the slave had to do was work, and his tasks were not very onerous, so the apologists held. Slavery created a harmonious society, more humane than the ruthless northern wage system. Slavery was, in fact, in perfect accord with scripture and even the Declaration of Independence, for slaves preempted the bottom of the social ladder and made possible the equality of white citizens. If the southern faith contained fallacies, southern whites, including those without slaves, thought it a creed worth dying for.

THE TERRITORIES AGAIN

Politics was no easy profession in the emotion-charged 1850s. Old leaders were gone: Calhoun died in 1850, Clay and Webster in 1852; after thirty years in the Senate, Thomas Hart Benton lost his seat in 1850; shorn of his influence, Martin Van Buren lived in semi-retirement in New York. Their replacements had a comparatively short apprenticeship for national leadership. Sam Houston came to the Senate in 1846, Stephen A. Douglas in 1847, William H. Seward in 1848, and John C. Frémont in 1850. In 1853 the senior member of the Senate had served there for only ten years, a striking illustration of the perils of sectional politics. The shrewd politician subordinated the principles of his party, and sometimes the needs of the nation, to the demands of his fickle constituency.

Franklin Pierce tried in vain to preserve the fragile Democratic unity that put him into the White House. He calculated his appointments carefully but could satisfy no faction completely. Stephen A. Douglas designed the Kansas-Nebraska Bill to restore direction and discipline to the drifting Democratic party. Douglas' measure provided territorial status for the region from the Indian Territory north to the Canadian border. The Missouri Compromise forbade slavery in the area, but Douglas substituted

The Kansas–Nebraska Act, 1854

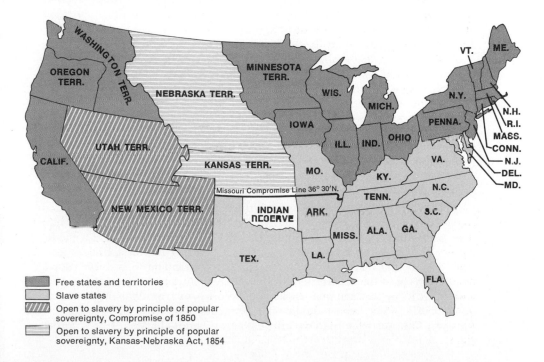

Free states and territories

Slave states

Open to slavery by principle of popular sovereignty, Compromise of 1850

Open to slavery by principle of popular sovereignty, Kansas-Nebraska Act, 1854

popular sovereignty for the earlier prohibition. Under pressure from south-ern senators, Douglas then accepted an amendment to the bill specifically repealing the Compromise of 1820. Another change split the area into two territories; the change seemed to promise that Kansas would be slave and Nebraska free, though this understanding was nowhere explicit.

The Little Giant realized that his bill might reopen sectional debate, but he decided to take the risk. Once every acre of American soil had terri-torial government Douglas believed the question of the expansion of slavery need never again arise. Moreover, territorial organization of the region west of Missouri and Iowa would create the possibility of land grants to a trans-continental railroad running west from St. Louis or Chicago; unless Kansas and Nebraska were formally established, a southern transcontinental route from New Orleans, which would run through territory already organized, had an advantage. The Northwest wanted a transcontinental; the South wanted the Missouri Compromise repealed; Douglas wanted to reunite the two sections in a vital Democratic party. He fully expected momentary acrimony to give way to permanent sectional peace, and he hoped, perhaps, to preside over the prosperous, happy nation that his Kansas-Nebraska Bill was to produce. Privately he assured northern malcontents that migrants from the Ohio Valley would outnumber slaveowners in Kansas and Nebraska; since the votes of these northern farmers would make the new states free, Congress could safely appease the South by repealing the Missouri Compromise. Democratic leadership drove the bill through the Senate with votes to spare and then through the more stubborn House.

If slavery had been an ordinary political issue, as Douglas thought it was, his scheme might have worked. Since he lacked any moral conviction about slavery, Douglas treated the subject rationally and was mystified when others did not. The South supported his bill grudgingly; the North, however, erupted. Dismay from Free-Soilers was predictable, but Douglas had not foreseen anger among his own Democrats. Denunciation came not only from state legislatures in New England, where abolition flourished, but from New York and the Northwest as well. Four antislavery congress-men joined two senators to issue an "Appeal of the Independent Democrats" that asked for immediate, emphatic, public opposition to "this enormous crime." The dazed Douglas himself remarked that his burning effigies lit the route from Boston to Chicago.

Both sections undertook to fill Kansas with partisans. Massachusetts chartered the New England Emigrant Aid Company to encourage and finance antislavery settlement. The company provoked resentment in the South, particularly in Missouri, where the defenders of slavery organized to repel the Free-Soil challenge. "Border ruffians" from Missouri rode into Kansas to elect a proslavery legislature, which promptly produced a model slave code for the territory. Wholesale fraud marked this first Kansas elec-tion and several of those that followed. The political process broke down completely because neither faction considered binding the results of elec-tions that its opponents won. Baffled governors sent from Washington could neither calm nor govern the quarrelsome territory.

So Kansans took matters into their own hands. In May, 1856, "border

Charles Sumner: abolitionist
from Massachusetts

ruffians" terrorized the free-soil town of Lawrence, burned the hotel that
served as unofficial headquarters for northern migration, and destroyed an
abolitionist press. A few nights later, an antislavery group directed by a
fanatic named John Brown revenged the deaths of two Lawrence residents
by executing five proslavery settlers at Pottawattomie Creek. Brown's victims had had no connection with the sack of Lawrence, but for Brown, who
fancied himself God's agent appointed to destroy slavery, no connection was
necessary. Sniping, arson, and guerrilla warfare persisted in Kansas through
the summer of 1856.

Civil strife in Kansas rekindled the controversy over slavery in Congress. Just before the attack on Lawrence, Charles Sumner, an abolitionist
senator from Massachusetts, delivered a tasteless speech denouncing "The
Crime Against Kansas." Sumner impartially indicted slavery, slave-owners,
and southern politicians, singling out Andrew P. Butler, a senator from
South Carolina, for particular contempt. A few days later Preston Brooks,
a South Carolina congressman and Butler's nephew, beat the Massachusetts
senator senseless on the Senate floor. Sectional rivalry had reached such a
pitch that Brooks, by virtue of thrashing a defenseless man eight years his
senior, became a hero in the chivalrous South, and Sumner, an irritating
prig, achieved instant northern martyrdom.

THE REPUBLICAN CRUSADE

Outrage at the passage of the Kansas-Nebraska Act cropped up
all over the North in 1854 and 1855. In churches, schoolrooms, taverns, law
offices, and courthouses in hamlets from Maine to Wisconsin, little groups
of angry citizens pondered a political crusade and fashioned the organization to lead it.

Like all American parties, the Republican party embraced diverging factions: conservative northern Whigs, who stood for the American system and the Union, stood with abolitionists, anything but conservative, who thought union with slave states immoral; immigrants, especially German-Americans, rubbed shoulders with advocates of restricted immigration; bereft of their program, which the new party appropriated, Free-Soilers joined Whig opponents under the Republican banner. Northern Democrats found the Republican party a welcome alternative to their floundering organization; of the more than forty northern Democratic congressmen who had heeded party leadership and supported the Kansas-Nebraska Act, only seven were reelected in 1854. All these factions submerged their differences in their common distaste for the Kansas-Nebraska Act and the expansion of slavery.

The American party also arose in the political confusion left by the Kansas-Nebraska Act. This organization was a cross between a political party and a fraternal order. Initially an anti-immigrant, anti-Catholic secret society, the Americans, or Know-Nothings, as Horace Greeley called them, entered politics in 1854. Many southern ex-Whigs eased their transition to the Democratic party by stopping briefly in the American party. The imagined threat of Roman Catholicism, however, failed to conceal the party's internal disagreement about slavery. When the southern wing tried to commit the American party to southern principles, "North Americans" broke away and then merged with Republicans.

Republicans won control of several northern statehouses and confidently prepared for the presidential contest of 1856. The platform affirmed the party's opposition to slavery and its extension, advocated the reenactment of the Missouri Compromise, favored the admission of Kansas as a free state, approved the construction of internal improvements, including a railroad to the Pacific, and hinted at the need for a tariff. John C. Frémont, the party's nominee, had no encumbering political record to alienate any voter.

Democrats found a less colorful but very safe candidate. Since they had enacted the Kansas-Nebraska Act, they had to stand for popular sovereignty, but they wisely chose not to flaunt it. The party passed over Douglas and Franklin Pierce to pick James Buchanan, a conservative Pennsylvanian with a long political career and little political record. Legislator, Secretary of State, Minister to London, Buchanan was a doughface who roused little enthusiasm and had few enemies. Millard Fillmore, the candidate of the American party, joined Democratic campaigners in prophesying disunion if Frémont should win. Southern firebrands promised that "immediate, absolute, eternal separation" would follow a Republican victory.

Frémont did not win. Buchanan held the South, his own Pennsylvania, and Illinois and Indiana, where Douglas and his allies had worked valiantly for the Democrats. Frémont carried New England, New York, Ohio, and the upper Northwest. If he could have added Pennsylvania and either Illinois or Indiana, the Republicans would have carried off the prize on their first attempt.

DEMOCRATIC UNITY TESTED

James Buchanan was not one to take responsibility for controversial decisions. The issue of territorial slavery had burned previous Presidents and legislatures. Buchanan let the Supreme Court take a turn. Through correspondence with two justices, he had influenced the Court's forthcoming ruling on *Dred Scott* v. *Sanford*, which would, he knew, limit congressional jurisdiction over the territories. The President promised in his inaugural address that he, "in common with all good citizens," would accept the Court's decision as a final settlement.

The facts of the case were well known. In the 1830s Dred Scott had accompanied his master from Missouri to Illinois and then to the Wisconsin Territory. Neither Illinois nor the territory permitted slavery, a technicality that both slave and master ignored. Both returned to Missouri where Scott remained a slave until his master's death. Complicated legal maneuvering, in which Scott himself was only remotely involved, resulted in Scott's suit for freedom, first in Missouri and then in federal courts, on the ground that residence in free territory had made him a free man. Missouri's highest court found, on the basis of Missouri law, that Scott was still a slave. A federal circuit judge ruled that no Negro was a citizen and that Scott consequently had no right to bring suit. The Supreme Court of the United States initially intended to issue a routine decision upholding the Missouri court and ignoring the controversial matters of Negro citizenship and the power of Congress to limit territorial slavery. But pressures within the Court convinced some justices to state their position fully to resolve the troublesome questions once and for all.

The *Dred Scott* decision, announced in March, 1857, produced everything but the calm Buchanan expected. Each justice wrote his own opinion, and even experienced constitutional lawyers had difficulty determining precisely what a majority had decided. Chief Justice Taney wrote the official "opinion of the court," which left little doubt about the two critical questions. First, Taney held, blacks had ever been inferior to whites and, free or slave, were permanently barred from citizenship. Second, Congress had no power to prohibit slavery in any federal territory. Slaves, Taney argued, were property and were therefore protected by the due process clause of the Fifth Amendment; Congress must respect and defend the slave owners' black property no less than any other property. The Missouri Compromise, repealed three years before, had always been unconstitutional. Five justices concurred with parts of Taney's opinion; one simply wanted to affirm the judgment of the Missouri court. Benjamin Curtis and John McLean dissented.

Curtis disagreed with both of Taney's major findings. Curtis cited evidence that blacks, including some in the South, had unquestionably exercised the rights of citizenship. And the federal Constitution, as Curtis read it, gave Congress unrestricted power over federal territories. He pointed out that several of the Founding Fathers, in 1820 and before, had approved legislation limiting the extension of slavery; indeed, before 1840 such congressional authority had been almost universally assumed. The Missouri Compromise was constitutional, Curtis held, and the power of Congress to permit or prohibit slavery unimpaired.

The *Dred Scott* case, which Buchanan had expected to settle everything, did not even settle the fate of Dred Scott, who was quietly emancipated. Neither decision nor dissent convinced anybody not already convinced. The ruling neither established nor protected slavery in any federal territory. Republicans conceded only the Court's ruling on the status of Scott himself; they appealed the rest of the decision to the court of northern public opinion, where the election of 1860 overruled Taney's judgment. Republicans argued that the *Dred Scott* decision left popular sovereignty as dead as the Missouri Compromise. For if Congress could not itself keep slaves from the territories, it could not logically empower the residents to do so.

Popular sovereignty failed its practical test in Kansas too. In June, 1857, convinced that the election would be unfair, Free-Soilers refused to vote for delegates to a constitutional convention. Consequently, proslavery representatives dominated the convention that assembled at Lecompton. They produced a constitution guaranteeing slave property and forbidding free blacks to settle in Kansas. The delegates evaded the spirit of popular sovereignty by asking the electorate to approve the Lecompton Constitution "with slavery" or "without slavery." Since the constitution protected slave-owners already in Kansas, Kansans could vote only to prohibit *further* slavery; the voters could not abolish slavery altogether. When Free-Soilers refused to vote, the version permitting future slavery carried by a large but fraudulent majority.

Buchanan owed his election to solid southern support, which his party had to preserve in order to survive. The South demanded the Lecompton Constitution. Buchanan proclaimed Kansas "as much a slave state as Georgia", and made the constitution a test of party loyalty. But it was a test northern congressmen could not take. Stephen A. Douglas, who believed popular sovereignty should rest on a full expression of the popular will, led congressional opposition. The rift between Buchanan and Douglas split the Democratic party beyond repair. The Senate accepted the Lecompton Constitution, but the House did not. Congress then offered Kansans a second opportunity to pass on the Lecompton document but made acceptance of the constitution a condition for receipt of a large federal land grant. In an honest election in 1858, Kansas overwhelmingly rejected both the constitution and the land grant that Republicans had correctly called a bribe.

The nation, and the staggering Democratic party, had taken yet another blow in 1857. A financial panic swept through the North late in the summer and continued into the early months of 1858; railroad construction ceased, blast furnaces shut down, unemployment mounted, and ships stayed at their wharves in Boston, St. Louis, and San Francisco. Unregulated American banks and the dislocation of the world economy resulting from the Crimean War were partly responsible for the crash, but speculation in land, slaves, and corporate stocks also had severely strained the nation's credit. Distressed northern manufacturers blamed the crash on the new low tariff passed by the Democratic Congress in 1857. No panic has ever helped a party in power, and renewed demand for a tariff, especially from Pennsylvania iron interests, increased the risks for the low-tariff Democrats.

The panic was less severe in the South. Southern banks survived while northern banks closed; southern businesses failed at less than half the rate of their northern counterparts. Although declining demand sent the price of cotton down from sixteen cents in September, 1857, to nine cents at the end of the year, planters simply stored their bales until prices went up in the spring. Ardent southerners argued that their crop was the key to national recovery, that their economy was stronger than the North's, that, indeed, the South would become even more prosperous if it seceded. "Cotton," proclaimed Senator Hammond early in 1858, "is king."

DEMOCRATS DIVIDE

Stephen A. Douglas returned to Illinois in the summer of 1858 to run for reelection to the Senate. His opponent was an awkward, gaunt, homely man, but Abraham Lincoln was also a sharp debater with a fron-

Abraham Lincoln, 1860, photo by Mathew Brady. Lincoln claimed that this portrait, widely circulated in campaign literature, helped make him President.

tiersman's sense of humor and a growing conviction that slavery was wrong. Lincoln cast himself as the underdog David challenging the Goliath of Illinois politics. Douglas, however, was never complacent; his opponent had been among the most important Whigs in Illinois, had almost joined Douglas in the Senate in 1850, and had enough stature in Republican politics to be a serious vice-presidential contender in 1856. Lincoln and Douglas debated up and down Illinois in a campaign as vital to the country as it was to either participant. The survival of northern Democrats and of the party as a national institution depended upon Douglas' ability to maintain a political middle ground between southern insistence upon the expansion of slavery and the Republican demand that the blight be restricted.

Lincoln cut away the middle ground at Freeport in the second debate. Was there any way, Lincoln asked, to reconcile popular sovereignty with the *Dred Scott* decision? Could settlers in any federal territory legally exclude slaves? Residents could effectively keep slavery out of any area, Douglas explained in what became known as the Freeport Doctrine, for without local police regulations "slavery cannot exist a day or an hour anywhere. . . ." The answer made sense; no slave-owner would risk his investment without the assured cooperation of local public officials. But that answer could not possibly satisfy the South; slaveowners wanted a firm guarantee of the permanence of slavery, no matter what a territory voted. That pledge Douglas could not give and still hold northern voters; without it, neither Douglas nor the party he led would have southern support.

Lincoln was no abolitionist. He repeatedly denied Democratic charges that he favored racial equality. But Lincoln did insist that slavery was wrong, and he promised that Republicans would *"make provision that it shall grow no larger."* Douglas successfully shifted the debate from moral rights and wrongs to democracy and union. He won reelection when his party narrowly secured control of the gerrymandered Illinois legislature. But Lincoln won a plurality of the vote and a national reputation. And his party made striking gains all over the North.

John Brown had never had much faith in politicians. The year 1859 demanded action, he thought, and he would arm the slaves to begin it. Brown proposed to capture the federal arsenal at Harper's Ferry, Virginia, and to distribute weapons to blacks who would win their own freedom. But, instead of slaves, southern militiamen swarmed to Harper's Ferry, and Buchanan sent Colonel Robert E. Lee with a small detachment of federal troops as well. Brown's invasion was soon confined to a small outbuilding and then snuffed out. Virginia tried the old fanatic for treason. Convicted and executed in 1859, John Brown became the first authentic martyr of the Civil War.

The effect of Brown's raid was far more ominous than the futile expedition itself. A wave of anxiety engulfed the South, and southern militiamen began to drill in earnest. Southerners tied Brown and violent abolition to the Republican party, in spite of constant Republican denials. The party's platform in 1860 explicitly denounced "the lawless invasion . . . of any State or Territory, no matter under what pretext. . . ." Republicans went further and affirmed "the right of each State to order and control its own domestic institutions. . . ." While the plank looked like a bid for southern votes, it

The last moments of John Brown, by Thomas Hovendon

was also a shrewd device to reassure northern conservatives who opposed all kinds of fanaticism.

The Republican platform in 1860 showed other evidence of political maturity. To the pledge to limit the expansion of slavery, Republicans added planks advocating a protective tariff, internal improvements, including a railroad to the Pacific, and a homestead law granting free federal land to western settlers. The delegates rejected as possible candidates William H. Seward, who had spoken of a "higher law than the Constitution" and of an "irrepressible conflict," and Salmon P. Chase, who had signed the flaming "Appeal of the Independent Democrats" in 1854; such men were too radical. Instead the convention settled on Abraham Lincoln, an opponent of slavery, but an economically conservative former Whig whose political hero was Henry Clay. Republicans had learned the lesson of 1856; they wrote a platform to please Pennsylvania and nominated a candidate from Illinois who had also lived in Indiana.

Democrats could not do anything right. At a first convention in Charleston the party could not agree on a platform. Douglas modified the Freeport Doctrine, but northern Democrats refused to guarantee absolutely that slavery could spread throughout the territories. Alabama's delegates walked out, and the rest of the lower South followed. What was left of the convention wrangled through fifty seven ballots and recessed without nominating anyone.

The respite merely made division permanent. Douglas Democrats could yield neither principle nor candidate; southern delegates were equally adamant. When the South was overruled on a series of procedural questions at the second convention, delegates from Virginia, North Carolina, and Tennessee withdrew. Delegates from California and Oregon followed, as well as most of those from Kentucky, Missouri, and Arkansas. Democrats from the upper South joined the cotton South in another convention that nominated John C. Breckinridge, Buchanan's Vice-President. Douglas' forces nominated the Little Giant and wound up their forlorn business. The Democratic party had completely come apart.

Still seeking to achieve compromise by skirting slavery, a group of border-state politicians of miscellaneous party affiliation established the Constitutional Union party. The party appealed to former Whigs and Know-Nothings and to cautious Democrats who thought both Douglas and Breckinridge too extreme. After adopting a few platitudes backing the Constitution, the Union, and the laws, the new party nominated John C. Bell, a former senator from Tennessee.

Early in the campaign Bell tried to combine all anti-Republican groups in support of his candidacy. The effort collapsed because of the intransigence of both northern and southern Democrats. Although Breckinridge himself

The Election of 1860

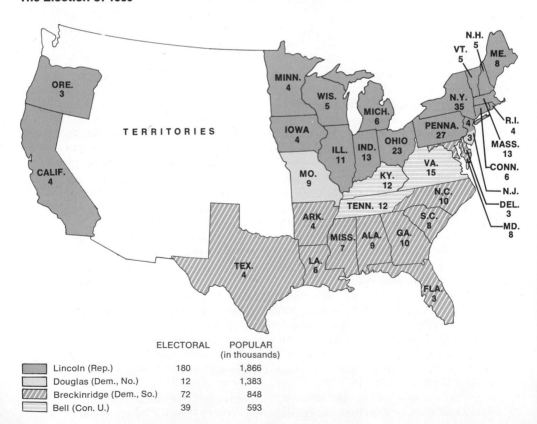

	ELECTORAL	POPULAR (in thousands)
Lincoln (Rep.)	180	1,866
Douglas (Dem., No.)	12	1,383
Breckinridge (Dem., So.)	72	848
Bell (Con. U.)	39	593

campaigned very little, his supporters stirred southern audiences with the vow that the South would prevail, in the Union or outside it. Lincoln also spent a quiet campaign; his previous speeches and the party's platform, he told interviewers, said all that needed saying. But Republicans mounted an active campaign on Lincoln's behalf; parades, floats, and fireworks brought out crowds for the party's orators, who promised a tariff here, a homestead there, and a railroad where it would do the most good.

Douglas conducted his own campaign. Contact with audiences in both sections led him to stress union, not his own candidacy. Douglas soon knew he would not be President; in every section, he was a second choice—to Lincoln in the North, to Breckinridge in the South, and to Bell on the border. More disheartening to Douglas was his discovery that neither North nor South seemed horrified by the increasingly casual references to division and war.

Douglas won 1,377,000 votes, only about a half-million behind Lincoln and considerably ahead of Breckinridge, who polled 850,000, and Bell, who received about 600,000 votes. Douglas carried Missouri and won the votes of three New Jersey electors. Bell won Virginia, Tennessee, and Kentucky; Breckinridge held the rest of the South. Lincoln won the northern states and the presidency. The split returns meant that Lincoln lacked a popular majority. Yet if the votes for his opponents had been cast for a single candidate, Lincoln would have lost only California and Oregon, and their loss would not have cost him the election. The clear and decisive result of the election of 1860 was that Abraham Lincoln would be President of the United States on March 4, 1861.

LINCOLN AND THE SECESSION CRISIS

While the deep South prepared to secede, James Buchanan, an ineffective lame duck, sat in the White House, and the President-elect put together a cabinet of contentious men representing all factions of his party. Few expected the prairie lawyer long to dominate Seward, designated Secretary of State, or Chase, who would take over the Treasury, or Simon Cameron, the wily Pennsylvanian who was to be Secretary of War. Little in Lincoln's long career promised either the personal strength or the political and administrative genius that he was to reveal at the White House. Lincoln had been a competent, shrewd, conservative politician of the second rank. The times required more than that.

South Carolina had promised secession if Lincoln won, and the legislature immediately called a convention to carry out the threat. The convention unanimously adopted an ordinance of secession on December 20, 1860. By the first of February, in spite of some support for compromise, Mississippi, Alabama, Georgia, Florida, Louisiana, and Texas had joined South Carolina. In early February delegates gathered at Montgomery, Alabama, and modified the Constitution of the United States for use by the Confederate States of America. The convention elected Jefferson Davis and Alexander H. Stephens to lead the new republic.

Buchanan pronounced secession illegal in one breath and in the next confessed his lack of power to prevent it. But even Buchanan drew a line: although Confederates took possession of federal property, including arsenals, all over the South, the President ordered the federal garrison to hold Fort Sumter in Charleston's harbor.

The upper South hesitated and conciliators in Washington frantically tried to devise in days the formula for union that had eluded them for years. Congressional compromisers, led by John J. Crittenden, a former Whig from Kentucky, suggested several constitutional changes to ease the crisis. A committee discussed amendments reviving and extending the 36°30′ line of demarcation between free and slave territories, guaranteeing the domestic slave trade, and forbidding Congress to interfere with slavery in the states. Jefferson Davis indicated that such terms might be acceptable, but Abraham Lincoln, fully aware both of principle and politics, urged Republicans in the Congress to make "no compromise on the question of extending slavery." Crittenden's committee adjourned in disagreement. A peace convention, sponsored by Virginia's legislature and attended by eminent and earnest men, sent Congress a program that differed from Crittenden's in a few details. The lower South boycotted the assembly and some Republicans joked about its resolutions. The nation awaited Abraham Lincoln—and war.

The President-elect was forced to sneak into Washington because his advisers feared assassination. But confidence rang in Lincoln's inaugural address. He reassured southerners that neither President nor party endangered "their property . . . their peace, and personal security." And he reassured the North as well: the Union was indissoluble; he would honor his oath to "preserve, protect, and defend" it.

Lincoln soon had a chance to prove his determination. By the beginning of April, Fort Sumter had become for both sides a symbol of federal authority. Major Robert Anderson, who commanded the fort, informed Washington that he needed supplies and reinforcements. Any expedition seemed likely to incite trigger-happy Confederates around Charleston. Most of the Cabinet advised against an attempt to relieve Anderson, and Seward even suggested that perhaps the Union could be restored by provoking a quick war, preferably with France or Spain. Lincoln decided to inform authorities in South Carolina that food was on the way to Major Anderson. Following orders from President Davis, South Carolinians demanded Anderson's immediate withdrawal. When it was not forthcoming, the ceremonial first shot was fired on April 12, 1861. Forty-eight hours later Anderson surrendered; the Confederacy had won the war's first military engagement.

Abraham Lincoln called for 75,000 militiamen to put down the rebellion and Jefferson Davis summoned 100,000 troops to secure southern independence. The border states could no longer hesitate. Ten days before the barrage on Fort Sumter, Virginia had voted decisively against secession; two days after Lincoln called for troops, Virginia seceded, and Arkansas, Tennessee, and North Carolina soon followed. Delaware remained loyal to the Union. After a riot occurred as Union troops marched through Baltimore on their way to the front, Lincoln used the army to hold Maryland. Kentucky and Missouri had pro-Confederate governors and pro-Union legislatures, an accurate indication of divided popular sentiment. Both states contributed troops to both armies, both served as battlegrounds, and both remained in the Union. The counties of Virginia beyond the Blue Ridge, which were relatively free of slaves and intensely loyal to the Union, seceded from the Old Dominion in 1861 and, as West Virginia, became a state in 1863. Lincoln's grip on the border states was less dramatic than a victory in the field, but it was in the long run far more important than the early Confederate military success.

Early southern victories confirmed prevailing Confederate optimism. For years the South had derided Yankees as pen-pushers and counting-house clerks; for years the South had claimed that it was more manly to grow cotton than to weave or market it; for years the South had believed in the perfect harmony of southern society and sneered at debilitating internal dissent in the North. So Confederates overlooked the fact that 22 million people lived in the North and only about 9 million, of whom 3.5 million were slaves, lived in the Confederate South. And eager Confederates ignored the North's overwhelming superiority in manufacturing, shipping, finance, and railroad transportation. Confident of the righteousness of their cause, southerners went gloriously to war.

But it was not a glorious war. Dreary, tedious, terrible, trying, bitter and unbelievably bloody—all these it was, but not glorious. To be sure, camaraderie among opposing pickets occasionally relieved the horror, and there were songs and campfires and parades and waving flags as well as bravery that passed comprehension. But the songs included stanzas like:

> I have read a fiery gospel, writ in burnished rows of steel:
> "As ye deal with my contemners, so with you my grace shall deal;
> Let the Hero, born of woman, crush the serpent with his heel
>   Since God is marching on."

And, as "The Battle Hymn of the Republic" revealed, there was a self-righteous identification of the cause with Christ and a pitiless determination to crush the satanic foe to lifelessness. Compassion and nostalgia and years have since sentimentalized the Civil War, and uniforms with bullet holes look more impersonal in museums than when mangled flesh protrudes. About 35 percent of the participants became casualties; more than a half-million Americans died, and 400,000 wounded survived.

The costs were undeniably high. But the war proved, in Lincoln's words, that a "nation, conceived in liberty, and dedicated to the proposition that all men are created equal" could indeed endure. Americans in the 1860s took a bold stride toward the ideal of human equality. Out of their war came a new nation, tempered in tragedy, that had resolutely settled a half-century of argument about the power of the central government and that had finally abolished slavery.

CIVIL WAR BEGINS

Few foresaw the long, agonizing struggle. Lincoln's initial call was for ninety-day volunteers; southern cavalrymen promised to have the horses home in the fall; spectators from Washington went out in carriages to watch the rebels lose the war at the first battle of Bull Run. But Win-field Scott, Lincoln's strategist, looked toward a war of attrition, one in which the North's superior resources, men, and money would eventually provide victory. Scott suggested an immediate blockade. Then he planned to use the army to cut the Confederacy into pieces, beginning along the rivers. Eventually the Union carried out Scott's "Anaconda plan," but not before a great many men had died in several futile attempts to win quickly by striking at the Confederate capital at Richmond.

Although the war between the capitals attracted the public's attention in the first years of the war, the struggle in the West was at least as important. Early in 1862, a Union army under Ulysses S. Grant moved south from Illinois and captured Fort Henry on the Tennessee River and a garrison of 12,000 Confederates at Fort Donelson on the Cumberland. Southern forces commanded by Albert Sidney Johnston regrouped in northern Mississippi and caught Grant's army by surprise just north of the Tennessee-Mississippi line at Shiloh. Johnston died in the fierce first day's action; northern reinforcements enabled Grant to drive off the Confederates on the second day. Casualties totaled about one-fourth of the 100,000 men involved in the gory battle.

The Union secured the lower Mississippi River in April, 1862, when forces under Benjamin F. Butler occupied New Orleans after David Farragut's gunboats had bombarded the city. But Union commanders were unable to press their advantage until the spring of 1863, when Grant besieged Vicksburg, Mississippi, the most formidable Confederate base on the river. Shortly after the surrender of Vicksburg on July 4, 1863, the Union controlled the Mississippi from source to mouth. In a series of bitter battles fought around Chattanooga, Tennessee, in the fall of 1863, Union forces broke the last remaining link between Richmond and the Confederate Southwest. By the end of the year, the western wing of the Confederate army was based in Georgia.

Meanwhile, the northern wing of the Confederate army, given superb tactical leadership by Robert E. Lee and Thomas J. "Stonewall" Jackson, repulsed forays into Virginia by northern forces. Lee and Jackson took uncanny advantage of the mistakes of the shifting northern command. Confederates compensated for smaller numbers by concentrating their forces to attain tactical superiority at a particular point, while otherwise avoiding contact.

Following the embarrassing retreat of sadly disorganized Union troops after the first brush at Bull Run in July, 1861, Lincoln put George B. McClellan in command of the Army of the Potomac. A fine administrator, McClellan drilled his troops into a disciplined army. But, his critics contended, once he had created the army, he did not want to spoil it with use, and McClellan's fumbling campaign in the peninsula of Virginia in the spring of 1862 gave substance to the charge. But Lincoln's replacements proved even worse, and he recalled McClellan to command late in 1862, when Lee began to advance into Maryland. In September McClellan caught Lee at Antietam Creek, where casualties on both sides exceeded 10,000 in the bloodiest day of the war. Perhaps a draw, perhaps a defeat for both armies,

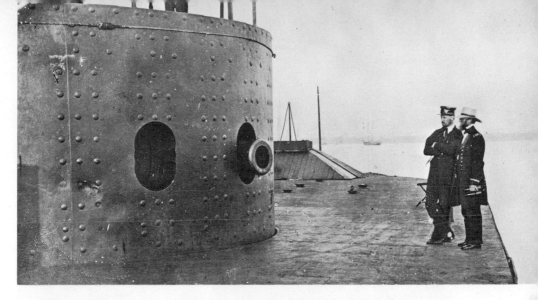

The *Monitor,* a northern ironclad vessel. The *Monitor* managed to keep the southern ironclad, the *Merrimac,* in port, but not until the *Merrimac* had disrupted McClellan's plans in 1862.

Antietam compelled Lee to abandon his invasion of the North, but so weakened McClellan that the Union was unable to pursue the retreating Confederates.

THE EMANCIPATION PROCLAMATION

If the Battle of Antietam had no victor, it was nevertheless decisive in one respect: Antietam was the occasion for announcing the Emancipation Proclamation. Initially Lincoln had made reunion the war aim to which all others were subordinate: "If I could save the Union without freeing *any* slave," the President wrote Horace Greeley in August, 1862, "I would do it; and if I could save it by freeing *all* the slaves, I would do it; and if I could do it by freeing some and leaving others alone, I would also do that." Lincoln himself would have preferred gradual, compensated emancipation and voluntary colonization of the freedmen abroad. But not even the loyal border states undertook gradual emancipation, and political pressure for abolition was growing in the North as the war continued. In the summer of 1862, even before his letter to Greeley, Lincoln had drafted the Emancipation Proclamation. On Seward's advice, to avoid the appearance of desperation, Lincoln decided to await a military victory to announce the change in Union policy. Antietam, though not precisely a victory, was made to serve.

The Emancipation Proclamation, announced in 1862, was to become effective on January 1, 1863. The President's war powers served as a shaky constitutional basis for his declaration that "all persons held as slaves within any state or designated part of a state, the people whereof shall be in rebellion against the United States, shall be then, thenceforward, and forever, free. . . ." As disappointed abolitionists pointed out at the time, the Proclamation freed slaves only in areas where Lincoln's decree had no

Antietam, 1862

effect; in the border states and in other areas under federal jurisdiction, slavery remained. But the Emancipation Proclamation unquestionably changed the war from a war for reunion to a war for a new union without slaves. Lincoln's proclamation doomed the whole degrading, anachronistic system, though it permitted loyal Union slave-owners a reprieve.

The Proclamation, and the battle at Antietam, had diplomatic repercussions too. Early in the war Confederates had hoped to secure military supplies, diplomatic recognition, and perhaps even intervention from Britain or France. For diplomatic purposes the Union had maintained that the war was just a domestic disturbance, that the Confederacy was not independent, and that the whole affair was of no interest to other countries. But Lincoln's formal announcement of a blockade early in 1861 unintentionally accorded the Confederacy status as a belligerent, and Britain's official proclamation of neutrality, to the Union's great annoyance, had the same effect. Late in 1861, the *Trent* affair added tension to already strained Anglo-American relations. An American warship stopped the British steamer *Trent* and took off two Confederate diplomats bound for Europe. The northern public treated the incident as a victory, but Britain backed its strong protest with military and naval preparation. Seward soon released the Confederates with a face-saving note, and Britain did not extend diplomatic recognition to the disappointed Confederacy.

When the war did not abate in 1862, Britain and France seriously considered recognition and perhaps intervention to force a negotiated settlement. British officials connived to sell the Confederacy fast, maneuverable vessels designed to destroy northern merchantmen. The *Florida* slipped out of England in March, 1862, and the *Alabama*, the most effective Confederate raider, set out a few months later. But the battle of Antietam and the Emancipation Proclamation changed the diplomatic situation. Antietam indicated that Lee could not win southern independence, and Britain shelved the idea of recognition and mediation. By making abolition the Union's avowed goal, the Emancipation Proclamation irrevocably tied British popular opinion to the Union's cause. Even when lack of cotton caused unemployment in depressed English textile cities, the sympathy of British working people for the Union did not abate. In 1863 the British government refused to permit delivery of the "Laird rams," English-made vessels designed to smash the Union's blockade. Confederate efforts to secure foreign intervention had failed.

GETTYSBURG AND SOUTHERN DEFEAT

Early in the summer of 1863, Lee decided to take the war to the North. After an impressive but costly Confederate victory at Chancellorsville, where Stonewall Jackson and more than 1,600 southern soldiers died, Lee headed into Pennsylvania. The Union Army, commanded by George G. Meade, stayed between Lee and Washington. Neither commander really chose the site, but the two armies squared off at Gettysburg on July 1. Meade held the high ground through three days of vicious fighting. More than 7,000 men died at Gettysburg, 4,000 of them Confederates, and more than 40,000 were wounded or missing. Lee retreated to Virginia, where in 1864 and 1865 he was only able to delay ultimate Confederate defeat.

To corner Lee in Virginia, Lincoln brought Grant in from the West. Grant left William T. Sherman the task of crushing the remaining Confederate army based in Georgia and commanded by Joseph E. Johnston. Sherman and Grant, with Lincoln's full support, determined to apply relentless pressure to the Confederate army, whatever the cost, and to use Sherman's force to divide the Confederacy again. Sherman left Chattanooga in May and slowly made his way toward Atlanta, which he captured on September 1, 1864. Sherman then detached his army from any northern base and began to live off the Georgia countryside on his march from Atlanta to Savannah, which fell before the end of the year. Although almost unopposed, Sherman's march left slaughtered livestock, smashed property, and hatred in its wake. When Sherman turned his army north and entered South Carolina in 1865, Carolinians paid dearly for having led the South to secession.

In Virginia both armies bled. One battle blended into another as Grant kept on coming regardless of his losses. The armies fought in tangled swamps at the Wilderness, in trenches at Spotsylvania and Cold Harbor, and finally settled down for a long siege at Petersburg. In the spring of 1865 Grant's unwavering pressure cracked Confederate resistance. Lee abandoned Petersburg and Richmond on April 2; one week later, at Appomattox Court House, it was all over.

No one knows what it cost. Statisticians have guessed at the extent of destruction; one estimate holds that southern wealth dropped by 43 percent but ignores the financial loss caused by abolition. And no statistic measures suffering. Confederates were never able effectively to breach the northern blockade, which caused mounting distress as the war went on. In 1864, when southern transportation had almost completely collapsed, short-

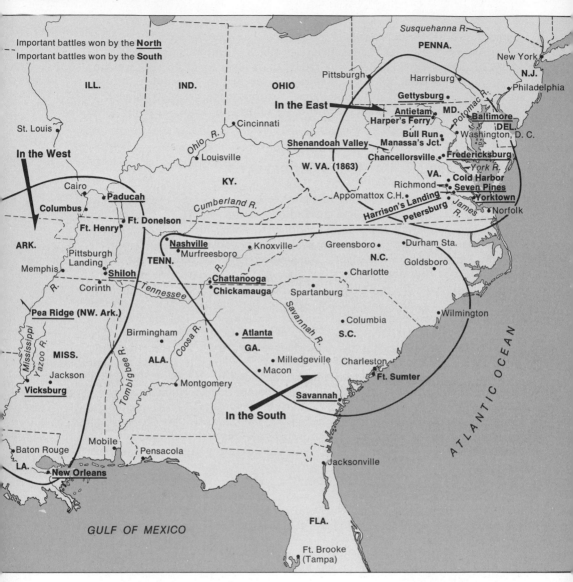

Important battles won by the **North**
Important battles won by the **South**

ages of metals, manufactured goods, clothing, and even food were felt all over the South. Nor was hardship confined to the armies or limited to the South. If destruction in the North was less widespread, Yankees too had empty sleeves, and northern homes had empty chairs.

BEHIND THE LINES

The Confederate nation failed with its valiant army. The task of launching a new state is formidable enough in peace; to organize, finance, and establish all the agencies of ordinary government in the midst of a war for survival was beyond the power of southern leaders. Some disillusioned southerners maintained that they had the wrong leaders, that Jefferson Davis spent too much time on details, meddled unduly with Lee's military plans, quarreled unnecessarily with his administration and the governors of the states. The charges were true—and probably irrelevant. All the charm, energy, and administrative skill in the world would have availed the South nothing once the blockade took effect and Grant and Sherman took over.

The southern economy showed the strain almost as soon as the war began. To put pressure on Europe to intervene, Davis forbade the export of cotton and thereby lost valuable foreign exchange. The Confederate congress displayed political cowardice and poor economic judgment by refusing until 1863 to enact a realistic tax program. The Union's blockade kept customs revenues to a minimum. Eventually the Confederacy taxed both property and income, but the measure was tardy and inadequate. Confederate bonds were speculative from the moment of issue and failed to raise much specie. Lacking other resources, the Confederacy had to print currency in ever larger amounts, a policy that brought serious inflation as early as 1862. Meaningless money and few goods combined to produce fantastically inflated prices and widespread discontent. Conscription, too, caused dissension, especially because slave-owners or overseers of twenty (and later, fifteen) slaves were exempt. That provision further alienated the nonslaveowning population, which had never been totally committed to southern independence.

Dissenters resorted to the traditional southern doctrine of state rights. Governors of several Confederate states undermined Richmond's policies. A governor of Alabama directed state officials not to collect taxes levied in Richmond. Several states officially opposed conscription on constitutional grounds. State judges used state law to release prisoners held under Confederate authority. In most such confrontations the Richmond government was helpless.

Abraham Lincoln had problems as well. Slavery, economic interests, and personal rivalries kept his party of the verge of division. Democrats, buoyed by success in the off-year elections of 1862, took advantage of wartime discouragement to promote their demand for a negotiated peace. The conscription law allowed men of money to hire a substitute or purchase exemption for $300. The Union, like its foe, was thus vulnerable to the charge that it was conducting "a rich man's war and a poor man's fight"; resentment of the inequitable draft law, racism, and other, more local, problems erupted in four days of serious rioting in New York City in July, 1863. Lincoln's critics, like those of Davis, charged that he exceeded his constitutional authority in using martial law and military courts to silence opponents or jail "Copperheads," as northern supporters of the Confederacy were called.

But the northern economy, stronger and more diverse than that of the South, was able both to supply the civilian population and to meet the demands of war. Republicans gained revenue and simultaneously fulfilled a campaign pledge by raising the tariff, first with the Morrill Tariff of 1861, and again in 1862 and 1864. A small income tax in 1861 also contributed to federal revenue. But war costs spiraled beyond tax resources, and the Union

Long ABRAHAM LINCOLN a Little Longer.

secured about ten times as much income from bond sales—about $2.6 billion—as from taxes. "Greenbacks," unsecured paper money, furnished another source of federal funds. The Treasury issued more than $400 million in greenbacks to meet wartime expenses. At its worst, the greenback dollar depreciated to about forty cents. The value revived with the success of the Union armies, and at the end of the war a greenback was worth about sixty-seven cents.

Congress also reorganized the Union's banking with the National Banking Act of 1863. To join the national system, banks had to invest one-third of their capital in federal bonds. Since these bonds paid about 7 percent interest, the investment was attractive. In addition, banks received national banknotes to 90 percent of the market value of their bonds. National banks were subject to some federal regulation, a provision that made many state institutions hold back. In 1865, however, Congress put a prohibitive 10 percent tax on the notes of state banks, and most of them became a part of the national system.

Republicans used federal lands to fulfill other campaign promises. In 1862 Congress pledged land grants and loans to finance the transcontinental railroad. In the same year Congress also passed the Homestead Act, which promised 160 acres of federal domain to a settler who lived on the land and improved it for five years. Finally, in the Morrill Act of 1862 Congress granted land to the states to endow colleges of agriculture and engineering.

While this legislation had a diverse political appeal—to manufacturing, railroad, business, and agricultural interests—the war was the overriding political issue until it ended. In 1864 Democrats nominated General McClellan on a platform that branded the war a failure and demanded a negotiated armistice. McClellan repudiated the platform but still appealed to those voters who were sick of the struggle. Although so-called Radicals in the Republican party were disgusted with Lincoln's slow acceptance of abolition and feared that he would be too lenient when the South surrendered, they could not unite on a single candidate to replace him. For a while in the summer, the President feared defeat in the election, but Sherman's success, especially at Atlanta, came opportunely;

55 percent of the electorate and a 212 to 21 margin in the electoral college returned Lincoln to office.

The meeting of Lee and Grant at Appomattox Court House was about a month away when Lincoln took the presidential oath a second time. His inaugural address sounded no note of triumph and betrayed no trace of satisfaction; he promised only continued resolution, humility, and compassion:

> With malice toward none, with charity for all, with firmness in the right as God gives us to see the right, let us strive on to finish the work we are in, to bind up the nation's wounds, to care for him who shall have borne the battle and for his widow and his orphan, to do all which may achieve and cherish a just and lasting peace among ourselves and with all nations.

Suggested Reading

Thomas J. Pressly, *Americans Interpret Their Civil War** (1954), provides a reliable introduction to the vast literature on this subject. Distinguished narratives include multivolume accounts by Allan Nevins, *The Emergence of Lincoln* (1950) and *The War for the Union* (1959–60), and by Bruce Catton, *Mr. Lincoln's Army** (1951), *Glory Road** (1952), and *A Stillness at Appomattox** (1954). A more general account is *The Civil War and Reconstruction* (1961), by James G. Randall and David Donald.

Lincoln's career is best traced in his writings, as edited by Roy P. Basler (nine volumes, 1953–55). Benjamin Thomas' *Abraham Lincoln** (1952) is the most satisfactory brief biography. Other useful biographies include *Stephen A. Douglas, Defender of the Union* (1959), by Gerald M. Capers, *Charles Sumner and the Coming of Civil War* (1960), by David Donald, and the multivolume study of Lee by Douglas S. Freeman (1934–35), who has also written *Lee's Lieutenants*, a study in several volumes (1942–44).

Roy F. Nichols, *The Disruption of American Democracy** (1948), traces the disintegration of the Democratic party. David Potter has written a model study, *Lincoln and His Party in the Secession Crisis** (1942), which is complemented by Kenneth M. Stampp's *And the War Came** (1950). Clement Eaton's *A History of the Southern Confederacy** (1954) is objective. Frank E. Vandiver's *Their Tattered Flags* (1970) is a more recent study of the Confederacy. The essays in David Donald (ed.), *Why the North Won the Civil War** (1960), are challenging and interpretive.

*Available in paperback edition

CHRONOLOGY

1864   Wade-Davis Bill, vetoed by Lincoln

1865   Lincoln assassinated; Andrew Johnson succeeds
Thirteenth Amendment abolishes slavery
Presidential Reconstruction: Amnesties for whites and enactment of Black Codes

1866   Civil Rights Act
Freedmen's Bureau

1867   Congressional reconstruction: Reconstruction Act imposes military districts on South; Tenure of Office Act

1868   Fourteenth Amendment ratified
Johnson impeached but conviction not secured
Presidential election: Ulysses S. Grant (Republican) defeats Horatio Seymour (Democrat)

1870   Fifteenth Amendment ratified

1870–71   Force Acts to combat Ku Klux Klan

1872   Presidential election: Ulysses S. Grant (Republican) defeats Horace Greeley (Liberal Republican, Democrat)

1876   Presidential election: Rutherford B. Hayes (Republican) defeats Samuel J. Tilden (Democrat) when a special electoral commission awards Hayes all 20 disputed votes in January, 1877

1883   Civil Rights cases

1895   Booker T. Washington addresses Atlanta Exposition

1896   *Plessy* v. *Ferguson* establishes doctrine of "separate but equal"

XII

RECONSTRUCTION

Reconstruction, Abraham Lincoln remarked as he received the news of Appomattox, "is fraught with great difficulty." The President's victory speech soberly emphasized the uncertain future, not the triumphant past, for Lincoln lacked specific programs for rebuilding his shattered nation. In the dozen years after Lincoln's death this national effort to reconstruct subtly changed to a search for peaceful accommodation. And the dilemmas Lincoln had foreseen endured, like the monuments both sections erected to the dead.

There are no monuments to Reconstruction, for nations do not celebrate their failures. Reconstruction just ended; it was never completed. Although the South rejoined the Democratic party and once more participated in the national political process, regional peculiarities have ever since set the section off from national politics. Although diligent southerners of both races slowly rebuilt their agrarian economy, industry rapidly transformed the rest of the country, creating problems and opportunities that much of the South did not share. Finally, although emancipation made racial equality possible, postwar generations never completed the task.

LINCOLN PLANS FOR RECONSTRUCTION

Lincoln foresaw the difficulty of reconstruction partly because he had to improvise a southern policy as Union armies began to occupy sections of the Confederacy. In 1863 the President promised amnesty to all southerners (except a few Confederate officials) who would swear allegiance to the Constitution and the Union. When the number of oath-taking voters reached 10 percent of a state's vote in the presidential election of 1860, military authorities were to permit the formation of a state government. Lincoln promised the executive recognition that signified the completion of reconstruction as soon as that state government abolished slavery.

But executive recognition, as the South was to discover repeatedly, was only one hurdle. Congress alone could permit southern states to rejoin the national legislature. Many Republicans in Congress thought the President too lenient and his conception of reconstruction too narrow. Charles Sumner, Thaddeus Stevens, Ben Wade, and other Republican critics who had earlier objected to Lincoln's cautious approach to emancipation were called Radicals. They believed that a victorious Union should punish rebellion and create a new pattern of southern life.

Radicals countered Lincoln's "ten-percent plan" with the Wade-Davis Bill, which Congress passed in July, 1864. Whereas Lincoln had been willing to accept a promise of future loyalty from a minority, the Radicals demanded proof of past loyalty from a majority. Before military occupation could give way to civil government, Radicals insisted, a majority of white male citizens must take an oath of past and future allegiance to the federal Constitution. No one who had supported the Confederacy could vote or participate in the formation of reconstructed state governments, which must abolish slavery, repudiate any debt incurred during the war, and deprive former Confederates of political rights.

Although Lincoln killed the Wade-Davis Bill with a pocket veto, he indicated a willingness to modify his own policy. The President did not insist on one method of reunion; if a southern state wished to reconstruct itself as the Wade-Davis Bill prescribed, Lincoln would not object. Lincoln's pose of flexibility conceded nothing, since no southern state would choose harsh congressional terms while the President's less demanding option was available. Radical sponsors of the bill responded to the veto with an indignant manifesto. The dispute over reconstruction, which divided Congress and the President more deeply than any other issue in American political history, had begun in earnest.

On the surface, the protracted debate centered on legal and constitutional questions. Were southern states still states with full constitutional rights? Or were they, as Thaddeus Stevens claimed, "conquered provinces," subject to the unlimited power of Congress to regulate federal territories? Was reconstruction a presidential function—for the executive power to pardon was clearly relevant—or could Congress assume full responsibility, since it must consent before a southern state could rejoin the national legislature?

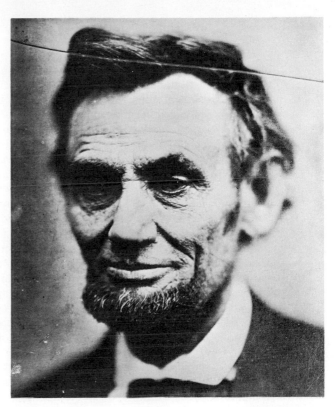

Lincoln's last portrait. Compare with the 1860 portrait (p. 209) for a visual indication of the strain of the presidency during the Civil War.

These questions, and dozens of others like them, disclose American political ritual. For at bottom, the questions of reconstruction were racial and economic, and at stake was the power to remake a great nation. But post–Civil War Americans, as their descendants have since, masked such visceral issues as racial equality and agrarian peonage with a constitutional façade that usually permitted civilized political discourse.

Abraham Lincoln knew that reconstruction was more than a constitutional nicety and dismissed the whole controversy over the legality of secession as "a merely pernicious abstraction." He thought reconstruction might be accomplished "without deciding or even considering" whether the Confederacy had ever been outside the Union. Lincoln hoped to subordinate dispute to agreement: "We all agree that the seceded states, so called, are out of their proper practical relation with the Union; and that the sole object of the government . . . is to again get them into that proper practical relation." Perhaps Lincoln, with his political genius, could have continued his uneasy coalition with the Radicals and still reconstructed the Union without bitterness. The assassin did not give him the chance.

THE RADICAL VIEW OF RECONSTRUCTION

Not all Republicans were Radicals in 1865, and not even all Radicals agreed on the entire program for remolding the South. At the very least, Radicals hoped to replace illiteracy and discrimination with education and tolerance. They proposed to educate, or coerce, the South toward com-

227

plete acceptance of emancipation and to finish that "more perfect Union" that the Constitutional Convention had begun.

The vision of some Radicals, of whom Thaddeus Stevens was most prominent, extended beyond social and political rights to economic equality for the freedmen. In place of ruined or neglected plantations, these Radicals saw economically independent farmers of both races tilling their own small farms. Stevens proposed to confiscate all southern land except individual holdings of less than two hundred acres. He suggested that some of the land thus obtained be granted to the former slaves who had worked it in order to assure their economic independence. The rest of the confiscated lands, Stevens said, should be sold at auction and the proceeds put toward reducing the national debt, establishing a fund for Union soldiers or their widows and children, and replacing northern property destroyed during the war. The South must pay for the hardship its war had brought. If the losers paid no reparation, northern taxpayers would in effect subsidize the defeated enemy by bearing the war's indirect costs. That situation, Stevens charged, was absurd.

Stern, unforgiving Thaddeus Stevens may have been right. Without economic security the freedom of the black man was not firmly based; peonage and slavery have much in common. Yet the radicalism of most of Stevens' Republican colleagues did not extend to the confiscation of slaveholders' plantations. Congress did not give farms to the freedmen, but it did temporarily support and protect them in their transition to freedom.

The Freedmen's Bureau, established about a month before the end of the war, was to provide this support. In the confusion immediately after Appomattox the bureau fed refugees of both races and helped them to relocate. It helped freedmen secure jobs and then supervised employers to prevent the concealed reestablishment of slavery. The agency also established and maintained schools and hospitals, in both of which the South had previously been deficient. And it attempted to protect the legal equality of blacks and to prevent social discrimination. But the Freedmen's Bureau did not function equally well in all places. Some agents were corrupt; some abused black trust; some used the political possibilities inherent in the bureau to promote their own careers.

Indeed, no part of Radical Reconstruction was free of political overtones. Thaddeus Stevens, forthright as usual, declared that any program must "secure perpetual ascendancy to the party of the union. . . ." The Thirteenth Amendment, Stevens pointed out, abolished the former practice of counting a slave as three-fifths of a person; consequently, the South, once readmitted, would be entitled to more congressmen than had represented the section before the war. More congressmen meant more electoral votes, thus endangering Republican control of the White House, for Democrats could fuse their northern minority with white voters of the South to create a national majority. Stevens' uncompromising demand for black suffrage was a function of his desire to perpetuate Republicanism through southern support, as well as a result of egalitarian convictions.

Stevens was probably honest in his conviction that the republic could not be entrusted to "whitewashed rebels" and those whom he regarded as apologists for treason. But his motive may have been less disinterested than he acknowledged, and some Republicans certainly hoped to use Reconstruction to serve themselves. Stevens, for instance, owned an iron mine in southern Pennsylvania that Confederates had damaged extensively during the war; his interest in compensating northern property-holders for wartime destruction may have been related to his own losses. Like other owners of iron mines, Stevens was also a confirmed advocate of the protective tariff; protection seemed to depend upon continued Republican supremacy, for Democrats had traditionally opposed the policy.

As Stevens' motives were mixed, so too were those of other Republicans. They believed in the comprehensive legislative program that the fortuitous secession of the South had allowed them to bring about—protective tariff, the national banking system, the Homestead Act, and federal grants to transcontinental railroads. Before the war southern Democrats had blocked this legislation. Postwar Democrats were still hostile to some of it, and were also flirting with various forms of economic heresy, such as the notion that national bonds should be redeemed in the inflated greenbacks with which they had often been purchased, instead of in gold as the bond promised. Northern businessmen, whose opinions weighed heavily with Republican politicians, preferred fiscal orthodoxy. Moreover, the North glimpsed industrial affluence in the future; it seemed no time for economic experimentation.

The white South was equally unready for social experimentation, and Abraham Lincoln may have agreed. Once a staunch Whig, Lincoln perhaps hoped to gain support for gradual change from the same coalition of moderates in both sections that had sustained his old party. Some Radicals so mistrusted the President that they welcomed Vice-President Andrew Johnson's succession. For Johnson, a self-made man from Tennessee and a thoroughly Jacksonian Democrat, seemed to have nothing in common with those substantial southerners whom Lincoln hoped might become the pillars of a southern Republican party. But to the surprised dismay of the Radicals, Andrew Johnson, who had never acted like a southerner during the war, seemed to join the Confederacy after Appomattox.

PRESIDENTIAL RECONSTRUCTION

The new President began immediately to exercise his power to pardon almost without limit. While Radicals fumed because the recessed Congress could not respond, Johnson encouraged amnestied southerners to establish new constitutions, hold elections, and complete reconstruction before Congress resumed in December, 1865. He insisted only that the South ratify the Thirteenth Amendment, repudiate the Confederate debt, and repeal the ordinances of secession. White southerners hastened to adopt Johnson's terms, which were surely among the most generous ever imposed upon a defeated foe. Although the President withheld political rights from a few prominent former Confederates, voters all over the South chose many of the same men who had led them out of the Union to lead them back in. Mississippi and South Carolina elected governors who had been Confederate generals; Georgia chose Alexander Stephens, the Confederacy's Vice-President, for the Senate of the United States. Neither the southern voter nor Andrew Johnson made any tactful gesture to quiet mounting northern suspicion that a costly victory was being cheaply given away.

Blacks, Radicals, and others who had added equality to the war aims of emancipation and union thought Johnson's terms too generous. A group of blacks in Virginia, for example, pointed out that Johnson's plan would subordinate both black and white supporters of the Union to those former Confederates who were organizing and dominating the state government. The President had left them, these freedmen complained, "entirely at the mercy of . . . unconverted rebels." Maintaining that they were " 'sheep in the midst of wolves,' " the blacks asked for "an *equal chance* with the white *traitors*" whom the President had pardoned. Without the protection of the ballot and federal arms to enforce equal rights, the freedmen feared their former masters would make freedom "more intolerable" than slavery.

Those whom Johnson pardoned did indeed try to preserve as much as possible of the prewar social order. Most white southerners were not ready to believe that legal freedom made their former slaves the equals of other men. So the Black Codes that southern legislatures adopted to replace slave codes made only grudging concessions to the new free status of the blacks.

These Black Codes permitted blacks to form families. One black might marry another, and black parents were responsible for their children. Most statutes also defined the legal rights of freedmen and sometimes made the black man almost the equal of the white man in court, although in some states blacks could not testify against whites.

But equality did not go beyond these provisions. Apprenticeship regulations bounded the economic and social freedom of young blacks; courts had to order the apprenticeship of unemployed young freedmen and give preference to their former masters. The resulting arrangement often differed little from slavery. Vagrancy regulations and laws forbidding disorderly conduct gave enforcement officers wide discretion and restricted the social and economic life of black adults. Any Mississippi black who lacked regular employment or could not pay the poll tax was guilty of vagrancy. Those convicted could be leased to employers who paid fines and costs; former masters again had preference and the result again might be only technically distinguishable from bondage. Even if a black obeyed all these statutes, other laws kept him out of the white community. The only black passengers permitted in first-class railroad cars in Mississippi, for instance, were maids, who were allowed to wait on their white mistresses.

The freedman's lack of land and money reinforced those provisions of the Black Codes that limited his mobility. Any black who lacked a contract certifying steady employment had to have a license. Contracts often specified annual wage payments, a practice that forced the employee into debt for expenses incurred while earning the first year's wage. And if he left his employer before the expiration of the year, he forfeited any wages earned up to that time.

RUIN IN DIXIE

Postwar economic distress impartially afflicted both black and white southerners and sharply limited the chance for anyone to get ahead. Losses, either through battle or through years of negligent cultivation, required capital to replace. Southern wealth had traditionally taken the form of land and slaves. Since slaves were gone, land had to serve as the basis for rebuilding southern prosperity. Yankee investors who might have advanced credit found their economic opportunity at home, where railroads and industry brought a larger and faster return at less risk than investment in southern agriculture.

Although some parts of the South escaped desolation, others had become wastelands. General Philip Sheridan's troops destroyed so much in the Shenandoah Valley that he boasted that even a crow would have to carry rations to survive a flight over the area. General William T. Sherman's army had left its mark along its route through Georgia and South Carolina. Where war had reached town, waste was sickeningly evident. One northern reporter described Charleston, South Carolina, as a city "of ruins, . . . of vacant houses, of widowed women, of rotting wharves, of deserted warehouses, of weed-wild gardens, of miles of grass-grown streets, of acres of pitiful and voiceful barrenness. . . ." But at least the houses and warehouses still stood in Charleston. Columbia, the same reporter noted, was a "wilderness of ruins, . . . blackened chimneys and crumbling walls." In the business district "not a store, office, or shop escaped; and for a distance of three-fourths of a mile on each of twelve streets, there was not a building left."

Damage in the countryside was less immediately visible, but not less economically severe. Even where plantation houses still stood, weeds ruined

Columbia, South Carolina, after the war

cotton fields as surely as they had Charleston's gardens. Throughout the rural South, men had to restore fertility to the soil, fences to the fields, and stock to the barns and to produce an initial crop for food and seed. When buildings had to be rebuilt, the hardship was compounded.

Some rural southerners at first avoided the task. To many newly emancipated blacks, freedom meant the right to leave the plantation, and this action upset the traditional pattern of southern agriculture. Gradually, sharecropping evolved to replace slavery as a method of harnessing labor. In this system, which spread throughout the South before 1880, impoverished landowners allowed impoverished tenant farmers of both races to work the land. Owner and laborer then shared the crop according to a formula that depended partly on prevailing rates in the community and partly on whether the tenant furnished his own seed and mule. Both parties often had to survive between harvests on credit advanced by the local store, so interest charges added to costs. Profits were frequently inadequate to carry either owner or tenant through the following season, when the cycle began again. In spite of important differences, sharecropping was in many respects more similar to prewar plantation agriculture than to farming in the rest of the nation.

Tenant farming enabled the South to use the land, but it produced a meager living for most southerners. The sharecropping system, like slavery,

A Georgia Plantation in 1860 and 1881

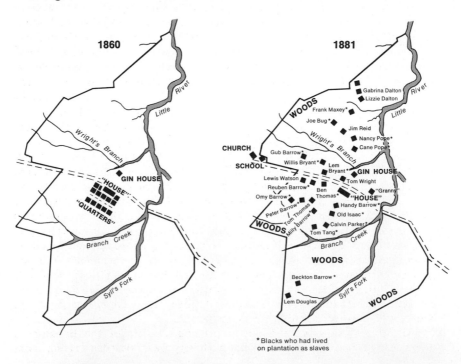

* Blacks who had lived
on plantation as slaves

discouraged agricultural innovation that might have helped the region develop more diversified farming. Sharecropping required the sale of a cash crop to pay bills already incurred. Creditors preferred the continued production of familiar crops to experimentation with new ones. Methods of cultivation were perhaps less efficient than those employed on large plantations before the Civil War. Plots were smaller; management was sometimes less competent and nearly always unable to purchase machinery, which was increasingly employed on northern farms.

CONGRESSIONAL RECONSTRUCTION

The economic transition from slavery to sharecropping was less dramatic and less frenzied than the political transition from Confederacy to reunited states. Once southern legislatures had been reestablished and federal elections held in 1865, Andrew Johnson was anxious to welcome the states back into the Union. Johnson's readiness to readmit the South was not shared by Congress, whose reaction to the Black Codes was prompt and hostile. Even Republican moderates were unconvinced that the governments Johnson had approved represented loyal, reformed, and contrite southerners.

Radicals renounced Johnson's work as a sham and urged Congress to undertake genuine reconstruction. The rebels had proudly reestablished "'the white man's Government,'" Thaddeus Stevens reported, and Congress should resolutely prove that such governments were entirely unacceptable components of the federal republic. Demagogues, including "some high in authority," he continued, with a barbed reference to the President, had appealed to the "lowest prejudices of the ignorant" to maintain the dominance of southern whites. Stevens held that the white race had "no exclusive right forever to rule this nation," nor could it convert "other races and nations and colors" to mere subjects. He did not shrink from the conclusion: this nation, he said, must be "the Government of all men alike. . . ."

Most Republicans stopped short of Stevens' stand. Yet if they were not ready to admit the black man to full political equality, as Stevens demanded, they did insist on more change than Johnson had required. So, in December, 1865, Congress refused to let southern legislators take the oath and sent them home. Congress then began work on two bills and a proposed constitutional amendment that became the congressional terms for reunion. The President vetoed both bills and encouraged those who opposed the amendment. His intransigence blighted any hope for a compromise program, for when moderate Republicans were forced to choose between Stevens' radicalism and the unreconstructed white governments Johnson had permitted, they chose radicalism. Andrew Johnson's political ineptitude and the adamant refusal of white southerners to concede to the blacks more than technical emancipation eventually drove the Republican party to Thaddeus Stevens and military reconstruction.

Moderates began with a bill to prolong the life of the Freedmen's Bureau and to give it a quasi-judicial authority over disputes arising from discrimination or denial of civil rights. The bill deprived state courts of jurisdiction in such cases, and specifically contradicted southern black codes by making punishable the sort of discrimination they permitted. Although the bill's sponsors thought they had secured the President's approval, Johnson vetoed the measure in February, 1866. The bureau, the President held, had grown out of the war's emergency and was based on the constitutional grant of power for war, which Congress could not legitimately invoke in peace. Once ordinary institutions, including civil courts, were reestablished, the bureau should disband.

Congress could not immediately assemble the majority necessary to override Johnson's veto, and moderates tried again to resolve the impasse with the Civil Rights Bill of 1866. The bill declared blacks to be citizens of the United States, thus burying the Dred Scott decision, and guaranteed "the full and equal benefit of all laws . . . for the security of person or property" to black citizens. Federal courts were to have jurisdiction over cases in which citizens had been deprived of equal rights. The bill received the support of every Republican in the House and all but three in the Senate. And Andrew Johnson vetoed it because it infringed the reserved powers of the states.

This time Congress overrode the veto and, for good measure, salvaged the Freedmen's Bureau bill too. To preserve its handiwork, Congress framed the constitutional amendment that eventually became the Fourteenth, which confirmed the status of the blacks as citizens and prohibited state legislation that denied equal legal protection to all citizens. Johnson could not prevent the submission of the amendment to the states, but his hostility encouraged southern states to reject it and temporarily blocked ratification. Tennessee, the President's own state, ratified the amendment and was rewarded by full restoration to the Union. Other southerners rejected the amendment and waited.

They waited too long, for the Congress that assembled in 1867 raised the price of readmission. In the crucial congressional election of 1866 Andrew Johnson had taken his cause to the country. His performance on the stump struck people as undignified and seemed as inept as his performance in the White House. Voters sent a new Congress to Washington with enough Radical votes to overwhelm the President.

The Radicals lost no time. In 1867 Congress passed a Reconstruction Act that combined ten southern states into five military districts and subordinated state governments to military commanders. The governments and constitutions Johnson had approved in 1865 were to be discarded and new constitutions granting suffrage to blacks and guaranteeing their equality were to be established. This legislation unquestionably mocked the traditional rights of the states, as both Johnson and the South claimed. The Radicals, however, were trying to crush traditions and had minimal interest in the constitutional pretenses of the defeated section. Radicals counted the doctrine of state rights an unmourned casualty of the Civil War.

Congress abridged the President's powers, as it had the rights of the states. Johnson's power to direct the army was limited by a requirement that all orders be issued through the General of the Army, who could not be removed or reassigned without the Senate's consent. The Tenure of Office Act required the Senate's approval for removal of any official for whom senatorial confirmation was necessary. Radicals hoped thereby to protect Secretary of War Edwin Stanton, who opposed the President's program, and whose support for military reconstruction was crucial.

The Radicals then turned to impeachment, both to remove the stubborn President and to warn future presidents. The charge against Johnson specified eleven offenses, most of which arose from his attempt to remove Stanton from the Cabinet. But, Thaddeus Stevens confessed, he did not mean to impeach the President for any particular offense or even for all of them together. Stevens meant to banish Johnson for his political mistakes, not for moral or legal lapses. Stevens wanted nothing less than to subordinate the President to Congress—to make future Presidents responsible to future Congresses—and impeachment was the means to his end.

The House debated all of Andrew Johnson's alleged crimes: his partiality toward the South, his public disrespect of Congress and its leadership, his drunken inauguration as Vice-President, his alleged complicity in Lincoln's assassination, and his deliberate violations of the Tenure of Office Act. The President was acquitted partly because the Senate found the bill of particulars too flimsy a basis for so unprecedented a step and partly because a few senators decided to support the independence of the executive branch rather than establish a precedent that might lead to a ministry responsible to the legislature, as is a parliamentary cabinet. The margin in the Senate was slim; Johnson survived by one vote. Thirty-five Republicans voted to convict; twelve Democrats and seven Republicans found for the President. After the roll calls in the Senate, Washington ceased to be the main forum for debate over reconstruction.

Thaddeus Stevens summarizes
the case for Andrew Johnson's
impeachment.

RECONSTRUCTION—A SOUTHERN VIEW

Radical Reconstruction, so the legend runs, was an undignified, corrupt, expensive, regrettable social experiment from which enlightened white conservatives freed the South in 1877. Blacks, their venal northern allies the carpetbaggers, and a few unprincipled southern opportunists called scalawags looted southern treasuries, discredited themselves, and demonstrated that the freedmen had no political capacity. The return to white control, many Americans have complacently believed, preserved the South from bankruptcy and barbarism.

Until recently, Americans have used Radical Reconstruction to confirm racial stereotypes that developed in the seventeenth century and persist in the twentieth. A simple illustration of the nation's stern judgment of that reconstruction has been the connotation and currency of the term "Black Reconstruction" applied to the period. D. W. Griffith's classic film *Birth of a Nation*, released in 1915, portrays the Southern white as the victim of Reconstruction. The narratives of professional historians, less emotionally charged and incomparably more dull than Griffith's movie, have too often made the same point.

This belief, like most myths, has a factual basis. Reconstruction did bring unprecedented taxes to the southern states, and not all the money was honestly spent. Blacks did not universally resist financial temptation, nor were they always dignified and wise in their legislative deliberation. Illustrative statistics abound. Florida spent more for printing in 1869 than the entire state government had cost in 1860. Sometimes bookkeeping was so casual that even a legislature could not calculate the state's debt; according to one estimate, South Carolina's debt tripled in three years, while another figure indicated that it had increased nearly six times. South Carolina also maintained at public expense a luxurious restaurant and bar that impartially dispensed imported delicacies to both black and white legislators.

But the term "Black Reconstruction" is misleading. Only in South Carolina did blacks ever become a majority of the legislature. They held high office elsewhere in the South—Mississippi sent two black senators to Washington—but they were by no means so dominant as the term "Black Reconstruction" implies. Many white officeholders, to be sure, did not belong to the social class that had ruled the prewar South; some were recently transplanted northerners, known as carpetbaggers. These white politicians had to have black support to succeed, but the simplistic picture of black rule is incorrect.

Nor is the myth of corrupt extravagance entirely justified. Rebuilding after a war is always expensive, and taxpayers always resent the bill. Further, Reconstruction governments not only had to restore public buildings and services; they also had to furnish new facilities and services that had been inadequate in most of the South. In many southern states, for example, public education for both races dates from these legislatures. For the first time, in some cases, states also accepted limited responsibility for the welfare of the indigent and sick. These were among the constructive accomplishments of the Reconstruction legislatures.

The notorious corruption of Reconstruction often came from the attempt by ambitious southerners to bring to the area the blessings of railroads and factories. Only the state commanded enough credit to entice the railroads that seemed to be the indispensable beginning of prosperity. Southern states issued bonds to finance railroad construction, but the proceeds sometimes vanished before the rails were laid. Fraud in the development of the American rail net was not peculiar to the South; in other states as well, public funds were converted to private use and politicians occasionally pocketed "fees" that might more candidly have been called bribes. Nor were corrupted legislatures confined to the South in the post–Civil War era. The peculation of southern legislators was trifling by comparison with scandals in the Grant administration.

Finally, not all corrupt southerners were black. Although some black politicians accepted bribes and some misused public funds, none stole as much as the white treasurer of Mississippi embezzled immediately after the state was supposedly saved from the irresponsible blacks. And for every purchased politician, there must have been a buyer. The fast-buck promoters of railroads and industries were whites, not blacks, few of whom were enriched by the plunder they had supposedly secured from public treasuries.

RECONSTRUCTION ENDS

Most southern whites resented any sign of racial equality and found black political participation particularly threatening. Although the Fourteenth Amendment extended most rights of citizenship to blacks and the Fifteenth Amendment gave them the franchise, white southerners did not always abide by these provisions. As Congress readmitted southern states to full membership in the union, the Ku Klux Klan and other terrorist bands perfected new ways to return the black man as nearly as possible to his old bondage.

These groups adopted mystifying hierarchies, rituals, and regalia, but no mystery shrouded their central purpose: they proposed to reestablish white supremacy by terrifying the blacks into giving up their quest for equality. The Klan and its imitators used direct, brutal, and highly visible methods: torch, lash, and rope were standard equipment. A frightened Louisiana tax collector wrote a northern senator that thirty-eight blacks in his district had recently met violent death. The lives of the "few white Republicans now left," he continued, were jeopardized. The official asked urgently for federal intervention, a plea that Congress met with the Ku Klux Klan Acts, or the "Force Acts," of 1870 and 1871. These measures set stiff penalties for those convicted of interfering with the right of any citizen to vote and permitted the use of troops against terrorists, as if they constituted a renewed Confederate rebellion.

The Klan was no match for the army; while troops remained in the

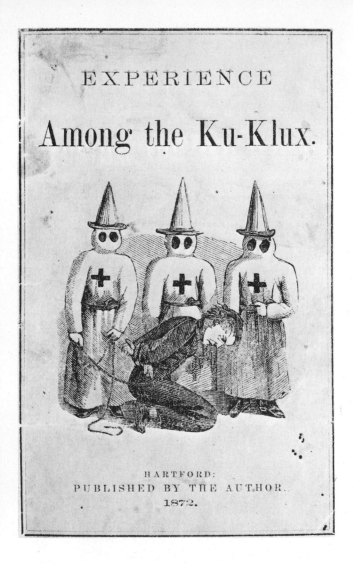

EXPERIENCE Among the Ku-Klux.

HARTFORD:
PUBLISHED BY THE AUTHOR.
1872.

South, federal law was outwardly obeyed. Had vigilant national administrations kept garrisons in the South for a generation, perhaps an equitably biracial society might have developed, even if racism remained. But within a decade after Appomattox, northern voters' interest in Reconstruction dwindled. Rutherford B. Hayes, the Republican presidential nominee in 1876, favored removing the occupying forces from the three unreconstructed states. His party ran its standard campaign, which blended emotional appeals to Union veterans with denunciation of Democratic "treason,"—a tactic known as "waving the 'bloody shirt' "—but this emotional Radicalism no longer produced a political mandate.

The voters in 1876 did not even produce a clear decision. The majority of the popular vote went to the Democratic candidate, Samuel J. Tilden, a financially conservative governor of New York who had successfully battled the notoriously corrupt Tweed Ring. Republicans conceded Tilden 184 electoral votes, while Hayes had won only 165 for certain. But Republicans also claimed the nineteen contested electoral votes from Louisiana, Florida, and South Carolina, where fraud and federal troops raised the Republican total, and one disputed vote of Oregon that had been awarded to Tilden on a legal technicality. Since the contested electors could determine the winner, public dispute was bitter and private bargaining intense.

To decide the dispute, Congress established a presumably bipartisan commission consisting of five members each from the House, Senate, and Supreme Court. The appearance of impartiality disappeared when the commission's one uncommitted member withdrew and was replaced by a convinced Republican. There was chicanery and intimidation on both sides, but the commission's award of all twenty votes to Hayes was unquestionably partisan and probably unjust.

Republicans paid a political price for the White House. Southern Democrats won assurance that federal funds would become available for construction of southern railroads, for improvements to southern harbors, and for projects that would make southern rivers more navigable and less apt to flood the countryside. In addition to capital for internal improvements, white southerners were to be given the respectability (and the salaries) of federal jobs. Hayes appointed David M. Key, a former Whig from Tennessee, as Postmaster General, the traditional post for the adminis-

The Election of 1876

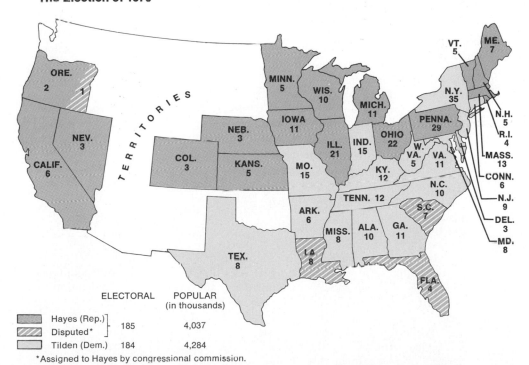

	ELECTORAL	POPULAR (in thousands)
Hayes (Rep.) Disputed*	185	4,037
Tilden (Dem.)	184	4,284

*Assigned to Hayes by congressional commission.

tration's patronage broker. Finally, civil government was restored through-out the South when Hayes recalled the last of the troops.

The experiment in Radical Reconstruction was over. Although the settlement in 1877 meant different things to different people, it clearly signalled a return to the politics of compromise. Republicans probably hoped that conciliation would persuade conservative southerners to make common cause with conservatives to the north. The promised flow of federal capital seemed to southerners to herald a "New South," where industry and transportation would complement agriculture and produce unparalleled prosperity. For blacks, however, the New South turned out to be quite like the old.

The tragedy of the Reconstruction is that so little was permanently accomplished. White southerners naturally wanted to preserve what they could of the sentimentalized past in which so many had taken refuge. Some were deceitful and harsh; most were unyielding on the central issue of white supremacy. Blacks understandably wanted to become wholly free Americans. In the attempt some were foolish and some corrupt, but most were humbly patient. Radicals wanted to reconstruct the South. Most expected the process to assure continued Republican supremacy; some intended to get rich; others meant to do full justice to the blacks. But Radicals retired or died, and their party soon found other causes more congenial than racial equality.

THE NEW SOUTH

Even while the politicians were preoccupied with Reconstruction, most of the rest of the nation had more important business to attend to. The North's business of the moment was industrialization. Prophets of the New South, like Henry Grady, editor of the Atlanta *Constitution,* urged their section also to pursue the profits of commercial enterprise and the promise of industrial plenty. Before 1900, the essential transportation was available; southern railroad mileage more than doubled in the 1880s alone, far exceed-ing growth in the rest of the nation. The pace of southern industrial devel-opment, though impressive, was less rapid.

Southern industry processed the region's agricultural staples and exploited such natural resources as bauxite, sulphur, and the oil of Texas and Oklahoma. Coal and iron deposits made Birmingham a major center for the production of pig iron. The American Tobacco Company, which James Buchanan Duke organized in North Carolina in 1890, brought new machines and new marketing techniques to one of the South's oldest crops. Textile mills sprang up in Georgia, Alabama, and the Carolinas, taking advantage of cheap labor and eliminating the need for transportation of raw cotton to northern mills. In 1900 investment in southern textile fac-tories had increased seven times over the total for 1880.

While the South wooed industry, tenant farming continued to burden the agricultural base of the economy. In some parts of Georgia, perhaps 1 percent of black farmers owned land in 1880; the blacks' share of total

Tenancy on Southern Farms

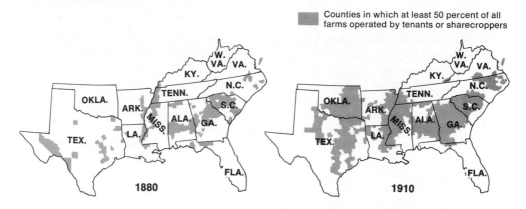

Counties in which at least 50 percent of all farms operated by tenants or sharecroppers

1880

1910

wealth in stock and soil was probably even smaller. Absentee land owner-ship and soil depletion through cash-crop farming increased along with sharecropping after Reconstruction. The lack of capital to buy fertilizer or to enable a shift to other crops doomed the South to soil-mining that could only bring diminishing yields and rural penury.

And the racial dilemma persisted with the poverty. The distinction between sharecropping and bondage was not apparent to many blacks. Blows hurt both pride and body, whether delivered by masters to slaves or by Klansmen to freedmen. Lacking troops to ensure equality, Hayes and his successors exhorted the South to respect the amendments and the civil rights laws, but presidential pleas were less effective than force. The "Redeemers," conservatives who ran the South for a generation after 1877, did not immediately disfranchise and segregate the black man. Rather they secured political support from freedmen, with promises, polite words, and a few local offices. Black support, in turn, helped these conservatives retain control when discontented whites in the 1880s and 1890s demanded increased public services, such as new schools. As rivalry among whites grew sharper, the votes of blacks in some areas were bought more or less openly, while intimidation in other places kept blacks at home on election day. When an honest count in a free election could no longer be assumed, white southerners blamed blacks, whose support was being corruptly sought, rather than white politicians who profited from public office. So the black man lost his right to vote in the cause of reform and honest elections; black men were disfranchised so that white men would no longer have to count one another out.

The North acquiesced to disfranchisement with only occasional bursts of self-righteous outrage. While in the House, James A. Garfield three times introduced bills to reduce the number of congressmen from southern states as the Fourteenth Amendment required. Garfield's bills failed to pass, and he dropped the crusade before he became President in 1881. In 1890, Henry Cabot Lodge, a young Republican congressman from Massachusetts, spon-sored a bill to permit federal supervision of federal elections. Some Repub-licans hoped, as had their predecessors during Reconstruction, to break the Democratic hold on the South with the black vote. But the Lodge bill failed to pass, and northern interest in helping southern blacks vote died with it.

One important northern newspaper consoled its readers with the observation that disfranchisement by law was less wrong than disfranchisement through terror.

The threat of renewed federal supervision made the South hasten to find legal means for securing exclusive white control of the political process. Between 1890 and 1905, various methods of restricting black suffrage were proposed, refined, and adopted. Some states used property qualifications and poll taxes, but these devices also excluded a great many poor whites. Literacy tests or tests requiring an "understanding" of selected passages from the state or national constitution left more discretion to the local examiners who administered the test. Louisiana permitted an exemption from such tests for those entitled to vote on January 1, 1867, or for sons and grandsons of such voters. Because blacks did not vote before the Reconstruction Act of March, 1867, Louisiana's "grandfather clause" exempted only whites. The president of the convention that proposed the change admitted that it seemed a bit ridiculous. But, he asked, "Doesn't it let the white man vote and doesn't it stop the negro from voting, and isn't that what we came here for?" No one could quarrel with results: the number of registered black voters in Louisiana promptly fell from over 130,000 to 5,320.

Although the Supreme Court of the United States subsequently invalidated the crude "grandfather clause" technique, other methods of disfranchisement survived the Court's scrutiny. The Court was also tolerant of the growing southern demand for social separation of the races. In 1873, in the Slaughterhouse cases, which did not directly involve the rights of blacks, the Court held that the Fourteenth Amendment protected only those rights derived from federal citizenship. Most civil rights, the Court decided, derived from state citizenship, and a citizen must appeal to his state to protect them.

In the Civil Rights cases of 1883, the Court held that the Fourteenth Amendment only prevented the discriminatory political acts of states, and did not outlaw social discrimination by individuals. Congress had exceeded its authority, then, in passing the Civil Rights Act of 1875, which required individuals to furnish equal access to such public facilities as inns, theaters, and transportation. In spite of a prescient and persuasive dissent from Justice John Marshall Harlan, the Court told blacks to appeal to state legislatures to secure equal public accommodations.

The Court's decisions permitted discrimination on racial grounds; southern legislatures in the next two decades gradually required the practice. Separate sections of public buildings or vehicles, separate schools, churches, lodges, and jails kept the races from social contact. And in 1896 the Supreme Court, in *Plessy* v. *Ferguson*, again went along. So long as the facilities were substantially equal, even if separate, the Court said no rights were abridged. Separation did not imply inferiority, the Court held, nor could either the Constitution or legislation "eradicate racial instincts or . . . abolish distinctions based upon physical differences. . . ." Justice Harlan was still unconvinced. "Our Constitution," he wrote, "is color-blind. . . ." The pose of equal accommodations for black citizens he called a "thin disguise" that would neither "mislead any one, nor atone for the wrong this day done. . . ."

Even before the Court accepted segregation, Booker T. Washington, the respected head of Tuskeegee Institute, indicated the black man's acceptance. At the Atlanta Exposition, where the New South displayed its initiative and its produce, Washington gave a widely acclaimed speech in which he appealed to his fellow blacks to learn trades, to become producing members of society, to earn—not demand—equality. He asked whites for help, for employment, for a chance to hew the wood and draw the water of the New South. But discussion of social equality Washington branded "the extremest folly," and he seemed to accept the Jim Crow laws that were requiring racial separation. "In all things that are purely social," said Washington with a superb metaphor, "we can be as separate as the fingers, yet one as the hand in all things essential to mutual progress."

Washington specifically did not accept disfranchisement and opposed any measure that permitted "an ignorant and poverty-stricken white man to vote" while it kept a "black man in the same condition" from the polls. But whites heard only Washington's seeming renunciation of equality. This was one time when they took the black man at his word.

Suggested Reading

Walter L. Fleming's *A Documentary History of Reconstruction* (1960), compiled nearly seventy years ago, has been reprinted and contains extensive source material for a study of the period. Kenneth M. Stampp's *The Era of Reconstruction** (1965) is a distinguished interpretive work that surveys the period, as does John Hope Franklin's *Reconstruction** (1962), and an older account by Paul H. Buck, *The Road to Reunion** (1937).

More specialized than these books are Howard K. Beale, *The Critical Year* (1930), which focuses on the election of 1866, C. Vann Woodward, *Reunion and Reaction** (1951), which analyzes the Compromise of 1877, and Joel R. Williamson, *After Slavery** (1965), which deals with the progress of the freedmen. W. E. Burghardt DuBois, *Black Reconstruction** (1935), stresses the positive accomplishments of the Radicals of both races. Fawn Brodie, *Thaddeus Stevens** (1959), illuminates all of Radical Reconstruction. Eric L. McKitrick, *Andrew Johnson and Reconstruction** (1960), documents Johnson's political ineptitude. Thomas F. Gossett's *Race: The History of an Idea in America** (1963) is a social and intellectual history of racism. Booker T. Washington argues his views in *Up From Slavery** (1901). In *Origins of the New South** (1951) C. Vann Woodward carries the history of the South from Reconstruction into the twentieth century.

*Available in paperback edition

APPENDIX

THE DECLARATION OF INDEPENDENCE*

The unanimous Declaration of the thirteen United States of America.

When, in the Course of human events, it becomes necessary for one people to dissolve the political bands which have connected them with another, and to assume, among the Powers of the earth, the separate and equal station to which the Laws of Nature and of Nature's God entitle them, a decent respect to the opinions of mankind requires that they should declare the causes which impel them to the separation.

We hold these truths to be self-evident, that all men are created equal, that they are endowed by their Creator with certain unalienable Rights, that among these, are Life, Liberty, and the pursuit of Happiness. That, to secure these rights, Governments are instituted among Men, deriving their just Powers from the consent of the governed. That, whenever any form of Government becomes destructive of these ends, it is the Right of the People to alter or to abolish it, and to institute new Government, laying its foundation on such Principles, and organizing its Powers in such form, as to them shall seem most likely to effect their Safety and Happiness. Prudence, indeed, will dictate that Governments long established should not be changed for light and transient causes; and,

* The original spelling, capitalization, and punctuation have been retained.

accordingly, all experience hath shewn, that mankind are more disposed to suffer, while evils are sufferable, than to right themselves by abolishing the forms to which they are accustomed. But, when a long train of abuses and usurpations, pursuing invariably the same Object, evinces a design to reduce them under absolute Despotism, it is their right, it is their duty, to throw off such Government, and to provide new Guards for their future Security. Such has been the patient sufferance of these Colonies; and such is now the necessity which constrains them to alter their former Systems of Government. The history of the present King of Great Britain is a history of repeated injuries and usurpations, all having in direct object the establishment of an absolute Tyranny over these States. To prove this, let Facts be submitted to a candid world.

He has refused his Assent to Laws the most wholesome and necessary for the public good.

He has forbidden his Governors to pass Laws of immediate and pressing importance, unless suspended in their operation till his Assent should be obtained; and when so suspended, he has utterly neglected to attend to them.

He has refused to pass other Laws for the accommodation of large districts of People, unless those People would relinquish the right of Representation in the legislature; a right inestimable to them and formidable to tyrants only.

He has called together legislative bodies at places unusual, uncomfortable, and distant from the depository of their Public Records, for the sole Purpose of fatiguing them into compliance with his measures.

He has dissolved Representative Houses repeatedly, for opposing, with manly firmness, his invasions on the rights of the People.

He has refused for a long time, after such dissolutions, to cause others to be elected; whereby the Legislative Powers, incapable of Annihilation, have returned to the People at large for their exercise; the State remaining in the mean time exposed to all the dangers of invasion from without, and convulsions within.

He has endeavoured to prevent the Population of these States; for that purpose obstructing the Laws for Naturalization of Foreigners; refusing to pass others to encourage their migrations hither, and raising the conditions of new Appropriations of Lands.

He has obstructed the Administration of Justice, by refusing his Assent to Laws for establishing Judiciary Powers.

He has made Judges dependent on his Will alone, for the tenure of their offices, and the amount and payment of their salaries.

He has erected a multitude of New Offices, and sent hither swarms of Officers to harrass our People, and eat out their substance.

He has kept among us, in times of Peace, Standing Armies, without the Consent of our legislatures.

He has affected to render the Military independent of and superior to the Civil Power.

He has combined with others to subject us to a jurisdiction foreign to our constitution, and unacknowledged by our laws; giving his Assent to their Acts of pretended Legislation:

For quartering large bodies of armed troops among us:

For protecting them, by a mock Trial, from Punishment for any Murders which they should commit on the Inhabitants of these States:

For cutting off our Trade with all parts of the world:

For imposing Taxes on us without our Consent:

For depriving us, in many cases, of the benefits of Trial by Jury:

For transporting us beyond Seas to be tried for pretended offences:

For abolishing the free System of English Laws in a neighbouring province, establishing therein an Arbitrary government, and enlarging its Boundaries, so as to render it at once an example and fit instrument for introducing the same absolute rule into these Colonies:

For taking away our Charters, abolishing our most valuable Laws, and altering fundamentally the Forms of our Governments:

For suspending our own Legislatures, and declaring themselves invested with Power to legislate for us in all cases whatsoever.

He has abdicated Government here, by declaring us out of his protection, and waging War against us.

He has plundered our seas, ravaged our Coasts, burnt our towns, and destroyed the Lives of our People.

He is at this time transporting large Armies of foreign Mercenaries to compleat the works of death, desolation and tyranny, already begun with circumstances of Cruelty and perfidy scarcely paralleled in the most barbarous ages, and totally unworthy the Head of a civilized nation.

He has constrained our fellow Citizens, taken Captive on the high Seas, to bear Arms against their Country, to become the executioners of their friends and Brethren, or to fall themselves by their Hands.

He has excited domestic insurrections amongst us, and has endeavoured to bring on the inhabitants of our frontiers, the merciless Indian Savages, whose known rule of warfare, is an undistinguished destruction of all ages, sexes and conditions.

In every stage of these Oppressions, We have Petitioned for Redress, in the most humble terms: Our repeated Petitions, have been answered only by repeated injury. A Prince, whose character is thus marked by every act which may define a Tyrant, is unfit to be the ruler of a free People.

Nor have We been wanting in attentions to our British brethren. We have warned them from time to time of attempts by their legislature to extend an unwarrantable jurisdiction over us. We have reminded them of the circumstances of our emigration and settlement here. We have appealed to their native justice and magnanimity, and we have conjured them by the ties of our common kindred, to disavow these usurpations, which, would inevitably interrupt our connexions and correspondence. They too have been deaf to the voice of justice and consanguinity. We must, therefore, acquiesce in the necessity, which denounces our Separation, and hold them, as we hold the rest of mankind, Enemies in war, in Peace Friends.

WE, THEREFORE, the Representatives of the UNITED STATES OF AMERICA, in GENERAL CONGRESS assembled, appealing to the Supreme Judge of the World for the rectitude of our intentions, DO, in the Name, and by Authority of the good People of these Colonies, solemnly PUBLISH and DECLARE, That these United Colonies are, and of Right, ought to be FREE AND INDEPENDENT STATES; that they are Absolved from all Allegiance to the British Crown, and that all political connexion between them and the State of Great Britain, is and ought to be totally dissolved; and that, as FREE and INDEPENDENT STATES, they have full Power to levy War, conclude Peace, contract Alliances, establish Commerce, and to do all other Acts and Things which INDEPENDENT STATES may of right do. AND for the support of this Declaration, with a firm reliance on the protection of divine Providence, we mutually pledge to each other our Lives, our Fortunes, and our sacred Honour.

THE CONSTITUTION

OF THE UNITED STATES OF AMERICA*

We the people of the United States, in Order to form a more perfect Union, establish Justice, insure domestic Tranquility, provide for the common defence, promote the general Welfare, and secure the Blessings of Liberty to ourselves and our Posterity, do ordain and establish this Constitution for the United States of America.

ARTICLE I

Section 1. All legislative Powers herein granted shall be vested in a Congress of the United States, which shall consist of a Senate and House of Representatives.

Section 2. The House of Representatives shall be composed of Members chosen every second Year by the People of the several States, and the Electors in each State shall have the Qualifications requisite for Electors of the most numerous Branch of the State Legislature.

No Person shall be a Representative who shall not have attained to the Age of twenty-five Years, and been seven Years a Citizen of the United States, and who shall not, when elected, be an Inhabitant of that state in which he shall be chosen.

[Representatives and direct Taxes shall be apportioned among the several States which may be included within this Union, according to their respective Numbers, which shall be determined by adding to the whole Number of free Persons, including those bound to Service for a Term of Years, and excluding Indians not taxed, three fifths of all

---

* The Constitution and all amendments are shown in their original form. Parts that have been amended or superseded are bracketed and explained in the footnotes.

other Persons.][1] The actual Enumeration shall be made within three Years after the first Meeting of the Congress of the United States, and within every subsequent Term of ten Years, in such Manner as they shall by Law direct. The Number of Representatives shall not exceed one for every thirty Thousand, but each State shall have at Least one Representative; and until such enumeration shall be made, the State of New Hampshire shall be entitled to chuse three, Massachusetts eight, Rhode-Island and Providence Plantations one, Connecticut five, New-York six, New Jersey four, Pennsylvania eight, Delaware one, Maryland six, Virginia ten, North Carolina five, South Carolina five, and Georgia three.

When vacancies happen in the Representation from any State, the Executive Authority thereof shall issue Writs of Election to fill such Vacancies.

The House of Representatives shall chuse their Speaker and other Officers; and shall have the sole Power of Impeachment.

Section 3. The Senate of the United States shall be composed of two Senators from each State, [chosen by the Legislature thereof,][2] for six Years; and each Senator shall have one Vote.

Immediately after they shall be assembled in Consequence of the first Election, they shall be divided as equally as may be into three Classes. The Seats of the Senators of the first Class shall be vacated at the Expiration of the second Year, of the Second Class at the Expiration of the fourth Year, and of the third Class at the Expiration of the sixth Year, so that one-third may be chosen every second Year; [and if Vacancies happen by Resignation, or otherwise, during the Recess of the Legislature of any State, the Executive thereof may make temporary Appointments until the next Meeting of the Legislature, which shall then fill such Vacancies].[3]

No Person shall be a Senator who shall not have attained to the Age of thirty Years, and been nine Years a Citizen of the United States, and who shall not, when elected, be an Inhabitant of that State in which he shall be chosen.

The Vice-President of the United States shall be President of the Senate, but shall have no vote, unless they be equally divided.

The Senate shall chuse their other Officers, and also a President pro tempore, in the absence of the Vice-President, or when he shall exercise the Office of the President of the United States.

The Senate shall have the sole Power to try all Impeachments. When sitting for that purpose, they shall be on Oath or Affirmation. When the President of the United States is tried, the Chief Justice shall preside. And no person shall be convicted without the Concurrence of two thirds of the Members present.

Judgment in Cases of Impeachment shall not extend further than to removal from Office, and disqualification to hold and enjoy any Office of honor, Trust, or Profit under the United States: but the Party con-

---

[1] Modified by the Fourteenth and Sixteenth amendments.

[2] Superseded by the Seventeenth Amendment.

[3] Modified by the Seventeenth Amendment.

victed shall nevertheless be liable and subject to Indictment, Trial, Judgment, and Punishment, according to Law.

Section 4. The Times, Places and Manner of holding Elections for Senators and Representatives, shall be prescribed in each state by the Legislature thereof; but the Congress may at any time by Law make or alter such Regulations, except as to the Places of Chusing Senators.

The Congress shall assemble at least once in every Year, and such Meeting shall [be on the first Monday in December,][4] unless they shall by Law appoint a different Day.

Section 5. Each House shall be the Judge of the Elections, Returns and Qualifications of its own Members, and a Majority of each shall constitute a Quorum to do Business; but a smaller number may adjourn from day to day, and may be authorized to compel the Attendance of absent Members, in such Manner, and under such Penalties, as each House may provide.

Each House may determine the Rules of its Proceedings, punish its Members for disorderly Behavior, and, with the Concurrence of two thirds, expel a Member.

Each House shall keep a Journal of its Proceedings, and from time to time publish the same, excepting such Parts as may in their Judgment require Secrecy; and the Yeas and Nays of the Members of either House on any question shall, at the Desire of one fifth of those Present, be entered on the Journal.

Neither House, during the Session of Congress, shall, without the Con-

sent of the other, adjourn for more than three days, nor to any other Place than that in which the two Houses shall be sitting.

Section 6. The Senators and Representatives shall receive a Compensation for their Services, to be ascertained by Law, and paid out of the Treasury of the United States. They shall in all Cases, except Treason, Felony, and Breach of the Peace, be privileged from Arrest during their Attendance at the Session of their respective Houses, and in going to and returning from the same; and for any Speech or Debate in either House, they shall not be questioned in any other Place.

No Senator or Representative shall, during the Time for which he was elected, be appointed to any civil Office under the Authority of the United States, which shall have been created, or the Emoluments whereof shall have been increased, during such time; and no Person holding any Office under the United States shall be a Member of either House during his continuance in Office.

Section 7. All Bills for raising Revenue shall originate in the House of Representatives; but the Senate may propose or concur with Amendments as on other bills.

Every Bill which shall have passed the House of Representatives and the Senate, shall, before it become a Law, be presented to the President of the United States: If he approve he shall sign it, but if not he shall return it, with his Objections, to that House in which it shall have originated, who shall enter the Objections at large on their Journal, and proceed to reconsider it. If after such Reconsideration two

---

[4] Superseded by the Twentieth Amendment.

thirds of that House shall agree to pass the bill, it shall be sent, together with the objections, to the other House, by which it shall likewise be reconsidered, and if approved by two thirds of that House, it shall become a Law. But in all such Cases the Votes of both Houses shall be determined by Yeas and Nays, and the Names of the Persons voting for and against the Bill shall be entered on the Journal of each House respectively. If any Bill shall not be returned by the President within ten Days (Sundays excepted) after it shall have been presented to him, the Same shall be a Law, in like Manner as if he had signed it, unless the Congress by their Adjournment prevent its Return, in which Case it shall not be a Law.

Every Order, Resolution, or Vote to which the Concurrence of the Senate and House of Representatives may be necessary (except on a question of Adjournment) shall be presented to the President of the United States; and before the Same shall take Effect, shall be approved by him, or being disapproved by him, shall be repassed by two thirds of the Senate and House of Representatives, according to the Rules and Limitations prescribed in the Case of a Bill.

Section 8. The Congress shall have Power To lay and collect Taxes, Duties, Imposts and Excises, to pay the Debts and provide for the common Defence and general Welfare of the United States; but all Duties, Imposts and Excises shall be uniform throughout the United States;

To borrow money on the credit of the United States;

To regulate Commerce with for-

eign Nations, and among the several States, and with the Indian Tribes;

To establish an uniform Rule of Naturalization, and uniform Laws on the subject of Bankruptcies throughout the United States;

To coin Money, regulate the Value thereof, and of foreign Coin, and fix the Standard of Weights and Measures;

To provide for the Punishment of counterfeiting the Securities and current Coin of the United States;

To establish Post Offices and post Roads;

To promote the Progress of Science and useful Arts, by securing for limited Times to Authors and Inventors the exclusive Right to their respective Writings and Discoveries;

To constitute Tribunals inferior to the Supreme Court;

To define and punish Piracies and Felonies committed on the high Seas, and Offenses against the Law of Nations;

To declare War, grant Letters of Marque and Reprisal, and make Rules concerning Captures on Land and Water;

To raise and support Armies, but no Appropriation of Money to that Use shall be for a longer Term than two Years;

To provide and maintain a Navy;

To make Rules for the Government and Regulation of the land and naval forces;

To provide for calling forth the Militia to execute the Laws of the Union, suppress Insurrections and repel Invasions;

To provide for organizing, arming, and disciplining the Militia, and for governing such Part of them as may be employed in the Service of the

United States, reserving to the States respectively, the Appointment of the Officers, and the Authority of training the Militia according to the discipline prescribed by Congress;

To exercise exclusive Legislation in all Cases whatsoever, over such District (not exceeding ten Miles square) as may, by Cession of particular States, and the acceptance of Congress, become the Seat of the Government of the United States, and to exercise like Authority over all Places purchased by the Consent of the Legislature of the State in which the Same shall be, for the Erection of Forts, Magazines, Arsenals, dock-Yards, and other needful Buildings;—And

To make all Laws which shall be necessary and proper for carrying into Execution the foregoing Powers, and all other Powers vested by this Constitution in the Government of the United States, or in any Department or Officer thereof.

Section 9. The Migration or Importation of such Persons as any of the States now existing shall think proper to admit shall not be prohibited by the Congress prior to the Year one thousand eight hundred and eight, but a tax or duty may be imposed on such Importation, not exeeding ten dollars for cach Person.

The privilege of the Writ of Habeas Corpus shall not be suspended, unless when in Cases of Rebellion or Invasion the public Safety may require it.

No Bill of Attainder or ex post facto Law shall be passed.

[No capitation, or other direct, Tax shall be laid unless in Proportion to the Census or Enumeration herein before directed to be taken.][5]

No Tax or Duty shall be laid on Articles exported from any State.

No Preference shall be given by any Regulation of Revenue to the Ports of one State over those of another: nor shall Vessels bound to, or from, one State, be obliged to enter, clear, or pay Duties in another.

No Money shall be drawn from the Treasury, but in Consequence of Appropriations made by Law; and a regular Statement and Account of the Receipts and Expenditures of all public Money shall be published from time to time.

No Title of Nobility shall be granted by the United States: And no Person holding any Office of Profit or Trust under them, shall, without the Consent of the Congress, accept of any present, Emolument, Office, or Title, of any kind whatever, from any King, Prince, or foreign State.

Section 10. No State shall enter into any Treaty, Alliance, or Confederation; grant Letters of Marque and Reprisal; coin Money; emit Bills of Credit; make any Thing but gold and silver Coin a Tender in Payment of Debts; pass any Bill of Attainder, ex post facto Law, or Law impairing the Obligation of Contracts, or grant any Title of Nobility.

No State shall, without the Consent of the Congress, lay any Imposts or Duties on Imports or Exports, except what may be absolutely necessary for executing its inspection Laws: and the net Produce of all Duties and Imposts, laid by any State on Imports or Exports, shall be for the Use of the Treasury

[5] Modified by the Sixteenth Amendment.

of the United States; and all such Laws shall be subject to the Revision and Control of the Congress.

No State shall, without the Consent of Congress, lay any duty of Tonnage, keep Troops, or Ships of War in time of Peace, enter into any Agreement or Compact with another State, or with a foreign Power, or engage in War, unless actually invaded, or in such imminent Danger as will not admit of delay.

ARTICLE II

Section 1. The executive Power shall be vested in a President of the United States of America. He shall hold his Office during the Term of four years, and, together with the Vice-President, chosen for the same Term, be elected, as follows:

Each State shall appoint, in such Manner as the Legislature thereof may direct, a Number of Electors, equal to the whole Number of Senators and Representatives to which the State may be entitled in the Congress: but no Senator or Representative, or Person holding an Office of Trust or Profit under the United States, shall be appointed an Elector.

[The Electors shall meet in their respective States, and vote by Ballot for two persons, of whom one at least shall not be an Inhabitant of the same State with themselves. And they shall make a List of all the Persons voted for, and of the Number of Votes for each; which List they shall sign and certify, and transmit sealed to the Seat of the Government of the United States, directed to the President of the Senate. The President of the Senate shall, in the Presence of the Senate and House of Representatives, open all the Certificates, and the Votes shall then be counted. The Person having the greatest Number of Votes shall be the President, if such Number be a Majority of the whole Number of Electors appointed; and if there be more than one who have such Majority, and have an equal Number of Votes, then the House of Representatives shall immediately chuse by Ballot one of them for President; and if no Person have a Majority, then from the five highest on the List the said House shall in like Manner chuse the President. But in chusing the President, the Votes shall be taken by States, the Representation from each State having one Vote; a quorum for this Purpose shall consist of a Member or Members from two-thirds of the States, and a Majority of all the States shall be necessary to a Choice. In every Case, after the Choice of the President, the Person having the greatest Number of Votes of the Electors shall be the Vice-President. But if there should remain two or more who have equal votes, the Senate shall chuse from them by Ballot the Vice-President.][6]

The Congress may determine the Time of chusing the Electors, and the Day on which they shall give their Votes; which Day shall be the same throughout the United States.

No person except a natural-born Citizen, or a Citizen of the United States, at the time of the Adoption of this Constitution, shall be eligible to the Office of President; neither shall any Person be eligible to that Office who shall not have attained to the Age of thirty-five years, and

[6] Superseded by the Twelfth Amendment.

been fourteen Years a Resident within the United States.

[In Case of the Removal of the President from Office, or of his Death, Resignation, or Inability to discharge the Powers and Duties of the said Office, the same shall devolve on the Vice-President, and the Congress may by Law provide for the Case of Removal, Death, Resignation, or Inability, both of the President and Vice-President, declaring what Officer shall then act as President, and such Officer shall act accordingly, until the disability be removed, or a President shall be elected.][7]

The President shall, at stated Times, receive for his Services a Compensation, which shall neither be increased nor diminished during the Period for which he shall have been elected, and he shall not receive within that Period any other Emolument from the United States, or any of them.

Before he enter on the execution of his Office, he shall take the following Oath or Affirmation:—"I do solemnly swear (or affirm) that I will faithfully execute the Office of President of the United States, and will, to the best of my Ability, preserve, protect, and defend the Constitution of the United States."

Section 2. The President shall be Commander in Chief of the Army and Navy of the United States, and of the Militia of the several States, when called into the actual Service of the United States; he may require the Opinion, in writing, of the principal Officer in each of the executive Departments, upon any subject relating to the Duties of their respec-

[7] Modified by the Twenty-fifth Amendment.

tive Offices, and he shall have Power to Grant Reprieves and Pardons for Offenses against the United States, except in Cases of Impeachment.

He shall have Power, by and with the Advice and Consent of the Senate, to make Treaties, provided two thirds of the Senators present concur; and he shall nominate, and by and with the Advice and Consent of the Senate, shall appoint Ambassadors, other public Ministers and Consuls, Judges of the supreme Court, and all other Officers of the United States, whose Appointments are not herein otherwise provided for, and which shall be established by Law: but the Congress may by Law vest the Appointment of such inferior Officers, as they think proper, in the President alone, in the Courts of Law, or in the Heads of Departments.

The President shall have Power to fill up all Vacancies that may happen during the Recess of the Senate, by granting Commissions which shall expire at the End of their next Session.

Section 3. He shall from time to time give to the Congress Information of the State of the Union, and recommend to their Consideration such Measures as he shall judge necessary and expedient; he may, on extraordinary occasions, convene both Houses, or either of them, and in Case of Disagreement between them, with respect to the Time of Adjournment, he may adjourn them to such Time as he shall think proper; he shall receive Ambassadors and other public Ministers; he shall take Care that the Laws be faithfully executed, and shall Commission all the Officers of the United States.

Section 4. The President, Vice-President and all civil Officers of the United States, shall be removed from Office on Impeachment for, and Conviction of, Treason, Bribery, or other high Crimes and Misdemeanors.

ARTICLE III

Section 1. The judicial Power of the United States, shall be vested in one supreme Court, and in such inferior Courts as the Congress may from time to time ordain and establish. The Judges, both of the supreme and inferior Courts, shall hold their Offices during good Behaviour, and shall, at stated Times, receive for their Services, a Compensation, which shall not be diminished during their Continuance in Office.

Secion 2. The judicial Power shall extend to all Cases, in Law and Equity, arising under this Constitution, the Laws of the United States, and treaties made, or which shall be made, under their Authority;—to all Cases affecting ambassadors, other public ministers and consuls;—to all cases of admiralty and maritime Jurisdiction;—to Controversies to which the United States shall be a Party;—to Controversies between two or more States;—[between a State and Citizens of another State;]⁸—between Citizens of different States,—between Citizens of the same State claiming Lands under Grants of different States, and between a State, or the Citizens thereof, and foreign States, Citizens or Subjects.

In all Cases affecting Ambassa-

⁸ Modified by the Eleventh Amendment.

dors, other public Ministers and Consuls, and those in which a State shall be Party, the supreme Court shall have original Jurisdiction. In all the other Cases before mentioned, the supreme Court shall have appellate Jurisdiction, both as to Law and Fact, with such Exceptions, and under such Regulations as the Congress shall make.

The trial of all Crimes, except in Cases of Impeachment, shall be by Jury; and such Trial shall be held in the State where the said Crimes shall have been committed; but when not committed within any State, the Trial shall be at such Place or Places as the Congress may by Law have directed.

Section 3. Treason against the United States, shall consist only in levying War against them, or in adhering to their Enemies, giving them Aid and Comfort. No Person shall be convicted of Treason unless on the Testimony of two Witnesses to the same overt Act, or on Confession in open Court.

The Congress shall have power to declare the Punishment of Treason, but no Attainder of Treason shall work Corruption of Blood, or Forfeiture except during the Life of the Person attainted.

ARTICLE IV

Section 1. Full Faith and Credit shall be given in each State to the public Acts, Records, and judicial Proceedings of every other State. And the Congress may by general Laws prescribe the Manner in which such Acts, Records and Proceedings shall be proved, and the Effect thereof.

Section 2. The Citizens of each State shall be entitled to all Privileges and Immunities of Citizens in the several States.

A Person charged in any State with Treason, Felony, or other Crime, who shall flee from Justice, and be found in another State, shall on demand of the executive Authority of the State from which he fled, be delivered up, to be removed to the State having Jurisdiction of the crime.

[No Person held to Service or Labour in one State, under the Laws thereof, escaping into another, shall, in Consequence of any Law or Regulation therein, be discharged from such Service or Labour, but shall be delivered up on Claim of the Party to whom such Service or Labour may be due.][9]

Section 3. New States may be admitted by the Congress into this Union; but no new State shall be formed or erected within the Jurisdiction of any other State; nor any State be formed by the Junction of two or more States, or parts of States, without the Consent of the Legislatures of the States concerned as well as of the Congress.

The Congress shall have Power to dispose of and make all needful Rules and Regulations respecting the Territory or other Property belonging to the United States; and nothing in this Constitution shall be so construed as to Prejudice any Claims of the United States, or of any particular State.

Section 4. The United States shall guarantee to every State in this Union a Republican Form of Government, and shall protect each of them against Invasion; and on Application of the Legislature, or of

[9] Superseded by the Thirteenth Amendment.

the Executive (when the Legislature cannot be convened) against domestic Violence.

ARTICLE V

The Congress, whenever two-thirds of both Houses shall deem it necessary, shall propose Amendments to this Constitution, or, on the Application of the Legislatures of two-thirds of the several States, shall call a Convention for proposing Amendments, which, in either Case, shall be valid to all Intents and Purposes, as part of this Constitution, when ratified by the Legislatures of three-fourths of the several States, or by Conventions in three-fourths thereof, as the one or the other Mode of Ratification may be proposed by the Congress; Provided that no Amendment which may be made prior to the Year One thousand eight hundred and eight shall in any Manner affect the first and fourth Clauses in the Ninth Section of the first Article; and that no State, without its Consent, shall be deprived of its equal Suffrage in the Senate.

ARTICLE VI

All Debts contracted and Engagements entered into, before the Adoption of this Constitution, shall be as valid against the United States under this Constitution, as under the Confederation.

This Constitution, and the Laws of the United States which shall be made in Pursuance thereof; and all Treaties made, or which shall be made, under the Authority of the United States, shall be the supreme Law of the Land; and the Judges in every State shall be bound thereby, any Thing in the Constitution or

Laws of any State to the Contrary notwithstanding.

The Senators and Representatives before mentioned, and the Members of the several State Legislatures, and all executive and judicial Officers, both of the United States and of the several States, shall be bound by Oath or Affirmation to support this Constitution; but no religious Test shall ever be required as a qualification to any Office or public Trust under the United States.

ARTICLE VII

The Ratification of the Conventions of nine States shall be sufficient for the Establishment of this Constitution between the States so ratifying the same.

Done in Convention by the Unanimous Consent of the States present the Seventeenth Day of September in the Year of our Lord one thousand seven hundred and Eighty seven, and of the Independence of the United States of America the Twelfth. In Witness whereof We have hereunto subscribed our Names.

Articles in Addition to, and Amendment of, the Constitution of the United States of America, Proposed by Congress, and Ratified by the Legislatures of the Several States, Pursuant to the Fifth Article of the Original Constitution.

AMENDMENT I[10]

Congress shall make no law respecting an establishment of religion, or prohibiting the free exercise thereof; or abridging the freedom

[10] The first ten amendments were passed by Congress September 25, 1789. They were ratified by three-fourths of the states December 15, 1791.

of speech, or of the press; or the right of the people peaceably to assemble, and to petition the Government for a redress of grievances.

AMENDMENT II

A well regulated Militia, being necessary to the security of a free State, the right of the people to keep and bear Arms shall not be infringed.

AMENDMENT III

No Soldier shall, in time of peace, be quartered in any house, without the consent of the Owner, nor in time of war, but in a manner to be prescribed by law.

AMENDMENT IV

The right of the people to be secure in their persons, houses, papers, and effects, against unreasonable searches and seizures, shall not be violated, and no Warrants shall issue, but upon probable cause, supported by Oath or affirmation, and particularly describing the place to be searched, and the persons or things to be seized.

AMENDMENT V

No person shall be held to answer for a capital or otherwise infamous crime, unless on a presentment or indictment of a Grand Jury, except in cases arising in the land or naval forces, or in the Militia, when in actual service in time of War or public danger; nor shall any person be subject for the same offence to be twice put in jeopardy of life or limb; nor shall be compelled in any criminal case to be a witness against himself, nor be deprived of life, liberty, or property, without due process of law; nor shall private property be taken for public use, without just compensation.

AMENDMENT VI

In all criminal prosecutions, the accused shall enjoy the right to a speedy and public trial, by an impartial jury of the State and district wherein the crime shall have been committed, which district shall have been previously ascertained by law, and to be informed of the nature and cause of the accusation; to be confronted with the witnesses against him; to have compulsory process for obtaining witnesses in his favor, and to have the Assistance of Counsel for his defence.

AMENDMENT VII

In suits at common law, where the value in controversy shall exceed twenty dollars, the right of trial by jury shall be preserved, and no fact tried by a jury, shall be otherwise reexamined in any Court of the United States, than according to the rules of the common law.

AMENDMENT VIII

Excessive bail shall not be required, nor excessive fines imposed, nor cruel and unusual punishments inflicted.

AMENDMENT IX

The enumeration in the Constitution, of certain rights, shall not be construed to deny or disparage others retained by the people.

AMENDMENT X

The powers not delegated to the United States by the Constitution, nor prohibited by it to the States, are reserved to the States respectively, or to the people.

AMENDMENT XI (1798)[11]

The Judicial power of the United States shall not be construed to extend to any suit in law or equity, commenced or prosecuted against one of the United States by Citizens of another State, or by Citizens or Subjects of any Foreign State.

AMENDMENT XII (1804)

The Electors shall meet in their respective States and vote by ballot for President and Vice-President, one of whom, at least, shall not be an inhabitant of the same State with themselves; they shall name in their ballots the person voted for as President, and in distinct ballots the person voted for as Vice-President, and they shall make distinct lists of all persons voted for as President, and of all persons voted for as Vice-President, and of the number of votes for each, which lists they shall sign and certify, and transmit sealed to the seat of the government of the United States, directed to the President of the Senate;—The President of the Senate shall, in the presence of the Senate and House of Representatives, open all the certificates and the votes shall then be counted; —The person having the greatest number of votes for President, shall be the President, if such number be a majority of the whole number of Electors appointed; and if no person have such majority, then from the persons having the highest numbers not exceeding three on the list of those voted for as President, the House of Representatives shall choose immediately, by ballot, the President. But in choosing the President, the votes shall be taken by

[11] Date of ratification.

states, the representation from each state having one vote; a quorum for this purpose shall consist of a member or members from two-thirds of the states, and a majority of all the states shall be necessary to a choice. [And if the House of Representatives shall not choose a President whenever the right of choice shall devolve upon them, before the fourth day of March next following, then the Vice-President shall act as President, as in the case of the death or other constitutional disability of the President.][12]—The person having the greatest number of votes as Vice-President, shall be the Vice-President, if such number be a majority of the whole number of Electors appointed, and if no person have a majority, then from the two highest numbers on the list, the Senate shall choose the Vice-President; a quorum for the purpose shall consist of two-thirds of the whole number of Senators, and a majority of the whole number shall be necessary to a choice. But no person constitutionally ineligible to the office of President shall be eligible to that of Vice-President of the United States.

AMENDMENT XIII (1865)

Section 1. Neither slavery nor involuntary servitude, except as a punishment for crime whereof the party shall have been duly convicted, shall exist within the United States, or any place subject to their jurisdiction.

Section 2. Congress shall have power to enforce this article by appropriate legislation.

[12] Superseded by the Twentieth Amendment.

AMENDMENT XIV (1868)

Section 1. All persons born or naturalized in the United States, and subject to the jurisdiction thereof, are citizens of the United States and of the State wherein they reside. No State shall make or enforce any law which shall abridge the privileges or immunities of citizens of the United States; nor shall any State deprive any person of life, liberty, or property, without due process of law; nor deny to any person within its jurisdiction the equal protection of the laws.

Section 2. Representatives shall be apportioned among the several States according to their respective numbers, counting the whole number of persons in each State, excluding Indians not taxed. But when the right to vote at any election for the choice of electors for President and Vice-President of the United States, Representatives in Congress, the Executive and Judicial officers of a State, or the members of the Legislature thereof, is denied to any of the male inhabitants of such State, being twenty-one years of age, and citizens of the United States, or in any way abridged, except for participation in rebellion, or other crime, the basis of representation therein shall be reduced in the proportion which the number of such male citizens shall bear to the whole number of male citizens twenty-one years of age in such State.

Section 3. No person shall be a Senator or Representative in Congress, or elector of President and Vice-President, or hold any office, civil or military, under the United States, or under any State, who, having previously taken an oath, as a member of Congress, or as an officer of the United States, or as a member of any State legislature, or as an executive or judicial officer of any State, to support the Constitution of the United States, shall have engaged in insurrection or rebellion against the same, or given aid or comfort to the enemies thereof. But Congress may by a vote of two-thirds of each House, remove such disability.

Section 4. The validity of the public debt of the United States, authorized by law, including debts incurred for payment of pensions and bounties for services in suppressing insurrection or rebellion, shall not be questioned. But neither the United States nor any State shall assume or pay any debt or obligation incurred in aid of insurrection or rebellion against the United States, or any claim for the loss or emancipation of any slave; but all such debts, obligations, and claims shall be held illegal and void.

Section 5. The Congress shall have the power to enforce, by appropriate legislation, the provisions of this article.

AMENDMENT XV (1870)

Section 1. The right of citizens of the United States to vote shall not be denied or abridged by the United States or by any State on account of race, color, or previous condition of servitude—

Section 2. The Congress shall have power to enforce this article by appropriate legislation.

AMENDMENT XVI (1913)

The Congress shall have power to lay and collect taxes on incomes, from whatever source derived, without apportionment among the several States, and without regard to any census or enumeration.

AMENDMENT XVII (1913)

The Senate of the United States shall be composed of two Senators from each State, elected by the people thereof, for six years; and each Senator shall have one vote. The electors in each State shall have the qualifications requisite for electors of the most numerous branch of the State legislatures.

When vacancies happen in the representation of any State in the Senate, the executive authority of such State shall issue writs of election to fill such vacancies: *Provided,* That the legislature of any State may empower the executive thereof to make temporary appointments until the people fill the vacancies by election as the legislature may direct.

This amendment shall not be so construed as to affect the election or term of any Senator chosen before it becomes valid as part of the Constitution.

AMENDMENT XVIII (1919)[13]

Section 1. After one year from the ratification of this article the manufacture, sale, or transportation of intoxicating liquors within, the importation thereof into, or the exportation thereof from the United States and all territory subject to the jurisdiction thereof for beverage purposes is hereby prohibited.

Section 2. The Congress and the several States shall have concurrent power to enforce this article by appropriate legislation.

Section 3. This article shall be inoperative unless it shall have been

[13] Repealed by the Twenty-first Amendment.

ratified as an amendment to the Constitution by the legislatures of the several States, as provided in the Constitution, within seven years from the date of the submission hereof to the States by the Congress.

AMENDMENT XIX (1920)

The right of citizens of the United States to vote shall not be denied or abridged by the United States or by any State on account of sex.

Congress shall have power to enforce this article by appropriate legislation.

AMENDMENT XX (1933)

Section 1. The terms of the President and Vice-President shall end at noon on the 20th day of January, and the terms of Senators and Representatives at noon on the 3d day of January, of the years in which such terms would have ended if this article had not been ratified; and the terms of their successors shall then begin.

Section 2. The Congress shall assemble at least once in every year, and such meeting shall begin at noon on the 3d day of January, unless they shall by law appoint a different day.

Section 3. If, at the time fixed for the beginning of the term of the President, the President elect shall have died, the Vice-President elect shall become President. If a President shall not have been chosen before the time fixed for the beginning of his term, or if the President elect shall have failed to qualify, then the Vice-President elect shall act as President until a President shall have qualified; and the Congress may by law provide for the case wherein neither a President elect nor a Vice-President elect shall have qualified, declaring who shall then act as President, or the manner in which one who is to act shall be selected, and such person shall act accordingly until a President or Vice-President shall have qualified.

Section 4. The Congress may by law provide for the case of the death of any of the persons from whom the House of Representatives may choose a President whenever the right of choice shall have devolved upon them, and for the case of the death of any of the persons from whom the Senate may choose a Vice-President whenever the right of choice shall have devolved upon them.

Section 5. Sections 1 and 2 shall take effect on the 15th day of October following the ratification of this article.

Section 6. This article shall be inoperative unless it shall have been ratified as an amendment to the Constitution by the legislatures of three-fourths of the several States within seven years from the date of its submission.

AMENDMENT XXI (1933)

Section 1. The eighteenth article of amendment to the Constitution of the United States is hereby repealed.

Section 2. The transportation or importation into any State, Territory, or possession of the United States for delivery or use therein of intoxicating liquors, in violation of the laws thereof, is hereby prohibited.

Section 3. This article shall be inoperative unless it shall have been ratified as an amendment to the

Constitution by conventions in the several States, as provided in the Constitution, within seven years from the date of the submission hereof to the States by the Congress.

AMENDMENT XXII (1951)

No person shall be elected to the office of the President more than twice, and no person who has held the office of President, or acted as President, for more than two years of a term to which some other person was elected President shall be elected to the office of the President more than once.

But this Article shall not apply to any person holding the office of President when this Article was proposed by the Congress, and shall not prevent any person who may be holding the office of President, or acting as President, during the term within which this Article becomes operative from holding the office of President or acting as President during the remainder of such term.

AMENDMENT XXIII (1961)

Section 1. The District constituting the seat of Government of the United States shall appoint in such manner as the Congress may direct:

A number of electors of President and Vice President equal to the whole number of Senators and Representatives in Congress to which the District would be entitled if it were a State, but in no event more than the least populous State; they shall be in addition to those appointed by the States, but they shall be considered, for the purposes of the election of President and Vice-President, to be electors appointed by the State; and they shall meet in the District and perform such du-

ties as provided by the twelfth article of amendment.

Section 2. The Congress shall have power to enforce this article by appropriate legislation.

AMENDMENT XXIV (1964)

Section 1. The right of citizens of the United States to vote in any primary or other election for President or Vice-President, for electors for President or Vice-President, or for Senator or Representative in Congress, shall not be denied or abridged by the United States or any State by reason of failure to pay any poll tax or other tax.

Section 2. The Congress shall have power to enforce this article by appropriate legislation.

AMENDMENT XXV (1967)

Section 1. In case of the removal of the President from office or of his death or resignation, the Vice-President shall become President.

Section 2. Whenever there is a vacancy in the office of the Vice-President, the President shall nominate a Vice-President who shall take office upon confirmation by a majority vote of both Houses of Congress.

Section 3. Whenever the President transmits to the President pro tempore of the Senate and the Speaker of the House of Representatives his written declaration that he is unable to discharge the powers and duties of his office, and until he transmits to them a written declaration to the contrary, such powers and duties shall be discharged by the Vice-President as Acting President.

Section 4. Whether the Vice-President and a majority of either the principal officers of the executive department or of such other body as Congress may by law provide, transmit to the President pro tempore of the Senate and the Speaker of the House of Representatives their written declaration that the President is unable to discharge the powers and duties of his office, the Vice-President shall immediately assume the powers and duties of the office as Acting President.

Thereafter, when the President transmits to the President pro tempore of the Senate and the Speaker of the House of Representatives his written declaration that no inability exists, he shall resume the powers and duties of his office unless the Vice-President and a majority of either the principal officers of the executive department or of such other body as Congress may by law provide, transmit within four days to the President pro tempore of the Senate and the Speaker of the House of Representatives their written declaration that the President is unable to discharge the powers and duties of his office. Thereupon Congress shall decide the issue, assembling within forty-eight hours for that purpose if not in session. If the Congress, within twenty-one days after receipt of the latter written declaration, or, if Congress is not in session, within twenty-one days after Congress is required to assemble, determines by two-thirds vote of both Houses that the President is unable to discharge the powers and duties of his office, the Vice-President shall continue to discharge the same as Acting President; otherwise, the President shall resume the powers and duties of his office.

AMENDMENT XXVI (1971)

Section 1. The right of citizens of the United States, who are eighteen years of age or older, to vote shall not be denied or abridged by the United States or by any State on account of age.

Section 2. The Congress shall have power to enforce this article by appropriate legislation.

Presidential Elections (1789–1968)*

Year and number of states	Candidates	Parties	Popular vote	Electoral vote	Percentage of popular vote[1]
1789 (11)	George Washington	No party designations		69	
	John Adams			34	
	Minor Candidates			35	
1792 (15)	George Washington	No party designations		132	
	John Adams			77	
	George Clinton			50	
	Minor Candidates			5	
1796 (16)	John Adams	Federalist		71	
	Thomas Jefferson	Democratic-Republican		68	
	Thomas Pinckney	Federalist		59	
	Aaron Burr	Democratic-Republican		30	
	Minor Candidates			48	
1800 (16)	Thomas Jefferson	Democratic-Republican		73	
	Aaron Burr	Democratic-Republican		73	
	John Adams	Federalist		65	
	Charles C. Pinckney	Federalist		64	
	John Jay	Federalist		1	
1804 (17)	Thomas Jefferson	Democratic-Republican		162	
	Charles C. Pinckney	Federalist		14	
1808 (17)	James Madison	Democratic-Republican		122	
	Charles C. Pinckney	Federalist		47	
	George Clinton	Democratic-Republican		6	
1812 (18)	James Madison	Democratic-Republican		128	
	DeWitt Clinton	Federalist		89	
1816 (19)	James Monroe	Democratic-Republican		183	
	Rufus King	Federalist		34	
1820 (24)	James Monroe	Democratic-Republican		231	
	John Quincy Adams	Independent Republican		1	
1824 (24)	John Quincy Adams	Democratic-Republican	108,740	84	30.5
	Andrew Jackson	Democratic-Republican	153,544	99	43.1
	William H. Crawford	Democratic-Republican	46,618	41	13.1
	Henry Clay	Democratic-Republican	47,136	37	13.2
1828 (24)	Andrew Jackson	Democratic	647,286	178	56.0
	John Quincy Adams	National Republican	508,064	83	44.0

* Before the passage of the Twelfth Amendment in 1804, the Electoral College voted for two presidential candidates; the runner-up became Vice-President. Figures are from *Historical Statistics of the United States, Colonial Times to 1957* (1961), pp. 682–83; the U.S. Department of Justice; and *New York Times Encyclopedic Almanac, 1972,* p. 101.

[1] Candidates receiving less than 1 per cent of the popular vote have been omitted. For that reason the percentage of popular vote given for any election year may not total 100 per cent.

Year and number of states	Candidates	Parties	Popular vote	Electoral vote	Percentage of popular vote
1832 (24)	Andrew Jackson	Democratic	687,502	219	55.0
	Henry Clay	National Republican	530,189	49	42.4
	William Wirt	Anti-Masonic	33,108	7	2.6
	John Floyd	National Republican		11	
1836 (26)	Martin Van Buren	Democratic	765,483	170	50.9
	William H. Harrison	Whig		73	
	Hugh L. White	Whig	739,795	26	49.1
	Daniel Webster	Whig		14	
	W. P. Mangum	Whig		11	
1840 (26)	William H. Harrison	Whig	1,274,624	234	53.1
	Martin Van Buren	Democratic	1,127,781	60	46.9
1844 (26)	James K. Polk	Democratic	1,338,464	170	49.6
	Henry Clay	Whig	1,300,097	105	48.1
	James G. Birney	Liberty	62,300		2.3
1848 (30)	Zachary Taylor	Whig	1,360,967	163	47.4
	Lewis Cass	Democratic	1,222,342	127	42.5
	Martin Van Buren	Free Soil	291,263		10.1
1852 (31)	Franklin Pierce	Democratic	1,601,117	254	50.9
	Winfield Scott	Whig	1,385,453	42	44.1
	John P. Hale	Free Soil	155,825		5.0
1856 (31)	James Buchanan	Democratic	1,832,955	174	45.3
	John C. Frémont	Republican	1,339,932	114	33.1
	Millard Fillmore	American	871,731	8	21.6
1860 (33)	Abraham Lincoln	Republican	1,865,593	180	39.8
	Stephen A. Douglas	Democratic	1,382,713	12	29.5
	John C. Breckinridge	Democratic	848,356	72	18.1
	John Bell	Constitutional Union	592,906	39	12.6
1864 (36)	Abraham Lincoln	Republican	2,206,938	212	55.0
	George B. McClellan	Democratic	1,803,787	21	45.0
1868 (37)	Ulysses S. Grant	Republican	3,013,421	214	52.7
	Horatio Seymour	Democratic	2,706,829	80	47.3
1872 (37)	Ulysses S. Grant	Republican	3,596,745	286	55.6
	Horace Greeley	Democratic	2,843,446	[2]	43.9
1876 (38)	Rutherford B. Hayes	Republican	4,036,572	185	48.0
	Samuel J. Tilden	Democratic	4,284,020	184	51.0
1880 (38)	James A. Garfield	Republican	4,453,295	214	48.5
	Winfield S. Hancock	Democratic	4,414,082	155	48.1
	James B. Weaver	Greenback-Labor	308,578		3.4

[2] Greeley died shortly after the election; the electors supporting him then divided their votes among minor candidates.

Presidential Elections (1789–1968) (cont.)

Year and number of states	Candidates	Parties	Popular vote	Electoral vote	Percentage of popular vote
1884 (38)	Grover Cleveland	Democratic	4,879,507	219	48.5
	James G. Blaine	Republican	4,850,293	182	48.2
	Benjamin F. Butler	Greenback-Labor	175,370		1.8
	John P. St. John	Prohibition	150,369		1.5
1888 (38)	Benjamin Harrison	Republican	5,447,129	233	47.9
	Grover Cleveland	Democratic	5,537,857	168	48.6
	Clinton B. Fisk	Prohibition	249,506		2.2
	Anson J. Streeter	Union Labor	146,935		1.3
1892 (44)	Grover Cleveland	Democratic	5,555,426	277	46.1
	Benjamin Harrison	Republican	5,182,690	145	43.0
	James B. Weaver	People's	1,029,846	22	8.5
	John Bidwell	Prohibition	264,133		2.2
1896 (45)	William McKinley	Republican	7,102,246	271	51.1
	William J. Bryan	Democratic	6,492,559	176	47.7
1900 (45)	William McKinley	Republican	7,218,491	292	51.7
	William J. Bryan	Democratic; Populist	6,356,734	155	45.5
	John C. Wooley	Prohibition	208,914		1.5
1904 (45)	Theodore Roosevelt	Republican	7,628,461	336	57.4
	Alton B. Parker	Democratic	5,084,223	140	37.6
	Eugene V. Debs	Socialist	402,283		3.0
	Silas C. Swallow	Prohibition	258,536		1.9
1908 (46)	William H. Taft	Republican	7,675,320	321	51.6
	William J. Bryan	Democratic	6,412,294	162	43.1
	Eugene V. Debs	Socialist	420,793		2.8
	Eugene W. Chafin	Prohibition	253,840		1.7
1912 (48)	Woodrow Wilson	Democratic	6,296,547	435	41.9
	Theodore Roosevelt	Progressive	4,118,571	88	27.4
	William H. Taft	Republican	3,486,720	8	23.2
	Eugene V. Debs	Socialist	900,672		6.0
	Eugene W. Chafin	Prohibition	206,275		1.4
1916 (48)	Woodrow Wilson	Democratic	9,127,695	277	49.4
	Charles E. Hughes	Republican	8,533,507	254	46.2
	A. L. Benson	Socialist	585,113		3.2
	J. Frank Hanly	Prohibition	220,506		1.2
1920 (48)	Warren G. Harding	Republican	16,143,407	404	60.4
	James N. Cox	Democratic	9,130,328	127	34.2
	Eugene V. Debs	Socialist	919,799		3.4
	P. P. Christensen	Farmer-Labor	265,411		1.0
1924 (48)	Calvin Coolidge	Republican	15,718,211	382	54.0
	John W. Davis	Democratic	8,385,283	136	28.8
	Robert M. La Follette	Progressive	4,831,289	13	16.6

Presidential Elections (1789–1968) (cont.)

Year and number of states	Candidates	Parties	Popular vote	Electoral vote	Percentage of popular vote
1928 (48)	Herbert C. Hoover	Republican	21,391,993	444	58.2
	Alfred E. Smith	Democratic	15,016,169	87	40.9
1932 (48)	Franklin D. Roosevelt	Democratic	22,809,638	472	57.4
	Herbert C. Hoover	Republican	15,758,901	59	39.7
	Norman Thomas	Socialist	881,951		2.2
1936 (48)	Franklin D. Roosevelt	Democratic	27,752,869	523	60.8
	Alfred M. Landon	Republican	16,674,665	8	36.5
	William Lemke	Union	882,479		1.9
1940 (48)	Franklin D. Roosevelt	Democratic	27,307,819	449	54.8
	Wendell L. Willkie	Republican	22,321,018	82	44.8
1944 (48)	Franklin D. Roosevelt	Democratic	25,606,585	432	53.5
	Thomas E. Dewey	Republican	22,014,745	99	46.0
1948 (48)	Harry S Truman	Democratic	24,105,812	303	49.5
	Thomas E. Dewey	Republican	21,970,065	189	45.1
	J. Strom Thurmond	States' Rights	1,169,063	39	2.4
	Henry A. Wallace	Progressive	1,157,172		2.4
1952 (48)	Dwight D. Eisenhower	Republican	33,936,234	442	55.1
	Adlai E. Stevenson	Democratic	27,314,992	89	44.4
1956 (48)	Dwight D. Eisenhower	Republican	35,590,472	457	57.6
	Adlai E. Stevenson	Democratic	26,022,752	73	42.1
1960 (50)	John F. Kennedy	Democratic	34,227,096	303	49.9
	Richard M. Nixon	Republican	34,108,546	219	49.6
1964 (50)	Lyndon B. Johnson	Democratic	43,126,506	486	61.1
	Barry M. Goldwater	Republican	27,176,799	52	38.5
1968 (50)	Richard M. Nixon	Republican	31,785,480	301	43.4
	Hubert H. Humphrey	Democratic	31,275,165	191	42.7
	George C. Wallace	American Independent	9,906,473	46	13.5

Population of the United States [1790–1970]*

Year	Total population (in thousands)	Number per square mile of land area (continental United States)	Year	Total population (in thousands)	Number per square mile of land area (continental United States)
1790	3,929	4.5	1930	123,077	41.2
1800	5,308	6.1	1931	124,040	
1810	7,239	4.3	1932	124,840	
1820	9,638	5.5	1933	125,579	
1830	12,866	7.4	1934	126,374	
1840	17,069	9.8	1935	127,250	
1850	23,191	7.9	1936	128,053	
1860	31,443	10.6	1937	128,825	
1870	39,818	13.4	1938	129,825	
1880	50,155	16.9	1939	130,880	
1890	62,947	21.2	1940	131,669	44.2
1900	76,094	25.6	1941	133,669	
1901	77,585		1942	134,617	
1902	79,160		1943	136,107	
1903	80,632		1944	133,915	
1904	82,165		1945	133,434	
1905	83,820		1946	140,686	
1906	85,437		1947	144,083	
1907	87,000		1948	146,730	
1908	88,709		1949	149,304	
1909	90,492		1950	151,868	42.6
1910	92,407	31.0	1951	153,982	
1911	93,868		1952	156,393	
1912	95,331		1953	158,956	
1913	97,227		1954	161,884	
1914	99,118		1955	165,069	
1915	100,549		1956	168,088	
1916	101,966		1957	171,187	
1917	103,266		1958	174,149	
1918	103,203		1959	177,135	
1919	104,512		1960	179,992	50.5
1920	106,466	35.6	1961	183,057	
1921	108,541		1962	185,890	
1922	110,055		1963	188,658	
1923	111,950		1964	191,372	
1924	114,113		1965	193,815	
1925	115,832		1966	197,859	
1926	117,399		1967	197,859	
1927	119,038		1968	199,846	
1928	120,501		1969	201,921	
1929	121,770		1970	203,185	57.4

* Figures are from *Statistical Abstract of the United States: 1969*, p. 5; and *New York Times Encyclopedic Almanac, 1972*, p. 146. Figures exclude Armed Forces abroad and after 1940 include Alaska and Hawaii.

Admission of States

Order of admission	State	Date of admission
1	Delaware	December 7, 1787
2	Pennsylvania	December 12, 1787
3	New Jersey	December 18, 1787
4	Georgia	January 2, 1788
5	Connecticut	January 9, 1788
6	Massachusetts	February 6, 1788
7	Maryland	April 28, 1788
8	South Carolina	May 23, 1788
9	New Hampshire	June 21, 1788
10	Virginia	June 25, 1788
11	New York	July 26, 1788
12	North Carolina	November 21, 1789
13	Rhode Island	May 29, 1790
14	Vermont	March 4, 1791
15	Kentucky	June 1, 1792
16	Tennessee	June 1, 1796
17	Ohio	March 1, 1803
18	Louisiana	April 30, 1812
19	Indiana	December 11, 1816
20	Mississippi	December 10, 1817
21	Illinois	December 3, 1818
22	Alabama	December 14, 1819
23	Maine	March 15, 1820
24	Missouri	August 10, 1821
25	Arkansas	June 15, 1836
26	Michigan	January 26, 1837
27	Florida	March 3, 1845
28	Texas	December 29, 1845
29	Iowa	December 28, 1846
30	Wisconsin	May 29, 1848
31	California	September 9, 1850
32	Minnesota	May 11, 1858
33	Oregon	February 14, 1859
34	Kansas	January 29, 1861
35	West Virginia	June 30, 1863
36	Nevada	October 31, 1864
37	Nebraska	March 1, 1867
38	Colorado	August 1, 1876
39	North Dakota	November 2, 1889
40	South Dakota	November 2, 1889
41	Montana	November 8, 1889
42	Washington	November 11, 1889
43	Idaho	July 3, 1890
44	Wyoming	July 10, 1890
45	Utah	January 4, 1896
46	Oklahoma	November 16, 1907
47	New Mexico	January 6, 1912
48	Arizona	February 14, 1912
49	Alaska	January 3, 1959
50	Hawaii	August 21, 1959

INDEX